THE UNIVERSITY UNFETTERED

THE UNIVERSITY UNFETTERED

PUBLIC HIGHER EDUCATION IN AN AGE OF DISRUPTION

IAN F. McNEELY

Columbia University Press *New York*

Columbia University Press
Publishers Since 1893
New York   Chichester, West Sussex

Copyright © 2025 Ian F. McNeely
All rights reserved

Library of Congress Cataloging-in-Publication Data
Names: McNeely, Ian F., 1971– author.
Title: The university unfettered : public higher education in an age of disruption / Ian F McNeely.
Description: New York : Columbia University Press, [2025] | Includes bibliographical references and index.
Identifiers: LCCN 2024039081 | ISBN 9780231218405 (hardback) | ISBN 9780231220583 (trade paperback) | ISBN 9780231562232 (ebook)
Subjects: LCSH: University of Oregon—Administration. | Public universities and colleges—Oregon—Administration. | Education, Higher—Aims and objectives—United States.
Classification: LCC LD4350.7 .M36 2025 | DDC 378.795/31—dc23/eng/20250117

Cover design: Noah Arlow
Cover images: Shutterstock

GPSR Authorized Representative: Easy Access System Europe,
Mustamäe tee 50, 10621 Tallinn, Estonia, gpsr.requests@easproject.com

For Karen Lenore McNeely

CONTENTS

Introduction 1

I STAKEHOLDERS

1 The Public 17

2 Students 49

3 Faculty 82

4 Administrators 109

II MISSIONS

5 Research 139

6 Teaching 168

7 Diversity 195

8 Impact 227

Conclusion 255

Acknowledgments 267
Sources 271
Notes 275
Index 317

THE UNIVERSITY
UNFETTERED

INTRODUCTION

It seemed as if a major disruption was about to come to American colleges and universities. Stresses and strains had been piling up for years. Then the global financial crisis struck in 2008, triggering fears of an economic meltdown unseen since the Great Depression. Even though the apocalypse never arrived, the Great Recession that followed was so named because it became a generation-defining event. Its impact was felt especially by young people at the cusp of adulthood, those either just entering or just leaving college. What would their collective decisions about the future mean for higher education? To be sure, it had long been a safe bet that students flock to college during downturns. Recessions are counterclyclical, pulling young people out of the job market and into the search for educational credentials. Still, the scale and scope of the world financial crisis were unprecedented. State budgets duly collapsed, which might have spelled disaster for the public universities that educate most of the country's students. Appropriations to public universities by state legislatures had been in decline for decades already, so this could have been a tipping point.

But sure enough, the students came in droves, paying high tuition, typically through loans backed by the full faith and credit of the federal government. Reassuringly, the 2010s turned out to be a boom time at many institutions. A flight to quality benefited established state schools at the expense of sketchy for-profit and online colleges that once seemed on the point of threatening the entire higher education establishment. Many of the for-profits went under, whereas most reputable institutions did much better than expected. Market competition reigned supreme—and public universities won.

Of course, we could not have known that at the time. Anxiety and, more positively, a hunger to reform the system set the tone. The whole decade unloosed a parade of reform proposals small and large, measured and deluded, all designed to capitalize on the pregnant uncertainty of the moment.[1] We saw everything from breathless prognostications of revolutionary reinvention[2] to earnest suggestions for improving teaching and research.[3] Exposés and critiques of waste, hypocrisy, underperformance, and exploitation[4] filled the shelves alongside cheerleading accounts of enduring collegiate values[5] and the ongoing prowess of American scientific research.[6] Toward the end of the decade, when things were a bit calmer, some realistic, even-handed appraisals of the "two cheers" variety did appear.[7] But prophecies of doom and foreboding continued to issue forth.[8] Throughout it all, many rank-and-file faculty members maintained a "this too shall pass" attitude, figuring that ivy-clad institutions had weathered storms for centuries and would weather this one too.

Some of the ideas bandied about during this time were staples that recur every generation or never go away: the idea that the humanities and the liberal arts would collapse before science, engineering, technology, and preprofessional fields; the idea that faculty tenure would be abolished as an un-American relic that coddles Ivory Tower leftists; the idea that big problems such as climate change required interdisciplinary solutions and the dismantling of departments, disciplines, and academic "silos"; and the idea that public accountability and public-spiritedness were being corrupted by private donors and the corporate management values they foisted upon us.

Other ideas were new to the moment, reflecting the blend of technological optimism and economic pressures that marked the early twenty-first century. One fad that fizzled was the proposal that traditional college degrees be "unbundled" into marketable badges and various à la carte career-ready credentials. But the biggest fever dream of the 2010s was the giddy prediction that MOOCs—"massive open online courses" reaching millions of students, each taught by a single faculty rock star—would force brick-and-mortar colleges to close up shop and throw the rest of the tweedy professoriate out of work.[9] In less radical forms, too, techno-utopianism thrived as online learning and the digitization of all knowledge promised to make students smarter, and to do so faster and cheaper than ever before.

While we were dreaming, a number of big decisions were deferred, not least of which was who would pay for it all. In 2012, student debt topped one trillion dollars for the first time. Some feared that, as had just happened in the 2008 mortgage security collapse, the student loan bubble was likewise about to burst. Over a decade later, that hasn't happened (at least not yet). What *has* happened is a doubling down on the notion that a college degree is the sine qua non of a dignified middle-class existence in the United States, and therefore worth almost any investment of money and time. In the early 2000s, well over 90 percent of Americans thought of themselves as solidly middle- or working-class. Since then, we have become a nation in which a bachelor's degree may not exactly guarantee steady and satisfying work, but *not* having one is a powerful predictor of diminished life chances, precarious employment, and even premature death—and only about 40 percent of American adults have a four-year degree.[10]

In the 2010s it became an article of faith that higher education credentials are indispensable to success in the so-called knowledge economy. Not coincidentally, those same years were extraordinarily polarized politically. Sometime during the Obama and Trump presidencies, higher education joined race, ethnicity, and income among the most reliable predictors of party allegiance.[11] The possession (or lack) of a bachelor's degree now marks one of the greatest economic, social, and cultural cleavages in the United States. As the COVID-19 pandemic of 2020–21 revealed, America is a society alarmingly divided, not just between right and left but between college-educated "knowledge workers" who can telecommute from their home offices and "essential workers" who show up in person to stock grocery shelves and drive garbage trucks.

The pandemic was another disruptive event, a shared global experience that upended higher education, not to mention daily life, even more directly than the 2008 financial crisis. Living and learning online for months during one's formative teen years has been an even more defining experience for the current generation of students than the Great Recession was for the prior one. But as soon as the pandemic ended, college life reverted to normal—outwardly, at least, while leaving traumas in its wake. Universities by and large snapped back to in-person teaching as soon as they could, sweeping under the rug clear evidence of a deep deterioration in student mental health and faculty and staff morale. We did learn one important thing from the pandemic: swapping out classrooms for Zoom squares and going fully online is not sustainable. But all that did was to pop the MOOC bubble, which any informed observer knew was a fantasy to begin with.

In the wake of a public health calamity, widespread exhaustion was the rule. A whiff of desperation hung around students, faculty, and staff who reluctantly returned to classrooms, offices, and labs. Meanwhile, right-wing provocateurs ginned up a familiar culture war over "political correctness," "wokeness," "critical race theory," and "diversity, equity, and inclusion" (DEI). It felt like a tiresome retread of 1990s-era debates over multiculturalism that have been revisited with scab-picking compulsion every few years since then. But flickers of McCarthyite paranoia showed this to be a genuine menace. In higher education, as in so much of our politics, we rehearsed vicious old battles—as if to give ourselves a reason to care passionately about yet another American institution that, it seems, we can neither love nor change nor do without.

If the period between the Great Recession and COVID-19 was a stress test for public higher education, we can now announce the results. Calls for revolutionary disruption failed utterly. Under immense pressure to bear heavy loads, our system of higher education remained recalcitrant to large-scale reform. Too much was at stake to experiment with major course corrections. Though there was no shortage of valuable ideas for fundamental change, most of them went nowhere. But piling more responsibility on colleges and universities worked all too well. As Americans continued to demand knowledge-based credentials, they looked to higher education to solve problems of economic precarity and threats to upward social mobility that had been festering since the late 1900s and became acute with the rise of globalized hypercapitalism in the early 2000s. Universities responded by cleaving to strategies that had worked well before, such as raising tuition and marketing to new consumers, but this came at the cost of overburdening students and their own employees. The nation was left with, at best, incremental changes to the old ways of doing things, plus an uneasy feeling that we had somehow lost the plot in our own national saga of higher education improvement.

Today we confront a disquieting loss of confidence in public universities: not only a crisis of morale within but also a faltering of faith without. Opinion surveys reveal that students and their parents increasingly doubt that college degrees will continue to provide a compelling return on investment as they have done in the past.[12] Across bitter partisan divides, adversaries converge on a gnawing suspicion that public universities have abandoned their public missions—or been forced to do so. It is high time for a reckoning.

Where is higher education headed now, after the tumultuous 2010s? One thing seems clear: the public university as we once knew it is gone and never coming back. After generations of fickle state support, public universities behave more and more like their private counterparts—charging what the market will bear, offering what consumers demand, competing relentlessly with peers, and managing their own priorities, strategies, and resources. But looking back on how we got here offers surprising reassurance. America's public universities emerged battered but intact after the 2010s, a decade of disruption bookended by a once-in-a-lifetime financial crisis and a once-in-a-century pandemic. Resisting widespread calls for fundamental reinvention or disruptive innovation, they hewed to their core missions. If anything, exposure to the rigors of competition and the discipline of the market only strengthened their commitments to the public good. What problems remain are ironically the by-products of misguided public pressures and outdated public policies. In this book I explain the paradoxical success of the public university, how it thrives in being set free from public control, and what must still be done to improve it.

The University Unfettered tells the story of a single public flagship institution that was a generation ahead of its peers in coping with state disinvestment and repositioning itself for an independent future. During the 2010s, it fought for and won the right to govern itself, triggered the dissolution of the state's entire university system, and reaped the largest private donation that had ever been bestowed on a public institution. But the drama of its internal transformation is even more significant for what it reveals about American higher education at large. The chapters guide the reader through eight fundamental questions about how *any* contemporary university juggles rival stakeholders and balances competing missions—questions about how money is spent, how education and knowledge are pursued, how decisions get made, and how internal and external constituencies influence them. Each chapter, one per question, blends deeply informed reconstruction of strategic decisions at one university with concise analyses of the entire sector, drawing from the ample scholarship on higher education policy, history, sociology, and economics.

For each question, the answer turns out to be some variant on: let the market decide; let the competition guide us; let us follow our peers and emulate our betters. Public universities used to adhere to nonmarket values and ideals of public service. But after a generation of financial austerity and inconstant political support, public universities now behave as semiautonomous agents, much like their private counterparts, in a marketplace where multiple values, missions, and priorities converge and sometimes conflict. As these institutions have come to mean different things to different people, rival values and visions have to be weighed against one another. Universities thus resort to competition and the logic of the market to sort out what their priorities ought to be. Each is in rivalry with its reputational neighbors, each is eager to move up relative to its aspirational peers, and each is fearful of moving down relative to ambitious up-and-comers. It follows that any given university can improve itself by matching its goals and practices to what other, better universities are doing—and that constant striving redounds to the benefit of American public higher education as a whole.

The unfettering of the public university is a story of crisis and turnaround revealed by an unprecedented look into how one institution reacted to multiple, cascading stressors. The resulting account is perhaps the first to explain the inner workings of any university as experienced by those who manage it. My surprising finding is that public universities have done remarkably well by their stakeholders despite public disinvestment—and where they still underperform on their various missions, well-intentioned public policy is as often the culprit as the remedy. Ultimately, only competition makes universities better, and only competition provides a source of real accountability to the public.

From this point forward, I will call this institution, simply, the "University"—capitalized—and its home state, similarly, the "State." The University is a public institution, so the sources I rely upon are in almost all instances open to the public, typically on websites accessible at the click of a mouse. I treat those sources as a historical archive, just as I would do (and have long done) in writing any other work of history.[13] Yet to preserve anonymity, I avoid naming names, and even when I do identify specific individuals, I confine myself to public figures (presidents and other senior leaders) and use pseudonyms. Anyone who is so motivated can, with a trivial amount of effort, determine both the identity of the University and the names of the key actors. But that might evoke misleading assumptions based on its reputation, location, brand, sports teams, or biggest donor. My reason for anonymization is not to be coy but to take the focus off the specifics and off the personalities. That way, I can concentrate on the larger picture, the bigger trends, and what is typical rather than what is unique about this one case. If I cannot tell my story without recourse to proper names, it is a good sign that I am not telling it correctly.[14]

The University is a major public research flagship with roughly 25,000 students and a wide range of both undergraduate and graduate programs spanning the arts and sciences and the professions but lacking medicine and engineering. Although it belongs to the prestigious Association of American Universities (AAU), the leading consortium of research universities in North America, the University by no means ranks among its largest, wealthiest, most productive, or most prestigious public, much less private, members. In *U.S. News and World Report* rankings, it usually comes in at the nice round number of 100, give or take. That makes it atypically privileged by the standard of the several thousand accredited colleges and universities in the United States, but otherwise *very* typical of the complex teaching- and research-oriented universities that we often think of when we look below the top tier of elite private universities and so-called public Ivies that dominate the headlines. Together, universities of this type educate millions of students and account for half of the nation's scientific and scholarly research. More so than the most elite colleges and universities, the graduates and the knowledge that these high-quality middle-tier institutions produce will determine the future of the American experiment in publicly supported mass higher learning.

The University has been a bellwether for a great many of the trends buffeting American higher education over the last generation. Since the 1990s, it had experienced both a steep decline and severe volatility in state funding and a commensurate reliance on hikes to student tuition. Such pressures came to a head during the Great Recession. Thus, in the early 2010s, the University's leaders orchestrated a dramatic divorce from their own boss—the State Board of Higher Education. That board was subsequently dissolved and replaced with an independent board of trustees serving the University alone. In the process, the entire state university system previously overseen by the State Board was dismantled and replaced with brand new governance. Vulnerable in the scramble for power, the faculty, tenured, tenure-track, and non-tenure-eligible alike, proceeded to unionize. This thoroughly recast the relationship between the University's administration and its most essential employees: its teachers and researchers. Meanwhile, the administration suffered remarkable turnover. Fully six presidents (three of them interims) and six provosts (chief academic officers) served between July 2009 and July 2022, together with an ever-changing cast of deans, vice presidents, and middle managers whose roles were often unclear but somehow always seemed to expand.

This was, in short, a period of incessant leadership upheaval, institutional improvisation, and financial and administrative reengineering that, although extreme by national standards, was hardly unusual among public research universities (and even some private ones) during this period of upheaval. On the contrary, the University only experienced more deeply the stresses and strains that its peers did elsewhere. And in the central paradox I confront in this book, it survived and thrived not just despite but because of it all. Whichever leaders were in the hot seat at any given time, they simply responded to market forces while dutifully and sincerely intoning their commitments to the public good. Robust student enrollments, vibrant faculty research, and record-setting philanthropic donations are among the positive legacies of a time when the institution was perilously exposed to the rigors of competition and the disciplining clash of rival interests. Today, the

University stands as *the* national proof of concept for the claim that public research universities should be emancipated to compete openly with their peers to achieve excellence—and that this is the best way for them to fulfill their historic public missions.

This book can be read with profit by anyone—whether student, parent, faculty member, administrator, trustee, policy maker, or layperson (American or otherwise)—with a natural curiosity about how universities work. No one, to my knowledge, has written about a university's inner workings in this way before: with deep empirical grounding in real-world conundrums and strategies, framed in historical and comparative contexts, and combining insider knowledge with a disinterested perspective.[15] I aim to demystify a campus world shrouded in high-minded ideals. I speak to any reader who has ever worked in a large, imperfect organization, navigated its complex politics, and struggled with how it both does and does not live up to its principles.

I hope this book will be especially useful to those who are already involved in university life and want to know how its ideals are translated into concrete decisions and enacted (or not) in practice. Faculty members will learn about political trade-offs and financial constraints that they may not understand and are socialized to be proudly disdainful about. Administrators will see how their activities, which are often confined to specific areas, fit within comprehensive institution-level and national contexts. Trustees and policy makers will learn about the inner workings of the universities they oversee. Laypersons from the business and professional worlds will find much to compare with the organizations they inhabit and lead. Academic leaders from other countries may find helpful insights on what is worth emulating, and not worth emulating, about American higher education.

I confess that I am profoundly ambivalent about what the public university has become. Politically, I admire European-style social democracy and the generous public benefits that it provides. But the United States is not now and never has been a social democracy. Instead, in the absence of an actual welfare state, American higher education has historically served as one of the nation's most powerful engines of prosperity and upward mobility. I thus find it deeply uncomfortable to endorse such a thoroughly market-driven vision of the university's role in society, the exclusions it entails, and the meanness of spirit and waste of resources that relentless competition can invite. Yet I am forced to concede that productive rivalry is one of the few constants in the history of higher learning—from the city-states of ancient Greece to the urban universities of the Middle Ages to the system of interstate competition in nineteenth-century Germany that spawned the modern research university, which directly inspired our own network of state universities in the United States. Globally, the American model is now spreading to Asia, just as it had once spread to America from Europe, and Europeans are scrambling to fortify their universities for global competition.[16]

One cannot dismiss the contemporary market-driven public university as a recent offshoot of neoliberalism, late capitalism, corporatization, privatization, or any other lapse from some alleged Golden Age of public munificence. It is if anything a reversion to type. Public leaders and supporters would do far better to cultivate and unleash the power of academic and institutional rivalry than to tame or control it. That has for centuries been the challenge for higher learning's patrons, and it will remain the public's task for the 2020s and beyond. In the conclusion, I have more to say about how public leaders and policy makers can continue to play their roles. I show how the fifty states can still reconcile institutional competition with civic values in a collective, continent-wide quest to better the quality of life through the pursuit of knowledge. In the meantime, I encourage you to delve into the specifics and peculiarities of my case study, for it shows how a single vanguard institution now stands as a model for others of its type. Having adapted to disruptive forces that continue to buffet higher education, that one university has already forded a divide that others will sooner or later have to navigate.

I

STAKEHOLDERS

Against all odds, public universities have done well by their stakeholders during an era of disruption that shows no sign of ending soon. The *public* itself, foremost among stakeholders, need not fear privatization. Despite a generation-long decline in state support and rising dependence on tuition and private philanthropy, universities are in no danger of abandoning their public commitments or losing their public character. *Students*, for their part, need not fear rising tuition. Despite unavoidable increases in the cost of higher education, the money that students (and their parents) spend is being used wisely and strategically to ensure that their investment pays off handsomely over a lifetime. The *faculty*—who are not just employees but the true keepers of the university's academic mission—need not fear the decline of their profession. Despite the replacement of tenure-track faculty with non-tenurable instructors, the American professoriate is robust and secure and simply becoming more differentiated in response to the many missions the university fulfills. And none of these groups should fear the expanding power of *administrators*. Despite headline-grabbing accounts of waste and excess that are to be expected in any large organization, the management of a competitive, multifaceted university requires lots of skilled leaders and staff.

Part I takes up these four stakeholder groups in turn. It shows how the faithfulness universities display toward each of them is ultimately attributable to market competition. Market competition gives universities actionable incentives to respond to stakeholder demands. Challenges remain, but they have proven to be manageable even during a decade of extraordinary stressors, so it is likely that they will remain manageable in the future.

1

THE PUBLIC

Have public universities lost public accountability and become privatized?

In the days before they fired The Hat, there was a run on fedoras at all the local haberdashers. The Hat had become the University's president in 2009, rapidly gaining deep support from big donors, sports fans, civic leaders, and jaded faculty alike—no mean feat. During his first years in office, he grew student enrollments, hired talented administrators, supported the humanities, bolstered diversity, cultivated politicians—including, initially at least, the new governor—and boosted the University's renowned athletics programs. However, The Hat ran afoul of the governor by protecting staff from state-mandated furloughs during the Great Recession. He also raised faculty salaries in the teeth of statewide budget cuts and an across-the-board salary freeze. In a highly competitive nationwide higher education market, he claimed that the University had to preserve its core talent. The tuition it was bringing in more than justified the added expense.

Most controversially, The Hat had spent two years taking on his own bosses on the State Board of Higher Education: the eleven politically appointed trustees overseeing all six of the State's public universities.[1] The State would be better off, he argued, if the University (and perhaps other public universities in the State) could be given its own Board of Trustees and be permitted to manage its own local affairs. His grand plan, "Preserving Our Public Mission Through a New Partnership with the State," envisioned a set of creative new mechanisms to ensure financial stability and preserve public accountability in exchange for autonomy and independent governance.[2] But The Hat had sharp elbows, he did not suffer fools, and his superiors on the State Board did not take kindly to the notion of their own powers being eliminated. When the governor withdrew his support, it was the last straw. Leading trustees from the State Board visited The Hat to offer him the chance to go quietly. Then all hell broke loose.

The story went public on the Tuesday before Thanksgiving 2011: The Hat must resign or face being fired by the State Board. Within a week, more than six thousand signatures had been collected in protest, mostly from faculty and staff, but also from students, community leaders, and ordinary citizens. The Hat was a true scholar, a student of ancient Sanskrit literature no less, and was beloved by the faculty. But he also had a folksy touch and a radiant charisma that outshone his almost aggressively plain appearance. Bald, he wore a tan fedora around campus in all kinds of weather. As word spread of his firing, a number of male supporters on the faculty, and not a few female ones, ran out and bought one—hence the run on the local haberdashers—and wore their hats to various campus protests and bullhorn events. Bowing to popular outrage, the State Board convened an extraordinary public meeting, televised live, in the State's largest city. Righteous advocates took two-hour bus rides to testify in person and to plead in heartfelt testimony for The Hat's reinstatement, but to no avail. Impassively, the State Board voted to fire him, without cause, on November 28, 2011, while he sat in the front row and looked on.

With the University community livid about his firing, politicians—for once—paid attention to the faculty, hoping to mend fences and turn around what had become a public relations fiasco for the State Board. Leading faculty were invited to meet with the governor in the state capitol and to fraternize with legislators at a cocktail hour afterward. Some were given a tour of his official mansion, including the gubernatorial bedchamber, and were introduced to his dog. But the faculty, acting officially through the University Senate, would not be placated. Just over one week after the news broke, on November 30, 2011, hundreds of faculty assembled on the floor of the basketball court to voice their outrage in a series of speeches. In what resembled a Maoist struggle session, the University system's chancellor was barraged, to his face, with an itemized list of sins and asked to reflect not just on his official actions but on his takeaways "as a human being" on the whole affair. A unanimously approved motion gravely intoned that the "Statutory Faculty condemns the Chancellor and State Board of Higher Education for their decision to terminate [The Hat] and for the process by which they reached this decision."[3]

The exact same thing had happened once before, twenty-four years earlier—almost to the day—on December 2, 1987, when the State Board had fired another popular president. That one, a veteran of the Manhattan Project, had become legendary for building the University's research facilities in the throes of the *last* major recession, during the 1980s. Yet he too had displeased the State Board by focusing on the excellence of the State's flagship institution, including its national reputation, rather than conforming to the more parochial needs of the State and its other universities. So the 2011 faculty resolution simply swapped out one president's name for another and otherwise copy-pasted the previous list of formal "Whereas..." complaints more or less verbatim. This was a structural conflict between the State and its flagship university, the resolution implied, and not just a clash of strong-willed personalities.[4]

Nationwide, too, the firing of The Hat was not an isolated incident but was a rupture, one among several in those years, of a seismic fault in the governance of public universities in the aftermath of the Great Recession. About six months later, the president of the University of Virginia, one of America's most distinguished flagships, was likewise summarily fired by its governing board, but that time, against all expectation, an outburst of faculty protest prevailed in having her reinstated. Leadership turnover at public flagship institutions, in states as varied as Texas, North Carolina, California, Missouri, Oregon, and Wisconsin, revealed a broader pattern, even though the circumstances were different in each case.[5] Major public research universities across the country had begun to find themselves in tension with the states that oversaw them. More deeply, *every* individual university's incentives to compete—for students, for faculty, for research grants, for big donors, for athletic glory, and for status, prestige, and rankings—came into conflict with the desires of policy makers and legislators, not only to support various institutions besides the flagships but to promote a whole series of other worthy goals, ranging from collaborating with K–12 and community college systems to producing graduates in key workforce development occupations to the care and feeding of struggling communities hosting the less prosperous regional colleges and universities.

The root cause of all these tensions was public disinvestment, with state funding for higher education being one of the first casualties of legislative budget cuts whenever recessions strike.

This was not just a sporadic cost-saving measure but a long-term, multigenerational trend; the erosion of states' financial support for their public universities has been dubbed "The Great Mistake" by the trend's harshest critic.[6] Equally important—and this is the other half of the question for this chapter—was privatization: universities' collective, long-term turn to private revenue sources in response to the steady erosion of public support, which threatened a commensurate reduction of public accountability. In this chapter, I first explore The Hat's New Partnership proposal and how it sought to salvage the University's public mission in the face of powerful trends toward privatization. I then widen the lens, looking at various other dimensions of privatization nationwide, from public policy to private philanthropy. The chapter concludes with a balance sheet evaluating the impact of the University's governance reform after The Hat was fired. I focus on the years since 2014, when an independent Board of Trustees was duly established at the University and the statewide system was dissolved.

What is most surprising is how little the precise details of governance actually matter beyond the critical fact of local institutional autonomy. Next to the power of the market forces that are created by student demand, which is the focus of chapter 2, what states do or don't do to regulate public higher education is of distinctly secondary importance.

THE NEW PARTNERSHIP

Cynics had greeted the New Partnership as nothing but a stealth bid to privatize the University—whatever "privatization" might be taken to mean. Largely, this fear reflected the long shadow cast by the University's largest benefactor, the Big Donor, a world-famous businessman who had long funded both academics and, more controversially, athletics. An outspoken critic of the State Board's failure to privilege the flagship and support research excellence, the Big Donor was widely but incorrectly suspected of harboring designs to remake the University in his own image. But the New Partnership was avowedly and consistently framed around public values. It sprang from the sobering recognition that the old ways of governing and financing public higher education were gone and never coming back. The white paper sketching out the plan opened with the contention that "the issue of how to preserve the public mission of America's great public higher education system is at the forefront of policy discussions in states across the country."[7] It proceeded to sketch a new model for flagship research universities, not just for one state but, ideally, for the whole nation. A bold three-part plan was laid before the public, one centered on autonomy (in the form of an independent Board of Trustees), accountability (in the form of publicly established performance goals), and a new public-private financing scheme. The University would achieve autonomy from the State in return for greater accountability to its public mission—and without additional cost. Op-ed writers, business leaders, lobbyists, and other state-level opinion makers were mobilized in support of this.

The proposal laid out a depressing picture of the State's leading university as a poster child for public disinvestment nationally. Given the needs of the State's knowledge economy, in competition not just with other states but with other economies worldwide, it was imperative to close the "degree gap" between the population's actual attainment of college degrees and its economically optimal level. By the State's own reckoning, nearly sixty thousand additional bachelor's degrees would need to be produced by 2025 to close that gap. Obviously that burden would fall heavily on the

University and on other public institutions. But among peer public research universities nationwide, the University ranked dead last in state legislative appropriations per student. Figure 1.1 illustrates the steady tuition hikes over the years and shows exactly where the University's money came from. After a generation of public disinvestment, the University now received a scant 9 percent of its revenues from the State—a shockingly low figure by both historical and national standards, and again, far lower than in most other states. This was an extreme example of what had undeniably become a trend across the country.

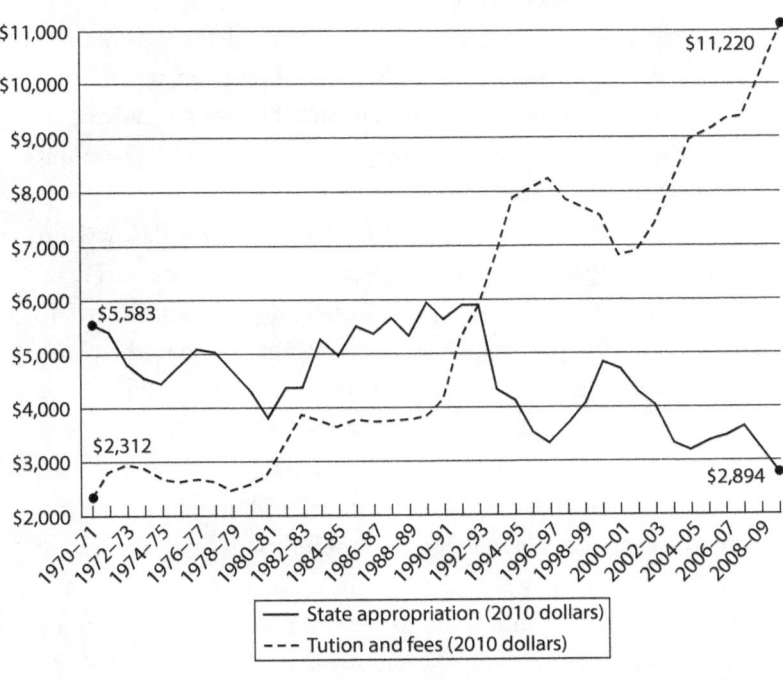

FIGURE 1.1 Tuition hikes compensate for state disinvestment.

Source: Office of the President, "Preserving Our Public Mission Through a New Partnership with the State," August 2010, https://perma.cc/VUU3-P6XW, 11.

Lack of predictability is, if anything, worse than cuts one knows are coming and here to stay. For years, the University had been bedeviled not just by *declining* state appropriations but also by *volatile* state appropriations. Because higher education is, for many states, the single greatest discretionary item, it tends to fluctuate the most when economic times are tough. K–12 education, Medicaid, prisons, pensions, and critical state services bear fixed costs regardless of the economic climate, but in recessions state income tax revenues plummet at the same time that unemployment insurance payments go up. State universities, the odd ones out, must therefore serve as a buffer. Yet, by their very nature, universities have to plan for the long-term future. Tenure-track faculty positions, academic degree programs, library collections, and research and information technology infrastructure are all predicated on time horizons measured in decades, and, in the case of campus buildings and architectural master plans, in centuries.

In direct response to this conundrum, the New Partnership offered a solution that was both elegantly simple and deliriously bold. This financial component, rather than its more conventional ideas for governance or accountability, formed the plan's most creative but also most controversial element. The white paper proposed that the entire state appropriation to the University—an amount that fluctuated significantly but historically ranged from $44 million to $75 million—be converted into debt service on a massive new public bond. The proceeds of that bond, backed by the full faith and credit of the State, would instantly generate an enormous nest egg for the University in the form of a flexible public endowment. Assuming a thirty-year maturity, similar to a home mortgage, a simple calculation at prevailing interest rates revealed that merely by maintaining its low baseline level of state appropriations—roughly $60 million in constant, non-inflation-adjusted dollars—the State could raise an $800 million endowment for the University in year zero. As a condition, the University promised to raise an equal amount in matching funds from *private* benefactors, bringing the grand total to $1.6 billion. It would then live on the combined endowment earnings in perpetuity, spending the proceeds conservatively at the standard rate of 4 percent. If invested wisely at an expected return rate of 9 percent, the endowment would easily outpace inflation over time. Meanwhile, the State's financial commitment would sunset completely when the bond was paid off in thirty years.

It seemed too good to be true: without adding any new money, but simply promising to pay off a routine bond debt that, in real terms, would become easier over time and ultimately disappear entirely, the State could put its premier research university on a stable financial footing forever. To be sure, this came at the cost of a thorough privatization, in the form of turning over the University's entire financial future to the tender mercies of the high-finance sector—one whose era-defining failures to manage money prudently had just been illustrated by the Great Recession. But the numbers actually penciled out. Even in a decade bookended by the dot-com bust of 1999–2000 and the world financial crisis of 2008–9, two events that shook the stock markets, a well-managed endowment would have produced *more* reliable funding than what the State legislature had appropriated during these same years.[8]

One small catch was locating some donor or donors with $800 million to spare. The Hat assured legislators and the public that this was the easy part of the job. Everyone assumed that he had the Big Donor and perhaps others waiting in the wings with checkbooks in hand. Concern therefore focused on what restrictions this or other benefactors might impose as preconditions for their donations, as private philanthropists (quite appropriately) do about 90 percent of the time. The New Partnership's scheme, after all, depended on the endowment being fungible: on its proceeds being used, say, to retrofit underground steam pipes and not just to put donors' names on fancy new buildings. The whole point of private philanthropy is to augment and enhance the core academic and administrative functions that are supposed to be supported by public funding and student tuition. To be sure, even if strings were attached to the private half of the endowment, the public half—the proceeds from the State's bond—would still be available for any appropriate purpose. And in theory, when private donations *can* be used for baseline operating expenses, for example, to pay for faculty and research facilities in marquee programs, they free up other funds to be used elsewhere, including in mundane, overlooked, underfunded corners of the university. None of this was made clear at the time, however. Regardless of what one suspected about the motivations of donors or the machinations of university leaders, free-floating anxieties about privatization ensured that public control of University finances seemed, as a matter of principle, about to be lost.

A bigger problem was how to ensure that the University remained accountable to the State. It seemed to many skeptical legislators that having secured a hefty $1.6 billion endowment, the institution would have every incentive to take the money and run. To allay such fears, the New Partnership promised two forms of robust public oversight. First, the University would be governed by a local autonomous Board of Trustees that, while assigned to one institution alone and not to the entire set of state universities, would nonetheless be publicly appointed by the governor and would bear fiduciary responsibility for upholding the University's public mission in service to the State. Not only that, but the local trustee board would also be subject to a higher coordinating board, likewise publicly appointed, overseeing higher education statewide. The coordinating board would focus on broad educational outcomes to benefit the State's citizenry and on ensuring that the local board—and any future boards that might be established at other state universities—remained accountable to policy goals determined by elected officials and government policy makers. In theory, this is how all public university boards work. In practice, public boards, like private ones, often include big donors, or at least figures with deep experience in the business world, who are therefore inclined to think in terms of profit and loss. Campus critics, suspicious of what seemed like a corporate-style board of directors, fastened on the question of whether faculty, students, and staff would hold seats on the board, and thereby be able to represent the University's internal constituencies. But that was hardly the biggest issue.

The second, more problematic, mechanism to ensure public accountability was a suite of proposed performance measures and goals. These would be crafted to ensure that the University remained committed to its public mission by, for example, remaining accessible and affordable to the State's citizens, contributing to its economic growth and workforce development, articulating its academic offerings with community colleges and regional universities to ease interinstitutional student transfers, and generally maintaining a full range of high-quality education and research programs. The New Partnership white paper held up the University of Virginia as a model public institution whose oversight board had recently adopted just such an approach. The whole issue of performance funding incentives—pegging state appropriations not simply to student enrollment headcounts but to measurable goals and quantifiable outcomes—has been debated for decades. That said, the underdevelopment of accountability mechanisms was the weakest aspect of the whole New Partnership proposal.

The University's Academic Council, a faculty body independent of the administration, was invited to weigh in on the scheme. Its report critiqued accountability metrics in its otherwise positive evaluation of the New Partnership. "We live in an age of accountability," it observed, in which policy makers and the public were no longer willing to trust that universities, their administrators, and their faculty were spending their money and time wisely, even in the core missions of teaching and research. Yet many worried that attempts to quantify these activities and attach incentives and imperatives to numerical results "will force us to measure things we cannot or should not measure."[9] This was about a decade after the Bush administration's No Child Left Behind Act of 2001, which promoted intrusive forms of accountability in K–12 education, specifically a fixation on standardized test scores. This proved so controversial that the act was gutted by bipartisan agreement in 2015. Yet by this time "key performance metrics" as well as other, customarily numerical, indicators of productivity and impact had gained currency in higher education. A private firm, Academic Analytics, had been founded in 2005 by ex-university administrators to provide data and consulting services to fellow administrators hoping to benchmark their universities' performance against others. The experience of other countries, however, notably the United Kingdom, offered abundant evidence that publicly established accountability metrics often create perverse incentives that cause institutions, and even individual faculty, to tailor their teaching practices and research agendas to whatever quantitative criteria are being evaluated and tested.[10] Such concerns were well-founded by 2011 in the United States as well.

The Hat was just as confident that the University would stack up well by whatever set of metrics the State cared to establish as he was that $800 million in private donations could be reaped in short order. "I don't really think that the state is likely to come up with silly metrics. And anything that's not silly, we're already measuring ourselves six ways from Sunday."[11] But the problem of accountability threatened to unravel the New Partnership. Aside from the vague implication that admonitions from on high would suffice to hold the University to its public commitments, the mechanisms of enforcement were hardly articulated at all. A draft legislative bill to enact the New Partnership did envision the use of "outcome-based" benchmarks rather than procedurally prescriptive micromanagement. A passing reference to "incentives" that could be used to encourage compliance, or punish failure, implied that there would be extra money available to steer local boards from the central perch of a coordinating commission, and in significant enough dollar amounts to influence the plans and behaviors of university administrators. But the notion of budgetary sweeteners contravened the proposed deal's central promise, which was to fix the State's appropriations at a constant low to moderate level and then to take its hands off of university governance almost entirely.

Accountability, in short, entailed a catch-22. Any scheme that was robust enough to satisfy the State had to have enough teeth to compel adherence to centrally determined policy goals, and any scheme that was robust enough to accomplish *that* objective would entail a level of intrusion into the University's teaching, research, and daily operations that was precisely what its leaders were trying to resist. But the New Partnership did not engage this challenge thoughtfully, either from the perspective of academic administrators within institutions or from that of policy makers overseeing them from outside.

Despite its flaws—sketchy in places, painted in broad strokes in others, and with some critical gaps unfilled—the New Partnership was both bolder and more realistic than the two alternatives on the table in the first decade of the 2000s. The first such alternative was the State Board's own proposal to convert the six state universities, plus the central bureaucracy that oversaw them, from a "state agency" into a formal "public university system."[12] That proposal's diagnosis of higher education's predicament aligned in many ways with The Hat's: given that State appropriations ranked so low in funding per student compared to other states, the least the legislature could do, if it was still intent on starving higher education for cash, was to cut the red tape. He who fails to pay the piper ought not presume to call the tune.

The State Board was right to point a finger at legislative micromanagement. At that time, it took 6,300 line items in the state budget to fund universities, in contrast to the undifferentiated block grants that the K–12 and community college systems enjoyed. These and other restrictions, on such mundane matters as procurement and risk insurance, needlessly fettered state universities' operational latitude. Worse, by lumping the universities in with other state agencies, the State could and often did divert student tuition payments to backstop budget holes in other state agencies entirely unrelated to education. It also collected, in its general fund, the substantial investment interest generated by all that tuition sitting in the bank. The State Board's proposal specified that tuition and tuition interest would be kept entirely within the university system. Finally, the new system would enjoy a range of major financial powers—to issue public bonds, initiate capital projects, and set tuition rates—all without legislative meddling. In exchange, it would enter into biennial performance compacts with the state government, replacing micromanagement with a small set of universally agreed-upon goals, such as boosting graduation rates and ensuring access to state citizens, while leaving the system free to reach them in its own way.

The State Board objected to the New Partnership because it focused only on one university and ignored the collective fate of the other five state schools. Indeed, one of the University's openly acknowledged goals had been to prevent the State Board from robbing Peter to pay Paul, by redistributing student tuition revenues from the (relatively) wealthy research institutions to the (undeniably) underfunded regional schools. That problem went back at least to the 1990s, when student tuition money and state appropriations were pooled together and then redistributed formulaically to individual institutions. Income redistribution, as any critic of socialism might note, stoked resentment, poisoned morale, and robbed local university leaders of incentives to improve their home campuses. That redistributive funding model was duly replaced around 1997 with the opposite model: a formula that ensured money would follow the students to whichever institutions they enrolled at. But it proved difficult to give the popular institutions enough new funds to meet student demand, and it was even harder, for political reasons, to claw money back from declining campuses in a zero-sum world.[13]

In short, before the New Partnership proposal came along in 2010, no one had any credible solutions to the underlying problem of public disinvestment. All the State Board's proposal could offer was to rearrange the bureaucratic deck chairs. Inasmuch as many other states had long since emancipated their public university systems from official state agency status, the State Board's proposal was already a generation or more behind the times. It offered a tepid, conservative response to the acute fiscal challenges and demographic pressures looming after the Great Recession. Politically, it appeared flat-footed and almost willfully obtuse next to the sexy New Partnership and its influential backers.

At the other extreme, the governor, like several other "education governors" of the time, issued a comprehensive bid to remake all of education in the State from top to bottom. To his credit, he had realized that the greatest educational problems hobbling the State's citizens pertained not to higher education but rather arose in early childhood, among deprived and underprivileged preschoolers. Thus instead of reforming only "K–12" education, he proposed that educators and policy makers all begin talking about "P-20": that is, including Pre-K (toddler care) as a run-up to kindergarten, but also, somewhat chillingly, lashing a struggling K–12 system to a still viable higher education system, not only at the undergraduate (years 13–16) but also the graduate school (years 17–20) levels. The seamless integration touted by the P-20 scheme seemed Orwellian, or at least counterproductive, given that U.S. universities still lead the world while America's K–12 education system notoriously underperforms systems in many far less wealthy countries in the developed world.

Those qualms aside, the governor's hope was simply to get most everyone through at least some college. Another catchy slogan, the "40-40-20" formula, enshrined into law as a formal goal of state government, held that by 2025, 40 percent of the State's adults should have a four-year bachelor's degree and 40 percent a two-year associate's degree, with the remaining 20 percent holding just a high school diploma. A plenipotentiary Education Board, run by a corporate-style Chief Education Officer, was established to orchestrate it all. Achievement compacts between the State and educational systems at all levels would spell out goals, promises, resource commitments, and evaluative metrics for everyone to see, while otherwise granting local boards and institutions ample operational freedom. Local trustee boards of the sort pushed by The Hat were most definitely possible under such a scheme. Governance would be at once "tight and loose": tight in its high expectations and high-stakes funding formulas, and loose in its low degree of managerial interference and local micromanagement.[14]

Perhaps sincerely, perhaps opportunistically, The Hat vocally aligned his plan with the governor's. There was nothing in the New Partnership that was incompatible with the overarching 40-40-20 vision. Indeed the governor's proposed achievement compacts, even though they too remained hopelessly sketchy, delivered precisely the accountability regime that The Hat had failed to spell out.[15] As it turned out, however, the whole scheme collapsed a few years later when the governor was forced to resign for steering lucrative state job opportunities to his long-term romantic partner (the same person who had once given the University faculty a tour of the governor's quarters and introduced them to his dog). The all-powerful Education Board expired a few years later.[16]

Nonetheless, the energy and idealism invested in the 40-40-20 goal turned out to be a political godsend at just the right time. It bought precious breathing room for The Hat's ideas to mature during the months and years after he was cashiered by the State Board. Hoisting a protective umbrella over the University's ongoing campaign for autonomy, the now ex-governor's commitment to rethinking education, and investing hopes, if not actual dollars, in college degree completion, allowed subsequent University presidents to cast independent governance precisely as a service to the State and its people rather than as an abandonment of public accountability and a public mission.

PRIVATIZATION AND PUBLIC ACCOUNTABILITY

How well did the New Partnership stack up as a diagnosis of the problems of public accountability and a remedy against the specter of privatization—on a nationwide level? That issue was a chief focus of debate in the 2010s among both concerned laypeople and higher education scholars. Contributors to that debate enunciated at least three basic views of the situation: that states had tragically abdicated responsibility for higher education, that states had retained and perhaps even improved their oversight abilities despite disinvestment, and that the whole issue was beside the point because universities had long since adapted to the new climate and accepted semiprivatization as the new normal.

Public Disinvestment

Christopher Newfield, perhaps the leading scholar in the rising field of "critical university studies," cast his own institution, the University of California, as an exemplary illustration of the first view: that public disinvestment is a disaster. Since the 1960s and the establishment of its world-famous Master Plan, California has served as *the* beacon of public higher education not only across the United States but around the world. Yet it had committed an epochal "great mistake" by starving its universities financially since the 1990s. Newfield identified five distinct trends fueling privatization both in California and to varying degrees nationwide: the shift from state support to ever-higher student tuition, the outsourcing of university functions to for-profit vendors, a shift in control from legislators and policy makers to wealthy private philanthropists, an abandonment of a substantive commitment to the university's public mission, and a redefinition of the educated person as a purely economic agent intent on maximizing their own human capital (rather than, say, seeking learning for its own sake—or as a means of participating in democratic citizenship).[17] Underlying it all was the selfsame ideology that had led to the Reagan-era dismantling of the American welfare state: a society-wide "risk shift" that converted public services into privately borne gambles: opportunities, such as investing in a college education, that could either pay off handsomely or not for individual consumers.[18]

Nationwide between 2007 and 2012—just before and after the Great Recession—per capita state funding for higher education declined by 23 percent nationwide, and tuition sticker prices rose even more, by 27 percent. But state disinvestment from higher education is a generations-long problem ultimately traceable to the citizen tax revolts that swept California and other states starting in the late 1970s. Typically through ballot initiatives that kneecapped government revenues, electoral tax and expenditure limitations have been shown to account for more than 50 percent of the decline in state appropriations in the last decades of the twentieth century. Admittedly, during the Great Recession states did increase their aid to financially needy students, but federal need-based aid, in the form of Pell Grants, had to increase even faster to compensate for the recession's adverse impact on state support.[19] In 2010, federal support surpassed state support per student for the first time in decades. This was due in part to Pell Grants earmarked for low-income students but also to subsidized loans and generous tax write-offs targeted at middle- and upper-middle-class families.[20] The steady increase in federal support over these decades has, in effect, liberated state governments—the one place where the costs of public universities can be directly confronted and regulated—from having to rein in tuition hikes. Instead, it foists the problem upon consumers in the form of student loan debt. Risk shift has taken other forms too, notably in the popularity of college savings (529) plans that took off during the 1990s stock market boom, which rely on a combination of parental self-discipline and investment performance to grow nest eggs for children as they mature into college. Again, risk shift, from public services to privately borne obligations (and opportunities), has been a hallmark of the broader dismantling of the U.S. welfare state since the 1980s.[21]

Performance Funding

An alternative view concedes that, although the adverse effects of public disinvestment are undeniable, states remain able to steer their universities and university systems and hold them publicly accountable through various technocratic governance mechanisms. The problem of public universities being short of money is nothing new after all. If anything, the financial leverage borne of scarcity *magnifies* states' abilities to command certain outcomes from higher education institutions. Ever since the recessions of the 1970s, policy makers have experimented with "performance funding" schemes as a superior alternative to the standard budgeting model, namely, handing over a fixed sum of money for each enrolled student, relying on a thicket of bureaucratic regulations to spell out "do's and don't's," and hoping that the money gets spent wisely.[22] The creative use of economic incentives to coax universities into competition for state funding leverages private capitalism's greatest tool, the quest for money, to promote identifiable public goods and values—at least in the view of performance funding's advocates.

The push for state-level performance funding has come in two major waves. The first, which began in the 1980s but crested in the 1990s at the height of "neoliberal" policy making in public management, added rather modest icing to a base-budget cake that otherwise remained tied to per-student enrollment formulas and political haggling. The second wave, which resulted from the Great Recession, was marked by much higher financial stakes and baked performance goals and monetary incentives right into universities' budgetary bottom lines. In neither period, however, has the measurable impact of performance funding schemes been clear or unambiguous.[23]

There are several reasons for the limitations of this approach. When it comes to student outcomes such as degree completion, small cash incentives ranging from 1 percent to 5 percent of overall university budgets are drowned out by the much larger compositional effect of incoming students' prior academic preparation. A study in one large state system found that student outcomes were the same whether performance funding had been introduced or not. Accountability metrics, when they are well-publicized among faculty and staff, do sometimes have a salutary effect on internal institutional cultures when academic policies and student services are retooled to meet states' policy goals. But knowledge about policy makers' performance expectations, much less the capacity to act on that knowledge, is highly uneven within and across individual universities. Then there are the unintended consequences: "creaming" the best students by only admitting those likely to succeed, turning underprivileged students away, and even diluting degree requirements to get more graduates through the system—not to mention diverting precious administrative resources toward the complex bureaucratic compliance infrastructure required to track the data that states ask for in the first place. In any case, flagships typically have the least trouble meeting statewide performance goals because they typically enjoy the pick of the best students and possess the best infrastructure to support them. It is the lesser regional institutions and community colleges that suffer the biggest performance gaps—and have the fewest resources with which to act.

Above all, there is the question of the political will to sustain performance funding long enough to condition future expectations. Since Tennessee led the way in 1979, thirty-eight states have experimented with performance funding. Of these, fully twenty-four discontinued those experiments, and twenty-two of those subsequently *reinstated* them. This whipsaw effect, not surprisingly, owed far more to constant shifts in political support and party control in state legislatures than to any sustained attempt to learn and apply the lessons of policy experimentation. Although performance funding remains popular, the jury is still out, after rigorous studies by economists, about its actual efficacy. Just as the New Partnership was tied to a doomed State-level reform scheme, political volatility remains the enemy of the long-term strategic planning that universities rely on, and volatility is a chronic problem of higher education politics in the fifty states. The time horizons required for performance funding to have a lasting effect on the behavior of universities, which plan for the long term, are simply longer than the democratic election cycle, which is (and perhaps ought to be) centered on immediate policy and political goals. Layered atop the systemic instability of higher education budgets as the wider economy bounces up and down, political fickleness renders performance funding a highly limited policy lever.

Adaptations to Privatization

From a policy perspective, the early 2000s were in many ways a lost decade before the flurry of public governance reform proposals of the 2010s, including the ones discussed here. In an epoch of fits and starts, public research universities have had several decades, starting with the tax revolts of the 1970s and continuing with the economic disruptions of the 1980s and 1990s—as in the case of the University of Michigan after the collapse of the automobile industry, or the University of California after the collapse of the aerospace industry—to adapt to a perennially straitened budgetary climate. Universities embraced a wide variety of privatization opportunities during these decades, sometimes strategically and sometimes like headless chickens.[24] Following the lead of private institutions, they mounted ambitious fund-raising campaigns, often in the billions of dollars. Master's programs for working professionals, business incubators and tech-transfer startups, licensing and franchising deals, retirement compensation incentives, real estate speculation, privatization of campus parking lots, and high school summer camps were but a few of the many external revenue streams they sought to tap into. Within institutions, resource-generating centers and institutes—because they are attractive to grant-making foundations, government agencies, and wealthy individuals—gained prestige and support relative to core academic departments and student services. And as chapter 2 shows in depth, many even applied the law of market competition to the internal budgeting of their own academic units.

Universities are inherently anarchic, decentralized organizations. They are as agile and opportunistic at the unit level as they are lumbering and conservative at the central level, and this is a key part of what makes them able to compete in the marketplace so successfully. But privatization only doubles down on this design feature by putting *money* on an increasingly level plane with *ideas* in internal competitions for administrative attention and financial support. The result, as two leading scholars observe, is "*more* anarchy and *less* organization at a time when leaders are trying to pursue the opposite. . . . when policy makers are trying to hold leaders more accountable."[25] That said, despite adding to the confusion of already confusing institutions, privatization and its attendant side effects have had reassuringly little impact on macro-level priorities. Public institutions adapted to state disinvestment by making major changes to their *revenue*-seeking activities, but they typically made few or no changes to their *spending* patterns. Unlike businesses, which feed profit centers and starve money-losing subunits, universities use aggressive cross-subsidies to direct money from revenue-generating programs to those that are mission-critical but less lucrative. Even as they coped with the decline and fluctuation in public funding, they retained whatever mix of teaching, research, and public service commitments they had before the privatization trend began.[26] All this suggests that even without the heavy hand of the state, public-spiritedness is to a large extent built into the DNA of public universities.

What *did* change was that the public mission would henceforth be privately funded on what seems to be a permanent basis. Having ridden out the worst years of the Great Recession, public institutions, at least the strongest of them, welcomed the year 2013 as finally marking a budgetary turnaround, five years after the onset of the financial crisis. State funding cuts had abated by that time, even if support remained at prerecession levels. In the interim, universities stabilized their finances and largely ceased to impose extra educational costs on students, which they had done previously. A durable new model—a new normal—had been established in which student tuition would occupy a permanently greater share of public universities' revenue streams: a hefty rise of some 10 percentage points relative to the pre-2008 period. At the same time, degree productivity went up sharply, proving that universities were succeeding in moving their students through college. They were now spending more per student, not just to offset lost state revenues but to enhance critical student services such as advising and counseling.[27] Well-resourced public institutions also began to mimic their private counterparts by offsetting a high tuition sticker price with generous markdowns in the form of need-based scholarships funded from internal sources, including other full-paying students' tuition. The "high-tuition, high-aid" model amounts to a form of progressive taxation, particularly on wealthy out-of-state and international students, who pay much higher tuition rates to subsidize the in-state students whose own tuition had long since ceased to cover the actual cost of their education.

Private Philanthropy

What about philanthropy as an ostensible driver of privatization—and as a force threatening to warp or subvert public universities' public character? The academic literature on the subject is surprisingly underdeveloped given how strongly some in academia feel about it. On top of an intense suspicion that private benefactors somehow exert a sinister influence on universities behind the scenes, many fret over the alleged infiltration of corporate values and business management practices in institutions that ought to be motivated by nobler ideals than bottom-line calculations. Pressures to adopt corporate practices are real, but they have other causes, which I explore in subsequent chapters. To the extent that donors do exert a discernible direct influence on core educational and research missions, scholars of the subject generally regard it as a positive one.[28] The main challenge for most schools is that they *lack* wealthy benefactors, not that they have to bend over backward to manage their egos and demands.

Big donors do tend to favor projects and ideas aligned with power and prestige in American society generally—science, technology, medicine, the study of capitalism, and the quest for solutions to "wicked problems" such as climate change or global peace.[29] In contrast, humanistic and qualitative fields do sometimes suffer, but these subjects often have their own patrons, for example, to support the study of particular ethnic groups, their languages, and their histories. In any case, many of the antidemocratic, distorting, systemically corrupting effects of private giving on public values in *other* spheres of American life are mitigated by the historic autonomy and byzantine structures of decision-making prevalent within universities.[30]

One of the main reasons, probably the principal reason, universities engage in elaborate multiyear "strategic planning" exercises is precisely to avoid being led around by mercurial donors with eccentric interests. That way, they can instead anticipate larger-scale needs, commit them formally to writing, and rely on these plans to nudge eager benefactors toward the most effective and appropriate uses of their generosity. For all the eye-rolling that strategic plans provoke, they form an invaluable counterweight to individual donor predilections, whether selfish or altruistic. Only in the larger and more systematic form of "advocacy philanthropy" practiced by large and influential nonprofit foundations, an example of which is explored in chapter 6, can outside money really be said to have warped the priorities of American higher education as such. Even then, these new forms of philanthropy consistently push in the direction of greater, not less, public accountability and public-spiritedness.

THE UNIVERSITY UNFETTERED

After The Hat was fired, it was up to a string of four more presidents to salvage the New Partnership in some form or another.

First up was a nationally distinguished academic leader, one who had led flagship campuses in both of America's two largest states, and who just happened to be a former University dean who had recently retired back in the State. Next up was a short-timer who, to his credit, clinched final legislative approval for the long hoped for independent Board of Trustees, but who suddenly resigned one weekend in August and left town before hardly anyone noticed he was gone. After another interim, the fourth president since 2009 (including The Hat), President Five took the helm in 2015. The first real hire of the new Board, President Five went on to a successful seven-year run. The University's new trustee governance structure during his presidency accumulated a substantial track record that is now ripe for preliminary assessment.

In the end, what the University got was independence but not a lot of extra state money. After the new Board of Trustees was officially empowered in 2014, the biggest lingering question was whether private donors would finally step forward to fill the gap. Indeed, in the fall of 2016, as if on cue, the Big Donor and his wife donated half a billion dollars for a brand new minicampus, a cluster of sleek glass buildings dedicated to applied sciences and marketable research innovations, built across the street from the University's main campus. A skybridge was built to connect the two, and President Five always answered—before even being asked—that the skybridge concretized how the new campus would redound to the benefit of the old one. That prediction has yet to be borne out one way or another. Regardless, this gift, along with a second half-billion follow-up, remained for five years the single largest private donation to a public university in U.S. history.[31] It also unlocked tens of millions in state bonds and further private donations earmarked for the new campus. A separate $425 million megadonation from a different donor followed in 2022 for a separate applied-research minicampus one hundred miles away from the main campus.

To judge by these two massive gifts, private philanthropy did not directly benefit the University's main campus, where the lion's share of teaching and research are carried out. But neither did they undermine it, or the institution's broader public mission, in any identifiable way. Some do criticize marquee projects like these as distractions from core university priorities and traditional academic goals, whereas others point out that the luster and renown they bring have salutary knock-on effects across the institution, in somewhat the same way that pretty peacock feathers signify the robust good health of the underlying bird. Whatever the case, looking at the other thirty-three thousand people who donated to the University in a marquee year dispels most concerns about whether philanthropy is beneficial: in 2021–22, $172 million was raised for student scholarships and other direct support, $235 million for faculty and academic programs, and $138 million for capital construction projects.[32] Such numbers speak to the deep positive impact that accumulated small to midsized gifts can have on students and core academic functions. Whatever else independent governance does or does not accomplish, the assurance that donor money remains under the oversight of a local board of trustees, pledged to support a single institution, is a powerful causal explanation for the growth in philanthropic support—at least for those lucky public universities prominent enough to enjoy a strong donor pool.

A trickier question is whether, under President Five and the new Board, the original performance outcomes championed by the New Partnership, or for that matter its two rival plans, were being met. With the old governor out, and his Education Board a dead letter, a new Higher Education Coordinating Commission (HECC) had been established to carry the torch of the

40-40-20 target, hold universities' feet to the fire in meeting that target, and run interference with the State legislature to prevent each individual institution from lobbying politicians for its own special needs. The new oversight body adopted a set of focused strategic initiatives to promote key policy goals. These included diversity, equity, access, affordability, and seamless articulation for transfer students moving from one state university to another. True to form, it also put performance funding formulas in place to incentivize the state's universities to take those goals to heart.[33] But as I show in chapter 7, that scheme exhibited the same limitations that other performance funding mechanisms exhibit.

The University's official summary of the first five years of independent trustee governance does make a strong claim for having met the State's performance goals. It boasts a significant 10 percent jump in four-year graduation rates, a marked increase in the racial and ethnic diversity of the student body, a dramatic increase in the proportion of Pell-eligible (financially needy) students, and a reduction in student-instructor ratios. It also touted series of successes in faculty research and contributions to the state economy, goals that are not explicitly quantified by the HECC but nonetheless speak to the University's ongoing, and substantial, public contributions. On the financial side, the record is mixed but still strong. The proportion of in-state undergraduates, who almost became outnumbered during the years when the University recruited large cohorts of out-of-state and international students to balance the books, fell from 67 percent before stabilizing at around 55 percent—very low by the standards of many public flagships, but still a majority.[34] State appropriations recovered significantly starting in 2012, and although tuition continued to ratchet upward, the *rate* of tuition increase noticeably flattened for both in-state and out-of-state students.[35] The University still lagged its national peers significantly when it came to state funding per enrolled student, but it was not worse off than it was before in this regard: peer institutions in other states simply adapted as well.

Tellingly, the Board of Trustees' five-year retrospective mentions the HECC only once, in passing, a testament to the State's diminished policy-making influence.[36] The impressive progress the University made in meeting benchmarks of public access and public service was instead largely self-imposed: an institutional commitment that was the product of President Five's personal initiative, publicly announced near the beginning of his tenure.[37] But such a commitment was not mutually exclusive with the wise political calculation that exceeding the State's performance benchmarks voluntarily is a canny way to forestall any future attempt to bake them into budgetary funding formulas or bureaucratic oversight structures.

The bargain had paid off: private philanthropy *did* materialize in the 2010s and at the same time the public mission was maintained. None of this is to deny the complex interplay of forces, statewide and intrainstitutional, policy driven and market driven, that led to this record of achievements—nor to downplay the persistent gaps and inequities that may yet render it unsustainable in the medium to long term. An underlying question remains whether these successes can be attributed to independent trustee governance or instead reflected other factors, such as President Five's fund-raising skills, the Admissions Office's successful wooing of better-prepared students, or simply the rising tide of economic rebound that lifted all boats—state tax revenues, parental college-savings plans, and donors' stock portfolios alike—after the Great Recession. But in retrospect, one counterfactual remains clear: given that the State's wider policy goals—the ex-governor's ambitious P-20 and 40-40-20 schemes—never came to pass, any governance reform that stopped *short* of local institutional autonomy would likely have dragged the University down with the rest of that failed agenda. Sixty or seventy years ago, when state university systems were first established, that kind of grand policy making might have stood a chance. The California Master Plan, adopted in 1960, succeeded wildly, for all its flaws and compromises, in establishing the kind of integration that (until recent decades) brought research universities, regional universities, and community colleges under an overarching public mission. But in the 2010s and beyond, with the level of complexity that public policy must confront, master planning is no more likely to succeed in higher education than it is, say, in health care or K–12 schooling.

Today's policy makers, acting in a sprawling environment decentralized over fifty states, can at best ride the waves, but cannot command the tides. They can make their public institutions either more or less hospitable to the consumer market, whether by subsidizing tuition or by providing perks, amenities, and facilities to students, faculty, and staff. They can push for higher graduation rates, more ethnic diversity and economic opportunity, academic programs that serve particular industries or other workforce development priorities, or other worthy (or unworthy) objectives. They can even micromanage the curriculum, police faculty time, and curb academic freedom if they so choose. But states are severely limited in the extent to which they can prescribe particular policy goals, however farsighted, because each state is in competition with the other forty-nine. Decades of tinkering with governance structures—whether trustee boards are centralized or localized, or whether state-level bodies have "coordinating" or "governing" powers, or whether simple per-capita formulas or elaborate performance funding schemes are used to set budgets—have done little to change that basic equation.[38] Even when it comes to something as fundamental as setting tuition, which is a core policy concern in any state, policy makers have to contend with the law of supply and demand that often undermines their best intentions. Campus-level leaders know this firsthand, which is why they often find themselves talking past their state-level overseers, and not infrequently incurring their wrath.

Looking to the future, a number of preconditions must continue to hold for the new high-tuition model of higher education to work, and they are by no means guaranteed. The public, both parents and students, must continue to regard a college degree as conferring a unique advantage in career success and life satisfaction—despite its mounting costs. State policy makers must learn the lessons of prior policy experiments and forswear capricious attempts at technocratic micromanagement. The federal government must continue to subsidize student loans on a grand scale. And a transitory demographic dip in the cohort of college-going students must be ridden out.[39] These are among the preconditions that held during the years covered in chapter 2, on students' collective market power.

2

STUDENTS

Why must tuition keep rising, and how do we know the money is being well-spent?

Perhaps the most radical answer to the question posed in chapter 1 is that U.S. higher education has essentially *always* been privatized. With the signal exceptions of the Civil War and the Cold War, when state and federal governments made historic investments and grand strategic plans for public institutions, our system has always been a "perfect mess" of free market competition embracing both the private and public sectors.[1] America's oldest colleges and universities were, after all, private institutions, and even now the Harvards and Stanfords of the world set the standard for excellence for both fellow private universities and leading public ones, notably the various states' research flagships.

Over the last century or so, this lightly regulated free-for-all has somehow managed to produce the world's most diverse collection of higher education institutions—crowned, at the top, by some of its very finest. Every university, public or private, now competes with every other university to the extent that its resources, mission, and geographic catchment allow. This is because private consumers, in the form of students and their parents, shop for the best institutions that their resources, life goals, and geographic horizons allow. The scramble for marketable, career-ready credentials, the quest for higher social status, and the willingness to splurge for the intangible benefits of the classic college experience are what ultimately drive the system. The supply of eager consumers, and the demands they make on the institutions they patronize, are the issues that preoccupy campus leaders on a daily basis at both public and private institutions. This is why, at public ones, administrators often find themselves at loggerheads with state-level policy makers who often have other values at heart.

Students have very little formal power at any university. They come and go each year, they customarily defer to the authority of faculty and administrators, and even those who dedicate their years to activism, protest, or various good deeds seldom make a lasting imprint on their alma maters. But their understandable concern for a return on their investment gives students commanding informal power. Students' collective choices as market consumers, which are made manifest in the copious amounts in tuition and fees they (and their parents) pay and in the majors and degree programs that they choose, are the most important influences on institutional decision-making at all but the best-supported public universities and all but the best-endowed private ones. For the broad middle of U.S. higher education, the overall quality of a university thus bears a critical and direct relationship to what its student body, taken as a whole, thinks they are actually getting for their hard-earned money. That calculation stands at the heart of the question, broken into two parts, at the beginning of this chapter: why tuition keeps rising and how it gets spent. The best way to answer the first part is to start with the second: to follow the student's tuition dollar as it wends its way through the university and, after that, to explain why that dollar buys less and less each year.

I begin by looking at the budgeting system or "budget model" introduced by the University at the beginning of the decade to allocate and trace the flow of student tuition. Then I compare this system with similar budgeting schemes widely employed across American higher education. This examination unfurls a revealing series of questions about how some parts of the university subsidize others, how academic administrators continually readjust and rebalance those cross-subsidies, and what values, trade-offs, and decisions go into calibrating just how much and how often this occurs. Only then does it become clear why rising personnel costs—specifically for the highly educated professionals the university produces, not just for the economy at large but for the higher education industry itself—are as much a feature of the system as a bug. That explains why tuition inexorably rises as university leaders try to balance the competing ideals of excellence and efficiency that this odd feature produces.

Throughout the chapter I focus on undergraduates as opposed to graduate or professional school students because undergraduates are far and away the prime concern of parents, policy makers, and the general public when it comes to debates about the affordability of higher education. I also confine my attention to tuition proper—what students pay to take classes and earn degrees—as opposed to fees, whether for housing, dining, health services, the recreation center, the student union, or computing services. Although fees, too, constitute a hefty and rising chunk of students' out-of-pocket expenses, most fee-based university services are budgetarily treated as "auxiliaries," which means they are separately accounted for and required to live within their own means, and their costs are more transparently pegged to the laws of supply and demand.[2] Finally, I bracket off the common practice of tuition discounting, pervasive in private institutions and increasingly common in public ones, whereby the advertised sticker price for any given student might be dramatically lowered by internal scholarships awarded for merit or need.[3] Attending instead to the headline tuition rate—even though this conceals the substantial bargain that many students receive in practice—provides a truer picture of the University's "general fund": the giant combined pool of student tuition and state appropriations that pays for the academic and educational core and its supporting infrastructure. Here is where the trade-offs between state dollars and student dollars, public goals and private interests, get worked out in practice.

A detailed examination of those trade-offs shows that university administrators do a remarkably conscientious job of allocating limited resources to academic priorities. Furthermore, it is the pursuit of academic excellence itself that drives those costs ever upward. Unexpectedly, spending practices at public universities turn out to be fully consonant with their academic missions, and with their commitment to stewarding tuition money to maximize students' return on investment.

HOW TUITION FLOWS

In July 2010, enjoying an influx of new students who streamed in with the Great Recession, the University introduced what it called the "New Budget Model" to get a better handle on its rapidly changing finances. The purpose of the budget model was to allocate undergraduate tuition more transparently and more predictably to the seven separate schools and colleges that formed the University's academic core, and at the same time to buffer that core against the ongoing volatility of state funding.[4] These schools and colleges included, in addition to professional programs in business, law, education, journalism, music, and design, a very large College of Arts and Sciences.[5] The College was itself subdivided into divisions for humanities, social sciences, and natural sciences, each of them individually larger than most of the professional schools and, as a whole, constituting anywhere from one-half to two-thirds of the entire academic operation, depending on whether one counted students' majors, the courses they took, or the budget dollars that paid for it all. For several years, the New Budget Model proved superb at distributing resources and delegating responsibility to the Schools for absorbing the growing student population. By the end of the decade, however, problems crept in as enrollments started to plateau, and it was ultimately abandoned as unworkable.

The New Budget Model

The core promise of the New Budget Model was to distribute undergraduate tuition on a purely formulaic basis to the academic units where undergraduates were being taught. This replaced the so-called incremental (aka "baseline plus begging") funding model typical of both the University and many of its peers, whereby each year preliminary budget drafts began with the previous year's amounts, and each School's dean lobbied the provost—the chief academic officer—to fund new projects, or, more commonly, simply to keep pace with the rising cost of recruiting and retaining high-quality faculty and staff. Such discussions had always involved careful scrutiny of enrollment figures—such as the number of credit hours, majors, degrees, and other indicators of productivity within each School—but they also included a large, subjective, political element. Academic judgments and values, after all, could never be entirely reduced to bottom-line calculations.

The New Budget Model replaced all that; its foundation was the 50-30-20 rule. This meant that the University would henceforth take the giant pot of undergraduate tuition money that it received and distribute 50 percent of it to individual Schools based on each one's share of overall undergraduate student credit hours.[6] Because students were charged tuition based strictly on the number of student credit hours they signed up for, this chunk of money had the virtue of tying *money* to *education* in a direct arithmetical relationship.[7] Out-of-state and in-state students did pay radically different amounts, but the University in effect split the difference between them. This enabled Schools to treat all students the same and not to worry about whether their courses and programs disproportionately served residents or nonresidents of the State.

The second half of the giant tuition pot was split into two unequal parts: 30 percent in proportion to the number of undergraduate majors each School enrolled, and 20 percent in proportion to the number of bachelor's degrees it produced. The thinking went that a School served its majors not merely by teaching them courses but by offering them other services, such as advising, enrichment, and community. So too, it should be rewarded not only for recruiting majors and pocketing their tuition money but also for seeing them through to graduation. The 30 percent and 20 percent components provided the Schools with an incentive not just to woo students and leave them to their own devices but to monitor, support, and guide them to successful completion of their college degrees.

One major challenge was that the College ended up massively subsidizing the other Schools under this formula. Because it offered the lion's share of the core general education curriculum, which required humanities, social sciences, and natural sciences courses of all undergraduates, the College prospered under the credit-hour-based half of the budget formula, but it suffered when the other half was distributed based instead on majors and degrees. For sound academic reasons, the professional schools also relied on the College for other foundational courses. Business majors had to take math and economics to improve their quantitative skills, and journalism majors were required to take history and literature to improve their writing. By pocketing a premium based on the number of majors and degrees, those professional schools profited disproportionately relative to the raw amount of instruction they offered. Conversely, even with the special boost offered by the "30-20" part of the scheme, others of the professional schools, notably the law school, lost money under the new formula.

As a noble fudge, a "general fund supplement" was introduced to hold all Schools harmless and spare any of them a debilitating budgetary shock, at least at the outset. This supplement was set at the exact amount required to offset the budget cut that the new 50-30-20 formula would otherwise have dictated in year one of the new model. With that number then fixed, only in *future* years of the scheme would the Schools win or lose money based on the incremental changes in academic activities incentivized by the formula, namely, offering more popular courses, signing up more majors, and graduating more students. Tellingly, the College's general fund "supplement" was a large *negative* number—on the order of $30 million in the mid-2010s, roughly $3,000 per major—which made clear the exact amount that it (plus a couple of other moneymaking Schools) was being required to cross-subsidize the less lucrative ones. This was not a surprise. Cross-subsidies are pervasive in higher education (as indeed they are in the business world) and are fully defensible for educational reasons; the general fund supplement simply made these transparent for the first time.

One ingenious feature of the New Budget Model was its attempt to tackle the problem, or at least the perception, of administrative bloat, which is the subject of chapter 4. Because executive administrators at the central level ultimately get to decide how tuition money is spent, it is often claimed that they starve core academic units to fund their own pet projects or, worse, to line their own pockets. Because aggregated tuition pools are so large at the central level as opposed to the School, much less at the departmental level—in the hundreds of millions of dollars—it does not even require a particularly conniving, dishonest, or weak central administrator to allow general fund revenues to be eaten away over time on perfectly worthy campus-level initiatives. To defeat this problem of moral hazard and impose fiscal discipline on themselves, the architects of the New Budget Model conceptualized central university costs—whether for utilities, office space, the library, student services, building maintenance, information technology, or HR and payroll operations—as a *tax* that it would levy on each individual School: initially a 28 percent flat levy based on the money that School actually spent.

The central administration received its own general fund supplement on the same hold-harmless principle as the Schools. Logically enough, it also lay claim to the entire appropriation from the state legislature to help fund central university functions and services. Together, then, the state appropriation, the taxes remitted by Schools, and the net of their general fund supplements (notionally zero, but fluctuating in practice) were pooled together into the master university-level general fund to support all manner of central services and facilities. This decision shielded the Schools from chronic volatility in state funding by having the University absorb these fluctuations centrally, where the problem could be more easily managed at scale.

The New Budget Model was criticized for failing to directly support research, graduate education, or interdisciplinary teaching and research.[8] Central planners were also chastised for hiking the internal tax rate from 28 percent to 35 percent, allegedly to feed their own bureaucratic ambitions, but in reality to compensate for an even larger than expected cut in state appropriations, plus various unanticipated rainy-day expenses.[9] Even under the most auspicious circumstances, it is difficult to peg the ideal mix of central and local expenses in advance, much less in the volatile aftermath of an epic recession.

The biggest negative effect of the New Budget Model was not a failure to plan but an unintended consequence of its own explicit intent. In making budgets and cross-subsidies transparent for the first time, it encouraged faculty and department heads to adopt for themselves the managerial profit motive that they incorrectly attributed to central administrators. Some were overly anxious about losing students and others were overly aggressive about marketing to them, but across the spectrum people assumed incorrectly that the whole institution had now been retooled around the 50-30-20 formula. This was especially true in the College, which had never entertained applying that formula internally to its own academic departments. The College's deans naturally scrutinized enrollment trends and routed new resources to areas of greatest demand, just as they had always done. But they made no formulaic decisions to tie crude enrollment figures to, for example, decisions to hire new faculty. Even though the College's own budget was determined by formulaic means, each of its dozens of departmental budgets continued to be hammered out through a traditional blend of qualitative and quantitative factors, academic judgments, and political negotiations. In effect, College deans acted on the principle of "from each according to their ability, to each according to their need."

It is only a slight exaggeration to say that the University's largest unit, comprising half to two-thirds of its academic mission, functioned as a communist economy within the capitalist competition among Schools inaugurated by the New Budget Model.

Responsibility Center Management

The New Budget Model gained national recognition for "unleashing the deans" to behave more entrepreneurially.[10] But the University had hardly invented this scheme out of whole cloth. The budget allocation philosophy called Responsibility Center Management (RCM), of which the New Budget Model was one instantiation, is in fact pervasive in academia. The basic idea behind RCM is to devolve responsibility to local units, in this case schools and colleges, by making their access to resources transparent and predictable. This includes carefully calibrating incentives at the central level to encourage frontline administrators, principally academic deans and department heads, to act in ways that support institution-wide values and priorities. Descended from corporate management techniques pioneered in the mid-1900s by behemoths DuPont and General Motors, RCM also closely resembles the famously decentralized "every tub on its own bottom" approach employed at Harvard since the early 1800s, wherein each separate college and school within that university functions as much as possible as its own financially autonomous domain. Spreading in the 1970s among other elite private universities, notably the University of Pennsylvania, RCM leapt to the public sector when Penn's provost moved to Indiana University. Adopted there in the 1980s, it has since caught on across the country, including at major public flagships in Michigan, Minnesota, and Virginia.

For public institutions especially, RCM offers a way to cope with declining state investment and harness other revenue, mainly but not exclusively student tuition, more efficiently and strategically. It also satisfies demands for accountability and transparency that come from policy makers and public watchdogs, including universities' own faculty members. RCM budget formulas force cost-benefit conversations about money and values instead of sweeping them under the rug, as is often the default temptation in higher education. Prematurely dismissed around 2000 as the latest in a series of "management fads" dating back to the technocratic social engineering experiments of the Kennedy and Johnson administrations, RCM's staying power more than two decades further on suggests that the trend is here to stay.[11]

The University's New Budget Model, which might be dubbed a hybrid variant, departed from classical RCM in two key ways. First, it only incorporated direct costs for faculty, staff, and miscellaneous services and office supplies because the University itself funded academic infrastructure and most central services. In contrast, classical RCM models attribute indirect costs for overhead, infrastructure, and at least some central services as much as possible to local units. Funding formulas might, for example, require metering departmental electricity usage and setting campus-wide rates for office space rental based on square footage, architectural quality, and even views of the campus quad. Not surprising, these can be tedious, error-prone calculations that are often subject to political haggling as each unit lobbies for special needs that are not adequately captured by the algorithm du jour. The University had avoided this problem by instituting a flat tax for overhead, and at a significantly higher rate than some peer institutions. It thereby recouped a large reserve of money for use by the center. That decision put space experts in charge of space planning, and technology experts in charge of technology planning, for example, rather than letting the invisible hand of market-savvy (but in practice uninformed) academic deans hold sway, as is the case at purer RCM institutions. To return to the analogy: if the University were a European country, it would be Denmark or Sweden—still capitalist, but with a heavy dose of socialistic central planning.

Second, on the more "capitalist" end of the spectrum, many RCM models actively incentivize local academic units to cultivate external revenue sources *besides* student tuition, by mounting their own marketing and recruitment operations rather than passively relying on central university admissions and communications offices to contact and woo prospective students. This might take a simple or even banal form, like a moneymaking summer camp or a conference and events series. At more ambitious universities, a school or college with an applied or pre-professional bent, for example in data science or counseling psychology, might launch a new professional master's degree, perhaps delivered in online format to cater to working adults, and then harvest the profits from that enterprise to fund faculty research travel, new computers, minority student scholarships, or any other worthy goal. The "eat what you kill" ethos of RCM in this turbocharged form is where the capitalistic core of this budget methodology becomes most evident. This is particularly so in private institutions that are already culturally conditioned to compete within the educational marketplace. But it is increasingly popular at public institutions as they scramble for new sources of income to compensate for declining state appropriations and the limits of what they can raise by hiking already sky-high tuition rates.

Whether pure or mixed in its expression, the capitalist ethos is what puts off many observers about RCM and other forms of incentive-based budget modeling. In this sense, RCM is to intra-institutional management what performance funding, as analyzed in chapter 1, is to institutions' external management by states. It is of a piece with an entire era of neoliberalism in public management: a decades-long campaign to leverage financial incentives and other quantifiable performance metrics, in tandem with the entrepreneurialism of faculty and mid-level academic administrators, using the mechanisms of an elaborately constructed market competition, all to serve idealistic, public-minded, and typically quite traditional academic and educational goals.

To be sure, cautionary tales abound of the perverse outcomes RCM has been said to generate. A college or department might launch large, crowd-pleasing general education courses to capture student enrollments; it might dumb down its own admission requirements to avoid driving off tuition-paying students; it might shy away from an intellectually valuable cross-disciplinary collaboration for fear of having to split the proceeds with a rival unit; it might hire cheaper and less qualified adjunct instructors to keep from spending money on expensive tenure-track faculty; it might inflate class sizes and student-faculty ratios; or it might develop its own in-house computer service center that competes with, and duplicates, central IT functions. It might even assess and rank faculty members based on their individual profitability rather than other, less monetized measures of teaching or research quality (as one public university in Texas notoriously tried to do[12]). All of these are documented dangers from several decades of experiments with RCM budgeting. Then again, many such behaviors long predated RCM; and for every horror story that RCM creates, there are untold successes that go unreported.

Harder to measure are the deleterious effects RCM has on morale, values, and institutional climate. Even laudable efforts at transparency and intellectual honesty, which after all stand at the heart of any university's academic values, can have the unintended effect of warping academic discussions and intensifying professional rivalries and resentments. Publicizing winners and losers, "profit" and "loss" centers, cannot help but create invidious distinctions of status and prestige, even if deans and administrators protest in the same breath that underlying intellectual and academic values can never be fully quantified, much less measured in dollars. Then there is the simple problem of misunderstanding and willful confusion. At the local level, many faculty who hear through the grapevine about RCM models fret that each individual department will not only be evaluated but also funded using the same formulaic criteria that are applied to schools and colleges at large. A needlessly skittish department might worry, for example, that by discontinuing a well-enrolled course for valid academic reasons, it might lose its Xerox machine; conversely, an inappropriately entrepreneurial department might dilute its undergraduate major requirements in a misguided attempt to capture more money for faculty travel. Such a tight coupling of academic decision-making and financial decision-making is rarely the case even in pure RCM implementations.

 RCM has proven difficult to implement even as it has been refined and popularized iteratively over several generations. To maintain the model long enough to reset expectations and change institutional cultures requires a level of sustained financial discipline that many universities find hard to pull off. Among other things, it requires that local units be allowed to keep the surpluses they generate and, conversely, be forced to make up any deficits they might run. Quite often, however, unanticipated needs at the central level compel universities to "sweep" hard-earned carry-forward surpluses from departments, which breeds cynicism and enmity. So, too, they often have to bail out academic programs that have fallen on hard times, whether through fiscal mismanagement or no fault of their own.

The keys to success, as judged by prominent examples such as the University of Michigan, are large size and lots of resources, which provide an ample buffer for the kinks to be ironed out, and—perhaps the most decisive factor—a culture of collegiality, cooperation, and problem-solving that allows academic administrators at all levels to override crude incentives and collaborate on shared institutional goals rather than besetting one another like profit-maximizing slaves to an artificial formula.[13] Scholars of incentive-based budgeting agree that academic administrators need, above all, to intone the ongoing importance of academic values and to show through their actions—not least the design of RCM budgeting formulas themselves—that they are willing to implement those values in practice. Merely enacting a new RCM scheme, even a successful one imported wholesale from another institution, is insufficient. The "care and feeding of the monster," as one scholar puts it, is a never-ending task.[14] The most durable and effective systems, such as the New Budget Model developed by the University, are hybrid approaches.

WHAT TUITION BUYS

Whatever its strengths and weaknesses, a cardinal virtue of RCM budgeting is the exercise in transparent accounting that it makes possible. This is the exercise to which I now turn, with the aim of exploring whether student tuition is spent wisely or wastefully.[15] To track the flow of tuition dollars at the University during the 2010s, let us begin with a thought experiment. Imagine that each individual academic department, whether history, physics, sociology, music, or accounting, is its own freestanding business enterprise. In this scenario, the University is simply a large shopping mall with many departmental storefronts, ranging from small jewelry carts to midsized clothing boutiques to big-box retailers. Each one runs its business by selling credit hours at a preset campus-wide rate, collecting tuition directly from the students it teaches, paying its own faculty and office staff out of that revenue, and using what remains for office supplies, computers, and incidental expenses such as the annual graduation ceremony. But first it has to fork over a large percentage of its gross income to the university—call it "rent and taxes"—to pay for the many centrally furnished facilities and services that it provides. These include classrooms, faculty offices, the library, heat, electricity, HR and payroll operations, and IT infrastructure—and, not least, the service of recruiting, advising, processing, and caring for the very students that are farmed out to academic departments in the first place.

To simplify the thought experiment, let us further imagine that all students are charged the same amount per credit irrespective of whether they are a state resident or not, even though in real life students at public universities pay greatly different tuition rates based on their residency status. This imaginary "composite" undergraduate student pays an amount per credit that averages out what in-state versus out-of-state students pay based on their overall proportions within the student body.[16] This is how Schools actually saw students under the New Budget Model. Figures derived from the actual budget values tabulated for each academic unit allow us to answer several important questions based on how a composite undergraduate's tuition money was spent in the middle to late 2010s.[17]

1. Do state appropriations cover the difference between in-state students' tuition and the actual cost of their education?

The answer is no: out-of-state students heavily subsidize in-state students, as they do at public universities most everywhere. The former paid well over three times as much as the latter for the exact same education and the exact same bundle of student services.[18] Is this because the State, through its legislative appropriation, covered the difference between what residents pay and the actual cost of their education—which is the way public universities were once thought to run? Only in a very limited sense. In the late 2010s, state appropriations to the University made up for only about one-third of the cost difference between an in-state student and the imaginary composite student.[19] The remainder was covered, principally, by out-of-state students: private consumers who by definition *chose* to move to the state and who elected to pay the going market rate (less whatever financial aid and scholarships they may have received) because they wanted to attend. This is one key reason the University's New Budget Model treated the State's appropriation as a contribution to academic and operational infrastructure. It dispensed with the fiction that it ever again could be conceptualized as paying down the differential between tuition and actual cost.

During this period, the State only provided 6 to 7 percent of the University's total revenues, which is a remarkably low figure by national standards albeit a simply more extreme version of a nationwide trend. Tuition, in contrast, accounted for 35 to 40 percent.[20] This makes it clear that precisely in order to serve its public mission, specifically its obligations to in-state students, the University had to cater to the demands and interests of its out-of-state population because they are the ones who balance the books. This is a dramatic illustration of the consequences of public disinvestment and the turn toward market-driven financing it brought about.

2. What percentage of a student's tuition dollar winds up in the pockets of the people who actually teach their courses, and how is the rest of it broken down?

Figure 2.1 (left) shows that 61 cents of a composite student's tuition dollar went directly to academic departments, schools, and colleges, and the other 39 cents went to the aforementioned "rent and taxes" payment collected by the central administration.[21] Figure 2.1 (right) shows that of the 61 cents, the lion's share went to pay salaries and fringe benefits to the people to do frontline work. Specifically, 49 cents went to faculty and graduate student instructors, 10 cents went to department and college staff (from front-desk receptionists to associate deans), and

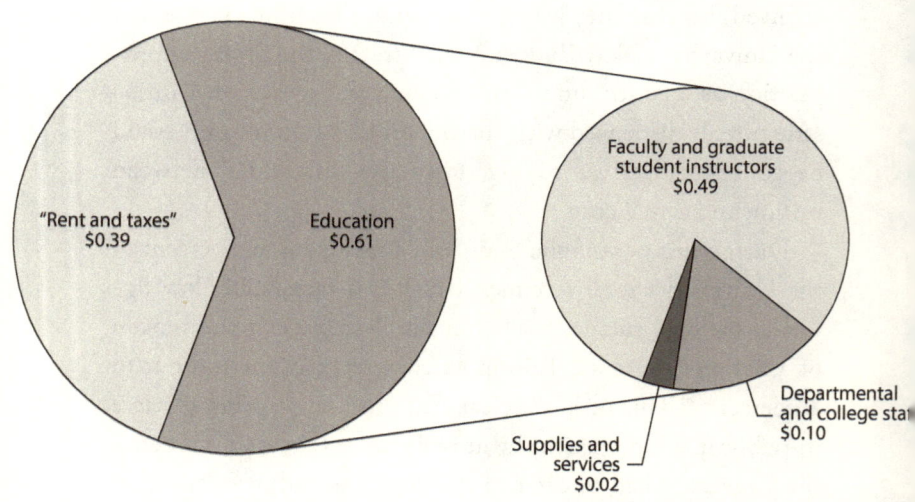

FIGURE 2.1 The tuition dollar: education vs. "rent and taxes."

Source: Office of Institutional Research, "Operational Metrics." University-wide and School-level figures on type I–III expenditures average of academic years 2016–17 through 2020–21.

only 2 cents went to various supplies and services, from computers to catering.

What about the "rent and taxes" portion? Because the University mingled student tuition together with state appropriations in its general fund to pay for central expenses, it is impracticable to trace what happened to a hypothetical tuition dollar. But figure 2.2 shows the breakdown of general fund expenditures for a typical year—again, excluding separately budgeted

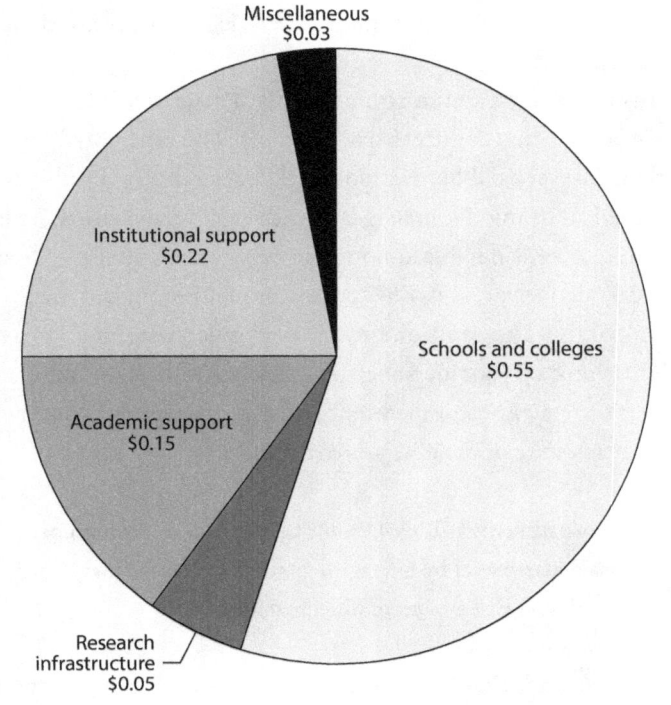

FIGURE 2.2 The general fund dollar: academic vs. nonacademic expenditures.

Source: Business Affairs Office. "Unaudited Financial Reports, FY21 Year End," 13, https://perma.cc/4BLF-VKTL, column on education and general expenditures, classifying each unit by academic or administrative function.

auxiliaries such as athletics, housing, and dining. It confirms, first, that Schools accounted for 55 cents of every general fund dollar spent, plus a modest 5 cents in support of research. Put another way, core academic functions account for half again as much as everything else. Of the remaining 40 cents, 15 cents went to various academic support functions, such as the library, the admissions office, and the dean of students' office, and a further 22 cents funded critical back-office functions including payroll, HR, information technology, facilities management, and police, plus executive leadership and "C-suite" offices for such things as fund-raising, communications, legal services, and budget planning.[22]

In chapter 4 on administrators, I take a deep dive into some of these latter, often controversial, expenses. The takeaway for now is that for every public relations flack, backslapping fund-raiser, or superfluous middle manager that the University hired, it also invested a considerable amount in academic advisors, library books and journals, and other critical student-support functions. Think of those 40 cents on the dollar in much the same way you might think of your personal finances: all told, it is not a bad amount to pay in combined rent and taxes, particularly for such a generous suite of benefits and services.

3. **Aren't students still paying to shore up money losing liberal arts departments by having their tuition diverted away from popular STEM and preprofessional fields?**[23]

One often reads that humanities and some social science departments are collapsing and dragging their home institutions down with them, whereas STEM (science, technology, engineering, and mathematics) fields, plus preprofessional fields such as business, are the real moneymakers and cannot be expected to subsidize their poorer cousins indefinitely. Surprisingly, it is often just the opposite.

Figure 2.3 compares costs per credit hour across Schools and College divisions, and figure 2.4 shows the expenditures per credit hour across select departments within the College. These figures dramatically illustrate what is a general rule at major public research universities: the arts and sciences subsidize the professional schools, and within the arts and sciences, the humanities more or less break even, the social sciences generate a profit, and the natural sciences run at a loss. (To be more specific, mathematics and psychology—the latter of which is sometimes treated as a natural science and sometimes as a social science—are

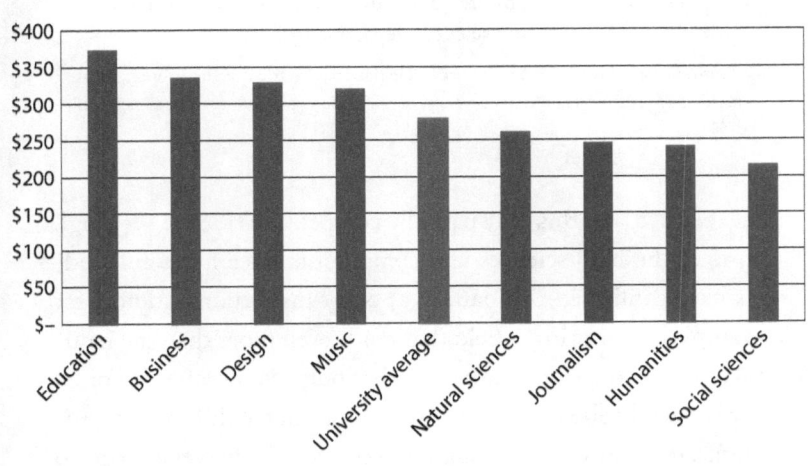

FIGURE 2.3 Expenditure per credit hour across Schools and arts and sciences divisions.

Source: Office of Institutional Research, Office of Institutional Research, "Operational Metrics." Primary operational metric #7 for the units indicated, average of academic years 2016–17 through 2020–21. The University's College of Education focuses on federally funded research grants rather than teacher training, which accounts for its outlier status as the most expensive School.

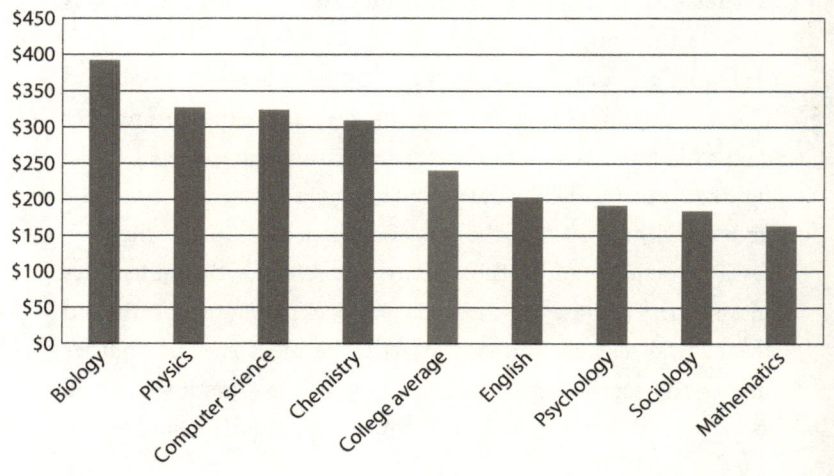

FIGURE 2.4 Expenditure per credit hour across selected arts and sciences departments.

Source: Office of Institutional Research, "Operational Metrics." Primary operational metric #7 for the units indicated, average of academic years 2016–17 through 2020–21.

inexpensive, and this only partially compensates for the *very* high costs of the hard sciences and computer science.) Careful studies have confirmed this pattern at other institutions, adding, for example, engineering, a field that tends even more than the natural sciences to generate expenses that outpace revenues.[24] For all the loose talk about closing down "unprofitable" liberal arts programs, in many cases it would be economically perverse to do so because they actually generate "profit" that can then be used to subsidize costly programs in STEM and professional fields that "lose" more money for each new student they enroll.

Admittedly, this odd reckoning of "profit" and "loss" in an avowedly noncapitalistic institution reflects the underlying absurdity of the student credit hour, a century-old accounting mechanism that, strangely, treats every hour of an educational experience—whether a giant introductory lecture class or an intimate seminar with a Nobel Prize winner—as having the same monetary value. Even setting aside that fact, however, the subsidization of STEM and certain professional fields by the liberal arts is only to be expected. Faculty in the former are in much higher demand, and many have lucrative alternative opportunities in the private sector. It is not so much that tenure-track scientists command vastly higher salaries than their liberal arts counterparts, although this is partly true (law and business professors are, in contrast, paid more exorbitantly), but rather that they teach less—which requires hiring a battery of non-tenure-track science instructors to take up the slack.[25] Moreover, science fields typically have much higher expenses for teaching laboratories and technology than is the case with liberal arts fields, where books and whiteboards often suffice.[26]

Some humanities programs do have a high baked-in cost. Personalized music instruction, for example, simply cannot be as "profitable" as the 500-person Introduction to Sociology lecture that functions as a cash cow by generating so many extra credit hours for the fixed cost of one faculty member. Admittedly, some shrinking humanities programs have also tipped into the red after decades of declining student interest. But by the same token, deans and administrators have had all that time to make continual adjustments year after year to maintain them at a steady or gently declining state. This was how the College shed 30 percent of its humanities majors in the 2010s without closing a single department, even as it simultaneously absorbed a 35 percent increase in natural science majors by hiring new faculty to teach them.[27] What feels to humanities faculty like a morale killing death by a thousand cuts is simply a form of relentless academic rightsizing that preserves intrinsically valuable academic programs while steadily trimming their costs—a process made all the more painful by the double standard that STEM fields do indeed enjoy greater and greater cross-subsidization as part of that same rebalancing. Although this disparity has provoked at least two generations of laments about the so-called crisis of the humanities, both the ongoing strength of humanities programs and the self-renewing vigor of these very critiques prove that these fields are not about to disappear anytime soon.

4. So—at long last—why does tuition go up every year?

As revealed by the answers to the previous questions, the quest for an answer takes us to the core of the university's academic mission, not to some side factors that might admit of an easy or radical fix. The University overwhelmingly spent student tuition money on frontline faculty; it kept "rent and taxes" to a reasonable level; it used most of *that* pot of money for core academic and infrastructural needs; and it made continual readjustments and recalibrations at every level to reconcile bottom-line monetary calculations with changing patterns of student interest and enduring academic values. There is little to no evidence of systemic waste, inefficiency, fraud, or abuse. And yet the cost of paying highly educated faculty and staff still seems to rise uncontrollably. It is the task of the next section to answer that question.

WHY A DOLLAR BUYS LESS EVERY YEAR

Professional economists have had several decades to study the problem of rising tuition and identify its underlying causes. What they have found is that the challenge of escalating costs long predates the epoch of public disinvestment, and it affects private institutions and public institutions equally and for much the same reasons. Runaway expense is, in fact, part and parcel of the same Golden Age that first made America's higher education system the best in the world. As early as the mid-1960s, at the height of public financial support by both federal and state governments, it was already clear that universities were victims of their own success: their financing threatened to become unsustainable.

In a now famous analysis from 1966, the economists William Baumol and William Bowen explained why knowledge-intensive service industries such as higher education and health care experience unremitting cost increases that far outpace regular inflation. Baumol used the performing arts as a case study. He pointed out that string quartets can never become more productive because they will always require four expert musicians, and those musicians cannot produce more quartets per hour simply by playing their instruments at a frantic tempo. What is now known as "Baumol's cost disease" was applied by his collaborator, Bowen, to higher education in 1968. Bowen calculated that if the average faculty member's salary keeps pace with the average autoworker's salary, growing at 4 percent a year, but that same faculty member cannot be expected to teach more students or conduct faster research—whereas automobile manufacturing most certainly *does* benefit from productivity increases—then higher education, just like string quartets or, say, haircuts, "is bound to become ever more expensive relative to other things." Reviewing nationwide cost trends from the mid-1940s to the mid-1960s, Bowen discovered a remarkably stable annual growth rate of 7.5 percent in the average cost per student, a finding soon dubbed "Bowen's Law." Regular baseline inflation accounted for only one quarter of that increase and was offset by virtually no measurable increase in the productivity of teaching and research.[28] A half-century later, growing labor costs, principally faculty, staff, and administrator salaries and fringe benefits, still account for the bulk of overall expense increases at colleges and universities.[29]

Cost increases may be acceptable and indeed desirable if the value of higher education also increases commensurately. The intrinsic benefit of acquiring knowledge and education might simply go up, much like the pleasure of consuming luxury goods such as string quartets. Or perhaps more pertinent, the added career income and even life expectancy that derive from a college degree might pencil out when taken as a purely calculated investment in an increasingly knowledge-centered global economy. That said, an irreducible tension remains at the heart of university budgeting as the cost of expert personnel continues to rise disproportionately relative to other economic goods and services. When the gap between baseline inflation and the cost of higher education widens too far—some suggest 3 percent as the upper limit of that gap—the growth of university budgets will inevitably outpace the resources likely to be available.

Given the chronic nature of the cost disease, if there was a magic bullet that could have been tried to increase labor productivity in academia, it would have been tried and implemented by now. At the very pinnacle of U.S. research universities' prosperity in the 1960s, talk of an impending "academic depression" did in fact become rife among policy makers and university leaders, showing that today's problems are not just a leftover trauma of the Great Recession. In 1971, the first of two Carnegie Commission reports brought this concern to widespread public attention, scrutinizing the finances of a range of institutions, including many of America's largest and most successful. Harvard, Chicago, and Michigan were all "headed for trouble," and Stanford and UC Berkeley were already in significant financial straits. This seems unbelievable in retrospect, especially given the massive endowments of prestigious private institutions today. In the public sector, the situation was much the same. In 1970, the University of California broke a century of tradition and for the first time charged students tuition.[30] (To recall that free attendance at UC was once a part of the social compact California made with its citizens is just as shocking as the notion that Harvard and Stanford were once strapped for cash.) Faced with the prospect of chronic penny-pinching, compounded by severe recessions in the larger economy in the early 1970s, institutions acted with alacrity and discipline to put their fiscal houses in order. Only two years after the initial alarm had been sounded, in 1973, many universities had already reached a plateau of "fragile stability" that they have remained perched on ever since. Austerity measures of all sorts, from deferring faculty hiring to paring back on office supplies, have remained an enduring part of administrators' tool kits, in every type of institution, private and public, for now over fifty years.

These findings have been reconfirmed for more recent decades as well. A typical university today devotes about 80 percent of its expenditures to labor costs, including salary and benefits for professors and other, often highly trained, professional and nonprofessional staff. And yet, compared to dentists, doctors, lawyers, and accountants, professors have not seen their salaries rise more than these other occupations, ones that also require very highly educated workers. (This is surprising: faculty are literally in the business of training all other university-educated professionals, so their incomes might even be expected to *lead* rather than lag their trainees'.) As in many service professions, productivity increases are either impossible or, when they are introduced, have the inescapable consequence of degrading quality. A professor who uses multiple-choice quizzes to teach larger classes is in this sense like a doctor who rushes through patient appointments or an attorney who cribs legalese from boilerplate wills.[31]

What about technology? In mainstream industries such as manufacturing and communications, innovations in robotics and fiber optics, for example, have enabled revolutionary increases in productivity. But in the professional service industries of medicine and law, technology has raised costs more than lowered them. The same holds true for college and university professors. Despite modest (and mostly illusory) productivity increases afforded by large-scale online teaching and learning, the steadily rising costs of *other* technologies essential to higher education, including high-performance computing and precision scientific research equipment, only compound the underlying dynamic of escalating labor costs across the higher education industry.

Critics rightly observe that faculty members' teaching loads have measurably declined in recent decades as many of them spend more and more time on research. Professors have also managed to transfer some of their prior advising and pastoral functions—in bygone centuries, they notionally served *in loco parentis* (in the place of a parent)—onto a burgeoning army of para-academic support staff. I turn to those objections in later chapters. For now, it is worth observing that the uptick in faculty "free" time for research is a manifestation of the same market forces that explain the uptick in faculty salaries. People who self-select into the professoriate typically value time more than money. Research time is, for the brilliant and diligent few, a hard-won luxury, comparable in value to monetary salary, for faculty who succeed in today's highly competitive academic job market. That de facto increase in in-kind compensation, moreover, has been matched by the ratcheting up of rigorous expectations and requirements for tenure and promotion.³² To save money, universities have also responded by greatly increasing the proportion of so-called adjunct and non-tenure-track faculty who only teach and do not do research. Wherever one looks, one sees universities making dynamic adjustments to stay one step ahead of market forces, while straining to avoid compromising either their academic values or their business models.

In sum, there is no pathology or dysfunction specific to higher education that accounts for the rise in costs in that industry—not lazy faculty, not overpaid administrators, not wasteful student amenities, not the absence of needed market discipline. Such rises are instead driven by the escalating expense of highly educated personnel, as a manifestation of what is an economy-wide trend in every globally competitive country. By the same token, that problem carries its own solution. Since the profound changes heralded by the knowledge economy have put an ever-greater share of disposable income in the hands of well-educated professionals, those professionals are now in a better position to finance their own children's education. When one focuses not on rising tuition as one factor in isolation but on the difference between tuition costs and disposable income, "there is no national affordability problem," conclude two expert economists. Consumers simply overestimate the actual cost of college, and universities do themselves no favors by underplaying just how much they write off their sticker price with scholarships and tuition discounting.³³

Surprisingly, tuition and fees actually declined in real terms across four-year public colleges and universities during the 2010s. Students took out far fewer federal loans and institutions significantly increased internal grants and subsidies to their own students. Those who did graduate with debt—only slightly more than half—did so with a significant but manageable $21,400 in loans, on average.[34] The overwhelming challenge facing higher education, then, is not one of cost but of access: America's increasingly affluent middle class can keep up, however grudgingly, with the rising cost of college, but those who are less fortunate increasingly cannot. Widening income inequality and a yawning wealth gap in turn have a cripplingly racialized dimension. This is the moral, political, and financial challenge that defines higher education today. (I tackle this in great detail in chapter 7.) But it remains an economy- and society-wide problem, not one created by the financing of higher education itself.

INSTITUTIONAL RESILIENCE

In 2018, the University abandoned the New Budget Model first instituted to ride out the Great Recession's aftermath. In its place it established a new Academic Allocation Model to parcel out resources based on substantive intellectual priorities rather than an institution-wide popularity contest driven by the choices of undergraduates. The shift to a more centralized and strategic budget system was less an admission of failure than an implicit declaration of a mission accomplished. RCM had done enormous service in focusing decision-makers at all levels on the core challenge of the 2010s: the need to offset declining state appropriations by attracting, retaining, and educating tuition-paying students. A few years further on, it was simply the right time to pivot toward other strategic goals, such as bolstering the University's research profile, and to update the budgeting process accordingly. Students fared well in the transition. Near the end of the decade, trustees approved a new program that locked in a set undergraduate tuition rate for five years for future cohorts. Although tuition would continue to rise, each successive cohort could now know, in advance, exactly how much their education would cost.[35]

Nationwide by the early 2020s, this picture of institutional resilience and financial stabilization turned out much the same, even if not all institutions were equally fortunate. The idealists and the realists may even be said to have converged on one cardinal point. The "great mistake" of public disinvestment has been avoided by those lucky institutions able to embrace the "perfect mess": those that, despite declining state support, proved able to raise tuition to keep up with the private pacesetters, even if they do still often trail them at a considerable distance. In an alternate universe, public research universities might have been forced to live within their means as determined by legislators in their home states, picking and choosing mission-critical priorities and making painful sacrifices under duress. This was indeed the story of a large number of regional and urban universities with less public cachet over the decade. But the top one hundred or so public research universities proved to be places where even those who are not wealthy enough to attend elite private institutions could still, proverbially, have nice things.

At the root of the many separate trends that drive and sustain upward pressure on costs is one unifying factor. Besides competition for the best faculty and students, surging demand for high-quality programs and amenities, and the aforementioned worldwide increase in the costs of highly educated labor, universities both public and private share an unlimited appetite for ways to improve and expand the search for new knowledge and new applications for that knowledge.[36] The quest for excellence means that they can *always* find good reasons to spend more money. Rising costs are not a function of profligacy or waste but of the perennial commitment to the pursuit of quality and excellence. Public institutions adapted to take advantage, as best their resources allowed, of the panoply of novel opportunities that are continually offered up by the system as a whole. New academic programs, new student amenities, new research agendas, and new technologies were the result. It was only natural that expenses grew as institutions pursued more of everything, all at once.

The rebound, flourishing, and expansion of public research universities in the 2010s is a classic illustration of the free market in action. Voting with their feet, and given a considerable boost by federal loans, students and parents decided en masse over the last decade, just as they had in decades before, that their investment in college is still worth it. Put more precisely: *enough* of them were sufficiently affluent, *despite* the escalating debt they were required to take on, to conclude that the benefits of the public research university experience outweighed the considerable costs. Universities, for their part, were only too happy to oblige because they too were bent on competitive self-improvement in a field of peers and rivals, each one striving for excellence on multiple dimensions. To the extent that declining state support crimped those ambitions, federally subsidized student loans filled the gap and fueled them to continue.[37]

The perverse outcome of all that competitive striving was a troublesome disconnect between institutional robustness and student indebtedness. But even the weight of that albatross might eventually be lessened. In 2022, a scholarly survey found that public opinion swung markedly toward a return to publicly funded higher education over the course of the prior decade. In 2010, those surveyed tended to see higher education as a responsibility of students and parents, but the public of 2020 had come to favor federal and state governments shouldering a significant share of that responsibility.[38] That shift helps explain widespread support for the Biden administration's decision to waive hundreds of billions of dollars in student debt at the stroke of a pen in 2022. Admittedly, that effort was aborted at the hands of the Supreme Court the following year. Yet the appetite for solutions to the student debt problem will no doubt remain undiminished as other political solutions are sought.

Whatever the fate of student loan policy, one thing remains clear. If ever-rising costs are the price we pay for ever-rising quality in public education, and most of that rise is attributable to the costs of highly educated professionals, the key question becomes how universities monitor, maintain, and improve the quality of their workforce. The next chapter focuses on the faculty: the people who actually deliver education, research, and knowledge.

3

FACULTY

How do universities manage the creative professionals who produce and impart knowledge?

Faculty across public higher education perceived the early 2000s as a time when they lost influence and their livelihoods became less secure. But at the University, it took a galvanizing event for them to do anything systematic about it. As soon as The Hat was fired, it became clear that a long-standing campaign to unionize the faculty would succeed. A handful of activist professors had been pressing for a faculty union for years, but without much success. Even the Great Recession, which depressed the faculty's hopes for raises while at the same time burdening them with more students to teach, had done little to improve the proposed union's popularity. Professors prefer to think of themselves as, well, professionals, not as common workers herded into a collective bargaining unit to speak for their interests.

But with The Hat gone, the calculation suddenly shifted. A president, their patron, a charismatic scholar-administrator—the one who had actually given them raises—had been publicly martyred; the hated State Board was still in charge; and the politicians had put the issue to rest and moved on. As a body, the faculty felt vulnerable and exposed but also newly powerful.

Here was a chance to take back control after years of feeling disempowered and disrespected by prior administrations and state boards alike. Whatever qualms they had about joining the ranks of organized labor seemed to be outweighed by the tangible, legally recognized bargaining power that a formal union could confer. This was a power that the University Senate, despite its historic role as the organ of faculty governance, and despite its fleeting renaissance as a conduit of faculty outrage against the State Board, could not offer.

Thus, in January 2012, a little more than a month after the Senate had risen up against the State Board, union organizers, themselves members of the faculty, began roaming the hallways of the academic departments, knocking on office doors to jawbone their colleagues into signing up for the cause. Emotions ran high. Some professors, particularly junior faculty, felt bullied into signing by their more senior colleagues. Others, including many of a left-wing bent, happily proclaimed their solidarity. The Senate hosted a forum offering a thorough airing of the pros and cons. The Blogger, a notorious anti-administration faculty gadfly who appears in the next chapter, posted color commentary on a daily, even hourly, basis.[1] Card check parties were held where faculty committed their intent in writing. The cards were then bundled together and submitted to the statewide labor relations board in March. A month later the new union was officially certified.

The shape the union took was unusual by national standards because it included both tenure-track professors and non-tenure-track instructors (a distinction defined later). Most faculty unions include only the latter. It might well have never secured the required majority vote of the combined professors and instructors had it not been for The Hat's firing and the catalytic effect that had on faculty activism. And it likely would not have succeeded in winning higher salaries and better working conditions, as it did during the 2010s, had its formation not coincided with a time of growth and prosperity fueled by tuition-paying students eager for the University's popular brand. The union's success was in many ways a fluke, the result of a very specific and very local competition for power.

For all its atypicality, the unionization drive at the University yoked together two of the most powerful trends affecting faculty across American academia: the adjunctification of the professoriate and the decline of shared governance. It revealed what had changed with the advent of a new millennium. A generation prior, in the 1980s and 1990s, the focus of debate had instead been on tenure. (While not a guarantee of lifelong employment, tenure protects those who have earned it from being fired except for very good reasons.) Exposés with titles like *ProfScam* and *Tenured Radicals* claimed that tenure coddles lazy faculty and incubates left-wing radicalism.[2] Although criticisms of tenure from outside academia never go away, the dominant issue of the 2000s and 2010s was instead whether tenure was being eroded from within: first, by the increasing role of part-time "adjuncts" paid by the course, often at a pittance, to deliver the university's central function of teaching; and second, by the increasing power of administrators who had seemingly arrogated to themselves a whole series of decisions that used to be collegially debated in "shared governance" with the tenured faculty.

Unionization's success showed that the vaunted traditions of shared governance, however important they remain to curriculum, academic quality control, and the university's intellectual mission, are no longer effective as a conduit for faculty power, if they ever had been.[3] Specifically, such traditions could not counteract the underlying driver of adjunctification: a chronic nationwide oversupply of highly qualified PhDs desperate for work given the paucity of tenure-track jobs available. In a university sector increasingly dominated by market power—the tuition-paying power of students, as shown in chapter 2, but also the highly competitive job market for faculty expertise, as shown here—the prospects for faculty senates as inherited venues for faculty-administration interaction remain severely limited whenever conflicts over real resources are at stake. Rather, at the University at least, only a deus ex machina in the form of labor relations law proved decisive in winning material gains and a louder voice for the faculty.

The takeaway for other institutions is that the raw and often destructive power of the free market can be channeled and tamed—even if traditional mechanisms of sharing power are no longer up to the task. Beyond the carefully choreographed and disingenuously high-minded culture of shared governance, a new script featuring a legally regulated conflict between "labor" and "management" brings questions of money and influence to the fore that have long been sidelined and denied. With the traditional idea of a unified faculty losing coherence, slow-acting trends in the market for academic talent provide reasons to believe that the system is on a course to righting itself. The American professoriate is simply becoming more differentiated and specialized than it has been in the past. New venues for faculty power and professional development can turn that diversity into a source of robust ongoing influence and, at the best run institutions, competitive advantage.

TENURE AND UNIONIZATION

To form a union under the State's labor law policies, organizers had to craft a bargaining unit encompassing different types of faculty and then persuade more than 50 percent of them to vote for it. Early on, they decided to fuse two different constituencies, tenure-track professors and non-tenure-track instructors, each with distinct and in some ways opposed interests. The organizers' grievances were, first, that because of decades-long public disinvestment, faculty salaries had for too long lagged those at peer institutions; and second, that because of high-handed and overpaid administrators, professors were being denied a voice in major strategic decisions and thus deprived of their traditional role in shared governance. That concern was primarily of interest to tenure-track faculty—the assistant, associate, and full professors who, after a six-year probationary period and a rigorous anonymous review by colleagues at peer universities, were either granted indefinite employment contracts or given one extra year to find work elsewhere.[4] Committed to a trifecta of teaching, research, and committee service, in which research excellence was by far the most important criterion, the roughly seven hundred professors constituted the core of the University's semipermanent instructional staff. Although some were bitter and others content, objectively they enjoyed stable working conditions that were largely under their personal control. Whether they felt they were paid competitive salaries or not, and whether they felt their role in shared governance was being respected or not, these faculty enjoyed enough job security and occupational freedom that few of them felt an existential need to form a union.

The same could not be said of the several hundred non-tenure-track instructors. This was a diverse group ranging from senior full-time lecturers to catch as catch can part-timers, all paid at different rates and hired and fired in different ways. These faculty delivered about half of the actual teaching at the University, and more than half in the College of Arts and Sciences, very much the largest academic unit. Between 2000 and 2010, the proportion of credit hours taught by professors dropped from 60 percent to only

44 percent. In 2010, instructors were even teaching more than half of the upper-division undergraduate credits, that is, the advanced courses that required the most faculty expertise. This shift in teaching responsibilities reflected the rapid hiring of non-tenure-track faculty to cope with the University's swelling enrollments after the Great Recession. But the decline in tenure-track teaching is a long-acting nationwide trend irrespective of any particular university's enrollment fluctuations.[5] Most everywhere, "adjunct" or, more broadly, "contingent" faculty had every reason to feel anxious, insecure, and even angry. The University had few uniform transparent policies on instructors' rate of pay, duration of employment, conditions for contract renewal, prospects for promotion, eligibility for benefits, working conditions, or access to technology, teaching materials, and office space. What policies could be found varied from unit to unit and were seldom even posted on university websites. Ironically, given union organizers' claims about administrative bloat, underinvestment in administration, including basic functions like HR and payroll, was in part to blame for the clumsily unprofessional way that instructors were treated.

Like contingent faculty across the United States, even some of the most senior instructors could technically be treated as casual employees by the central administration, however valued and secure they may have felt in their home departments. An experienced, accomplished, and beloved lecturer in organic chemistry, for example, might enjoy as little contractual protection against dismissal or arbitrary treatment as an adjunct instructor hired off the street to teach conversational English to the University's swelling population of international students. The challenge was that this large group—about seven hundred people, roughly the same size as the tenure-track faculty—was disparate and hard to organize. About half focused primarily on instruction, and the other half served in various laboratories and research centers and did little or no teaching. A great many were long-standing

University citizens, but others were poorly paid part-timers with only weak or transitory ties to the institution or to the academic profession itself. They had everything to gain from unionization, but few means of communicating with one another to form a common interest, much less forge a shared bond with the tenure-track professors whose employment conditions and higher professional status were so markedly superior to their own. The union's goal was to change this, but it faced an uphill battle.

In April 2010, one year into The Hat's tenure as president, the University Senate conducted a straw poll that seemed to spell the end of the unionization drive. In the wake of the poll, The Blogger opined that union organizers would soon close up shop. "Mainly I think people decided that the President was not just all hat."[6] Boasting a healthy response rate of nearly half of the 2,300 faculty and staff members surveyed, the poll offered a detailed snapshot of faculty opinion revealing a lack of cohesion and common interest. Not surprisingly, a solid 55 percent majority of the professors opposed unionization, more than twice as many as the 23 percent who supported it (the rest were undecided). Conversely, a similar proportion of instructors, 58 percent, supported the union, likewise outnumbering opponents, at 24 percent, more than two to one. Support among the non-tenure-track ranks was ambivalent, however, whereas opposition among the tenure-track ranks was often passionate. Anonymously submitted comments revealed a spectrum of attitudes still tipping decidedly, at that point, toward skepticism about faculty unionization.[7] A sample of typical comments follows:

TENURE-TRACK OPPOSITION

- An irrevocable step toward mediocrity.
- Fatal to research university status.

- I prefer to represent myself as an individual professional.
- Will prevent faculty from negotiating raises and other benefits on an individual merit-based basis.
- Happy with the current structure, which is merit-based.
- Tenure protects us; we do not need a union.
- Faculty should govern the university, and a union does little to affect the growth of administration.
- The idea of unionized tenure-track faculty appalls me.
- A union may be a good idea for non-tenure-track faculty but it is NOT for tenure-track faculty.
- There is no need for us to unionize. We have a new administration that is more transparent and is working to get our salaries to equal the average of our comparators.

TENURE-TRACK SUPPORT

- A counterweight to the administration, which gives primary weight to fund-raising, regardless of the purpose for which those funds are donated.
- The athletic department is out of control.
- Increasingly "business-style" administrators who govern in an authoritarian way with little or no meaningful input from faculty.

NON-TENURE-TRACK OPPOSITION

- The last thing we need is another layer of bureaucracy.
- I represent myself adequately and have no difficulty communicating with my superiors.
- The idea seems too abstract to make a decision one way or another.
- The faculty is the governing body of the university. As the governing body, the faculty should not be part of a union.

NON-TENURE-TRACK SUPPORT

- The only option for us to gain transparency for our terms of employment at the University.
- More equitable pay.
- The University needs to look at all of its employees equally, otherwise it will continue to take advantage of lower pay for non-tenure-track faculty.
- The administration does not inspire confidence.

The surprising success of the card check campaign amid such deep-seated hesitation reflected more than the temporary galvanizing effect of The Hat's firing. It sprang from the realization, through that catalytic event, that even tenure-track professors were vulnerable. They could no longer defend their individual interests as autonomous negotiators, nor rely on university administrators to assert their collective interests vis-à-vis state higher education leaders. Deeper still, the decisive swing toward unionization in early 2012 registered a slow-acting tectonic shift in the academic labor market. For very different reasons, tenure-track professors and non-tenure-track instructors had converged in their sense that the traditional roles of faculty were undergoing alarming changes nationwide, and that local action was needed as a bulwark against this threat.

THE ACADEMIC LABOR MARKET

The adjunctification of the American professoriate is a worrisome trend that reliably commands the headlines, and with good reason. But the deeper, more subtle story of the past generation has been an overall reconstitution of the profession by erosive forces within the academic job market. Although the percentages of *full-time* instructors, and for that matter graduate student assistants, have remained essentially stable over the last several decades, that same time period has seen a steady decline in the proportion of professors among universities' instructional staffs. That decline has been almost exactly matched by a dramatic upturn in the number of *part-time* adjuncts, those who are hired on a per-course basis as the need arises.[8] Put another way, the ranks of tenure-track faculty remain constant in absolute terms, but they have been steadily shrinking in relative terms as university enrollments have grown. By one estimate, the number of professors stayed at about 400,000 between 1975 and 2011, whereas the number of instructors (both full- and part-time) jumped from less than 300,000 to well over a million during this same period.[9] And among these, adjuncts are by far the most vulnerable and most often exploited. Horror stories abound of "freeway fliers" who piece together adjunct gigs at multiple institutions in the same metropolitan area, scraping by on ridiculously low wages of only $2,500 to $3,000 per course. National newspapers often run poignant accounts of adjuncts who died penniless, diseased, and alone after teaching loyally for decades at one institution without health care or pension benefits.[10]

It comes as no surprise, then, that nationwide, about one quarter of all faculty are unionized, and adjuncts, more so than full-time non-tenure-track and certainly tenure-track faculty, stand at the center of contemporary unionization efforts.[11] Organizations such as the Coalition of Contingent Academic Labor (COCAL) and the New Faculty Majority—the latter's name a gesture to the quantitative predominance of non-tenure-track faculty in the United States—show that adjunct unionization is not merely a local but a coordinated national effort, often spearheaded by adjuncts themselves.[12] At a time of rising labor activism in the public, clerical, and service sectors, national labor organizations, from the American Federation of Teachers (AFT) to the Service Employees International Union (SEIU) and even the Teamsters, have lent their organizational, legal, and political expertise to the cause. To be sure, their prospects of success are limited in right-to-work states, and also by a 1980 Supreme Court decision that enabled *private* universities to bar faculty unions.[13] But in the rest of academia, unionization has now become the only game in town for faculty of whatever rank or status who seek an organized alternative to the tender mercies of the academic job market. They have now joined the many graduate student unions, long influential at public flagships in Michigan and California, who in recent years have made inroads at such prestigious private institutions as Yale and New York University.

It was not supposed to turn out this way. In a now famous demographic forecast from 1989, William Bowen, the same scholar who a generation earlier had helped diagnose the "cost disease" of ever-rising expenses, predicted that the late 1990s and 2000s would witness a *dearth* of qualified faculty relative to the number of entry-level assistant professor jobs available. Analyzing faculty retirement patterns, student enrollment trends, the production of new PhDs, and the shifting popularity of various academic fields, Bowen and his coauthor even claimed that faculty shortages would be most acute in the humanities and social sciences—the very fields, unlike STEM and professional disciplines, that are today most acutely plagued by adjunctification and casualization.[14] Some argue that Bowen's analysis became a victim of its own success: many would-be PhDs who might otherwise have pursued other careers heard of the study's findings and elected to go to graduate school, confident that they would be employable upon finishing their degrees. Many times in history, however, the popularity of advanced higher education, and the intrinsic attractions of the academic life, have led to chronic imbalances between the supply and the demand for faculty labor, supporting a structurally chronic buyer's market that benefits universities looking for inexpensive instructors. What was atypical, even unprecedented, was the short boom time for American academics after World War II, christened the "Academic Revolution" by two influential analysts in 1968, that shaped expectations of ample tenure-track employment, not to mention the rosy mythology of shared governance. That mythology has now outlasted the subsequent weakening of the academic job market for several decades running.[15]

Just as the academic job market weakened in the 1990s in defiance of Bowen's prediction, one commonly reads that universities were colonized by corporate-style "neoliberal" managers who systematically pursued adjunctification—and undermined shared governance—as part of a deliberate stratagem to gain greater control over faculty labor at a time of public disinvestment and financial austerity. It is more accurate to say that the shift from full-time professors to full-time instructors and especially to part-time adjuncts was a by-product of *un*coordinated and *un*systematic management of faculty labor, especially at large universities and most especially at flagship research universities. In a nutshell, the administrators who are responsible for local hiring decisions at the departmental and college levels are not the same administrators who are responsible for institution-wide financial and personnel planning. The widespread introduction of Responsibility Center Management (RCM) budgeting during the 1990s, analyzed in chapter 2, only exacerbated the disconnect between central and local management. As a result, universities backed into a reliance on non-tenure-track faculty inadvertently and planlessly, through a series of locally rational decisions to plug various gaps in teaching needs rather than as part of a coherent managerial philosophy.[16]

What also changed during this time, at least at top research universities, was that the dwindling proportion of those who did still enjoy tenure came to enjoy even greater autonomy than they had before. The gulf separating star faculty from the rest widened appreciably. Uncomfortably for the tenured minority, it is their very privilege that creates disparities between available teachers and needs for instruction that are pervasive yet unpredictable. Top faculty enjoy the ability to take sabbaticals or go on leave for prestigious fellowships, to offer courses in their preferred specialties and effectively refuse to teach undesirable service courses, and to be paid and promoted based on their research productivity rather than on their popularity among tuition-paying students. These and other perquisites have expanded, not contracted, over recent decades, creating many of the instructional gaps that have to be filled by deans and department heads, sometimes at the last minute, scanning piles of adjuncts' résumés for any qualified warm body to take over a class.

More broadly, recent decades have seen a large-scale restructuring of the American faculty as a whole. One now sees a greater differentiation among the faculty at large, both nationwide and within single institutions. The proliferation of different ranks and statuses, a divergence in pay and working conditions between marketable and nonmarketable disciplines, and nagging inequities based in gender, race, and ethnicity—inequities that have grown more apparent as the professoriate diversifies—together amount to a progressive loss of coherence across the profession as a whole. The very prosperity and growth of American colleges and universities, fueled by an influx of new students, has introduced a greater division and specialization of labor, just as Adam Smith would have predicted for any growing industry. The proliferation of new fields of study and new types of teaching has had the unintended effect of undermining the unity of the traditional tenure-track faculty role. What is happening now is a pervasive "unbundling" of the classic trifecta of research, teaching, and service, with the turn toward specialized teachers and specialized researchers of various stripes. Faculty members' functions are being recombined and restratified depending on their particular value to their institutions as measured by whatever salaries are dictated by subspecialized job markets.[17] The possession of faculty status per se means less and less in such a world.

The forces of differentiation and fragmentation have given a small number of star faculty enormous negotiating power as individuals but have eroded faculty power and influence at the aggregate level. Remarkably, average faculty salaries have remained stagnant in real terms since the late 1970s, and professors continue to trail other educated professionals in salary (even if generous fringe benefits at wealthier universities, not to mention the freedom to set one's own schedule, compensate for this lack).[18] This finding discredits the notion that tuition increases, inasmuch as they are driven in part by the cost of faculty, result from faculty being coddled or excessively overpaid. Faculty report working just as hard if not harder than in previous generations, at an average of fifty or more hours per week.[19] The salary premium afforded by unionization also remains modest and uneven, and it is largely confined to those fields in the humanities, arts, and social sciences where faculty cannot typically find lucrative work in nonacademic fields. In contrast to scientists, engineers, and health care professionals, collective bargaining is the only effective redress for such faculty.[20] Meanwhile, the flat overall picture of faculty compensation masks widening gaps among different faculty subgroups based on institutional type and, most of all, disciplinary specialty.[21] If, in generations past, economics professors made only somewhat more than English professors, the law of supply and demand now enables the former to command vastly higher salaries, often 50 percent to 100 percent higher, than colleagues who are comparably qualified and comparably senior. Such disparities were magnified in the aftermath of the Great Recession because the more lucrative fields were quicker to recover from a downturn momentarily experienced by all.

An exhaustive recent study of the American professoriate concludes that, as a whole, their situation is precarious, fluid, unstable, and fragmented. At a granular level, larger economic forces are pulling different faculty in different directions: "Differentiation as shaped by market forces has only increased; and there is no sign that the trend is abating. . . . For full-time faculty and with even greater vengeance for part-time faculty, the market rules."[22] The megatrend of market-driven individualization is a more all-encompassing challenge even than the headline-grabbing problem of adjunctification that accompanies it.

A HOW-TO GUIDE FOR FACULTY MANAGEMENT

Given the parlous state of faculty power and influence in the early 2000s, it is all the more noteworthy that unionization at the University succeeded so thoroughly in bucking the national trend. The inaugural Collective Bargaining Agreement (CBA) showed that it was possible for faculty to attain through labor negotiations what had been denied them by the invisible hand of the academic job market. A 130-page document hammered out over several months of negotiations between union representatives and University administrators, the CBA was a model of its kind. Stripped of all the legalese found in any union contract, it might well have been entitled "A University Administrator's How-To Guide for Faculty Management."[23] Covering working conditions, salary raises, faculty review and promotion, and the union's rights and prerogatives as a bargaining entity, the document provided a new foundation for faculty-administration relations after years of chronic strife.[24] Its basic architecture remained unchanged well into the next decade. Over that time, it reshaped shared governance, midwifed a thorough professionalization of non-tenure-track faculty, and changed the way faculty in all classifications and ranks were managed across the institution.

Shared Governance

The new lingo and honest open conflict of formal bargaining provided cathartic relief from the passive-aggressive interactions endemic to traditional shared governance, where rivals cloak self-interest in the rhetoric of academic idealism. Despite predictable posturing on both sides in public, with union leaders issuing crowd-pleasing denunciations of administrators' alleged neglect of the university's prized teaching staff, and administrators, in return, solemnly intoning that they were honor bound to rise above the fray and act in the University's best interests, in the trenches, the two teams on opposite sides of the bargaining table proved pragmatic and constructive in their engagement.

The CBA distilled best practices shared widely across American academia, made newly explicit what had all too often been left confusingly implicit, preserved room for local judgment and discretion even in the act of codification and standardization, and instituted incremental but significant improvements to faculty management processes and policies that balanced individual faculty members' rights with the institution's broader interests. Thus the article on faculty tenure mandated processes followed by every major research university—such as the consultation of anonymous expert reviewers from other major universities—but added new mechanisms for post-tenure review to ensure that tenured faculty remained productive throughout their careers. Such reviews, which can be paper tigers elsewhere, became more robust as the union contract was periodically renegotiated.

Most consequentially, the CBA inaugurated new mechanisms of shared governance that supplemented but did not supplant those of the University Senate. Its centerpiece was an entirely new process for creating academic policies of all sorts. This enshrined the academic department, not the Senate, as the fundamental unit of formal faculty participation in their own governance and management.[25] Under various articles, departments were required to draft their own policies for the promotion and tenuring of faculty members; the allocation of teaching, research, and committee service duties; the criteria for merit raises; and departments' own internal governance. In the new system, the dean or provost could override departmental proposals, up to and including a wholesale revision of proposed drafts, although this was quite rare.

For many traditionalists, tenure is a sine qua non of shared governance. Even though all employees theoretically enjoy academic freedom and the right to speak truth to administrative power, in practice they may be cowed by the fear of retribution. The new protections changed all that. By prescribing formal channels of consultation with all faculty, plus a formal grievance process whereby faculty of any rank or classification could involve union mediators to intercede with administrators, the CBA weakened the practical necessity of yoking shared governance to the protections of tenure.

The dynamic interaction between administrators and departmental faculty within the guardrails of a new negotiating process also forged a balance between uniform standards and a deference to local disciplinary conventions. In other union contexts, union leaders often insist on standardization and uniformity in the interest of ensuring equity among workers, and managers fight to preserve discretion and flexibility to reward the highest-performing individuals. At the University, however, as often as not it was union leaders who insisted on local discretion and individual merit and administrators who touted the benefits of equity and uniformity. The end result was a series of several hundred publicly posted policies giving every faculty member, department head, and dean a set of flexible rules to follow whenever questions or conflicts arose on personnel and salary matters.[26]

The Professionalization of Non-Tenure-Track Faculty

If the CBA mainly reconfirmed and refined the existing treatment of tenure-track professors by following best practices at peer institutions, its treatment of non-tenure-track instructors marked a real watershed. The union settlement became a national model by giving job security, professional status, material support, and, above all, a career ladder with explicit promotion and merit standards to the University's many faculty members who were ineligible for tenure. Like its peers, the University had every incentive to drag its feet on the treatment of its instructors. The enrollment growth of the late 2000s and early 2010s illustrated how administrators were too busy hiring such faculty to cover classes to attend to the finer points of their working conditions and management. Without the legal mandates that came with the unionization process, it is difficult to imagine that the University ever would have undertaken such a systematic effort to professionalize its contingent faculty on its own initiative.

The CBA started by delineating the various titles and ranks, drawing a newly firm separation between "instructors," those who taught important courses that could be expected to be offered every year, and "adjuncts," those hired for avowedly temporary assignments or because of their special expertise (for example, local architects to teach practical design courses that the regular architecture faculty did not).[27] Within the rank of instructor, a three-stage career ladder was established to mimic the progression from assistant to associate to full professor that tenure-track faculty already enjoyed.[28] Although they lacked both the informal status and the formal job security conferred by tenure, instructors won a robust voice in the governance of their departments and of the wider university. They were no longer relegated to second-class citizenship but rather were valued for their specific (if still subordinate) roles in the institution. In a military metaphor, tenure-track professors were sometimes described as the officer corps and non-tenure-track instructors as noncommissioned officers.

Most important, instructors were granted year-long or multiyear contracts, depending on their seniority, instead of being contracted term to term as had previously been the case. The University was also required to give notice of renewal or nonrenewal as early as May 1 of the prior academic year, well before course enrollment figures could be forecasted. This shifted the burden of risk for unfilled courses from individual instructors to the University itself. In later CBA iterations, the University was required to provide a detailed rationale whenever it failed to renew the contract of an experienced instructor, and its ability to cancel classes at the last minute was similarly curtailed. It was also barred from either rehiring adjuncts indefinitely without giving the Union sound academic reasons or replacing a dismissed qualified instructor with an adjunct within a period of three years. That provision gave the institution an incentive to think long and hard before letting a qualified instructor go for financial reasons.[29]

Finally, in 2021, during the pandemic, instructors gained yet more protection: the entire procedure whereby they were periodically either renewed or not renewed was scrapped in favor of the presumption of continuous ongoing employment.[30] This avoided the problem faced by even the highest-performing senior instructors that whenever their contract renewal year happened to coincide with a momentary enrollment dip or a budget cut, the case for renewing their jobs suddenly became more tenuous. Rather than having to bite their nails, it was, again, the institution that had to bear that risk. Instructors still did not enjoy anything like tenure but, like other professional staff in the university, they could expect that their jobs would continue indefinitely until such time as their programs were discontinued or their job performance became unsatisfactory.

Inevitably, there were winners and losers as a result of these changes. Deans and department heads making hiring decisions, when faced with unstable enrollments or unpredictable finances, erred on the side of caution. They sometimes let qualified faculty go while they still had the chance, before such faculty rolled over into a more protected contractual status. Adjuncts who performed well *and* whose courses were popular might be nonrenewed if a recurring budget was not available for their particular position. Instructors' ability to piece together different assignments across the university, a key source of institutional flexibility often welcomed by instructors and administrators alike, was now hemmed in by restrictions designed to protect such faculty from exploitative treatment but which, in practice, limited even mutually agreed-upon special arrangements.

Most uncomfortably, the implementation of the CBA coincided with the cresting of the post-recession enrollment surge. From 2009 to the mid-2010s, the University had staffed up rapidly with non-tenure-track instructors because it could not hire tenure-track professors fast enough to keep up with the influx of new students. But as that surge plateaued, the University simultaneously faced new contractual requirements to either issue instructors multiyear contracts or phase out their positions. It often chose the latter option. Thus, on one day, the University's College of Arts and Sciences sent out more than one hundred pink slips to instructors, most of them perfectly qualified. Contrary to the widespread suspicion that universities seize on opportunities to replace real faculty with adjuncts, it was precisely the University's commitment to rebalancing *back* toward tenure-track professors that led administrators to take that course even in cases where it would have been easier and more profitable to continue relying on qualified non-tenure-track instructors. When this crunch period arrived, union leaders and administrators agreed that protecting established faculty of either tenure category would entail a sacrifice in flexibility and openness toward those with less seniority. By raising the drawbridge on newer, younger, part-time hires to protect established full-time members, the faculty union behaved just like unions in other occupational sectors, and in full partnership with management.

Competition vs. Solidarity

Because it entailed major new resource commitments, not just new policies and more professional treatment, unionization recast the management of faculty in ways that neither union organizers nor administrators initially predicted or necessarily would have welcomed. CBA implementation created a ratchet effect whereby generous salary increases called forth new scrutiny of faculty productivity and that dynamic pushed personnel decisions previously made at the local levels up toward the central administration. Nonetheless, when resources were tight, labor and management consistently agreed that the surest way to recruit, retain, and reward high-quality faculty was to measure their contributions with reference to their peers, both locally in departments and at comparable universities nationwide. Even in a unionized context, competitiveness rather than solidarity was the value that both sides prized in crafting policies to reward faculty.

Among the most hard-fought union victories was a series of salary increases that did a great deal to close the pay gap between the University's faculty and their counterparts elsewhere. For years, faculty leaders and administrators had gone back and forth about just how much the faculty was underpaid relative to peer institutions, but no one denied the basic fact of the matter. Administrators were themselves eager to pay market rates to recruit and retain a higher caliber of faculty, thereby improving the luster of the institution. Even if they could not afford to be so single-mindedly focused on faculty compensation as union leaders were, they had every incentive, particularly after gaining an independent trustee board and the right to set tuition, to steer more of that tuition money in the faculty's direction. By the end of the 2010s, the University had made major strides forward, paying its faculty 90 to 95 percent of the peer average.[31]

Under the new system of shared governance, decisions about compensation increases blended local judgment with institution-wide standards. Each academic unit was tasked with codifying and quantifying the specific types of activity—whether research grants in the sciences, or scholarly books in the humanities, or juried concert performances in music—seen as most meritorious in a given discipline. A smaller amount was set aside for equity adjustments to mitigate salary compression and inversion, compensating senior faculty who had missed out on regular raises over decades relative to junior faculty hired more recently at market rates. Administrators focused primarily on recruiting new junior faculty and retaining the very best senior faculty, leading them to prioritize merit increases, whereas union leaders focused on the interests of the long-serving rank and file and argued more for equity and across-the-board raises. Yet despite minor philosophical differences, both sides agreed on the primacy of merit. So, too, by pegging both merit and equity increases to department-level rather than institution-wide pools, the CBA recognized and reinforced wide divergences in salaries from field to field. Had the union instead insisted on equal pay for equal work—English professors after all worked just as hard as economics professors—it is likely that they would have faced a crippling backlash. Gross market disparities among disciplines were instead codified in the union contract.

The University incurred significant, albeit predictable, ongoing financial burdens as a result of unionization. A regime of hefty salary increases, on a regular schedule and under transparently negotiated criteria, replaced the past practice of administrators using irregular windfalls to sneak in ad hoc raises while the State Board and the Legislature were not looking. Here, finally, is a straightforward causal explanation for why tuition steadily increased at the University in the 2010s. The fact that faculty salaries, representing a very large share of the institution's total expenditures, were now subject to formal collective bargaining negotiations enabled the University to tell students just how much of their tuition increase was being used to pay their own professors and instructors—a number on the order of $15 million in one typical bargaining cycle.[32]

The flip side of major salary increases was a dramatic tightening of faculty workload expectations that, more than any other policy, strained the new shared governance process enshrined by the CBA. Under the agreement, departments were tasked with drafting their own workload policies—including the number of courses taught, research expectations, student advising duties, and committee work—after receiving input from the administration. Naturally, many departments proposed that they could do a better job teaching their students and/or produce more research if only their teaching loads could be reduced. Deans retorted that across-the-board reductions in course offerings would break the bank. A number of contentious meetings culminated in a compromise whereby each arts and sciences department was granted a basket of course releases to distribute to tenure-track faculty as they saw fit.[33] More controversially, the teaching load for most non-tenure-track faculty was set at three courses per term irrespective of past practice. That act was a dramatic case of classic union-style standardization that painfully cranked up the workloads of a small but significant number of senior instructors. It met with protest from the union.[34]

The combination of financial and managerial tightening required to meet the CBA's obligations reverberated across the administration, contributing to the ultimate replacement of the former RCM budget model. No direct line of causation links the demise of the New Budget Model to the unionization of the faculty, but as faculty management became subject to formal agreements mandating regular salary increases, multiyear contracts for instructors, and other resource commitments, it became critical for decisions about faculty hiring to be made not by local managers but by central administrators with a comprehensive view of the institution's finances. Decisions about hiring instructors steadily migrated from department heads to deans, and decisions about hiring professors steadily migrated from deans to the central administration. Recall that in the early part of the decade the New Budget Model had vested hiring power for both faculty types in the deans. It also flowed enough tuition that they in turn felt free to delegate to department heads the authority to hire instructors as their teaching needs dictated. As the costs of faculty salary increases mounted in the later 2010s, however, triggering chronic budget deficits in some of the schools and colleges, deans and department heads came under the watchful eye of central budget managers and lost that flexibility.

As an unintended but logical consequence of faculty unionization, the standardization of faculty workloads replaced a less tightly monitored regime based on the presumption of good citizenship and on collegial negotiations among deans and department heads. This introduced a whiff of corporate-style productivity metrics and surveillance mechanisms into the daily lives of tenure-track and non-tenure-track faculty alike. That said, there remained a built-in firewall against intensive micromanagement in the need to match working conditions at rival universities. Union and administration leaders consistently agreed that to compete in the national job market for faculty, the gold standard ought to remain whatever other leading public research universities were doing to cultivate and reward their own faculty talent. This ensured that the University's teaching staff would continue to enjoy the occupational freedoms and perquisites that their counterparts did at other American flagships, and not devolve into mere laborers.

LESSONS

The story of faculty unionization and its aftermath at the University in the 2010s contains several broad lessons for American academia as a whole. First, adjunctification is not some coordinated plot by cost-cutting administrators intent on breaking the resistance of a tenured old guard to neoliberal management techniques. Rather, it is precisely the result of uncoordinated, locally rational decisions in an academic job market where tenured top performers enjoy great advantages but younger and less privileged faculty face a chronic excess in the supply of highly qualified competitors.

Second, tenure may be shrinking but it is not going away. Tenure can be reconfirmed and strengthened for the significant minority of the faculty still hired for the trifecta of research, teaching, and service. Far from protecting the lazy or eccentric, tenure substitutes intellectual competition for economic competition; it selects for, and then rewards, a certain type of creative professional driven more by peer recognition than monetary compensation; and it ensures that faculty work for their professions, not for their institutions—and those are all good things for the creation of knowledge. But tenure need not be normative or universal. Non-tenure-track instructors and researchers can most certainly enjoy the benefits of belated professionalization, including job security, a career ladder, merit raises, academic freedom, a voice in major decisions, and fair and transparent standards of treatment.

Third, a robust hybrid model that includes both types of faculty may prove the most viable model in the long run. The terms and expectations of faculty work will likely continue to expand in unforeseen ways to accommodate the highly differentiated roles that faculty now play. So long as robust policies are in place that protect the ability of every faculty and staff member to speak out on matters of intellectual and institutional importance, that new faculty model may withstand public scrutiny far better than the motivated reasoning that causes defenders of tenure to conflate it with academic freedom.

Fourth, shared governance, like tenure, may be reconfirmed and strengthened by faculty unionization, and not threatened by it. Senates can continue to focus on curriculum, academic quality control, and other spheres of intellectual judgment. But in a world where the market reigns supreme over the treatment (or mistreatment) of faculty, shared governance is ineffective in gaining tangible benefits in working conditions. Bargaining for collective power in an otherwise individualistic market competition is the function for which unions are tailor-made.

And finally, fifth, unions are perfectly compatible with academic quality when they insist on the same competitive, individualistic standards that university administrators do: they too subscribe to a vision of excellence through competition that animates every other corner of university life.

4

ADMINISTRATORS

Why do the ranks of university administrators keep growing, along with their powers?

"Administrators Gone Wild," a not so subtle reference to "Girls Gone Wild," a series of sexist spring break party videos popular in the 1990s, was among The Blogger's first posts on the subject of administrative bloat in 2011. In it, he vented the familiar claim that administrators were an expanding, malevolent, corrupting influence on university life. "Dude just couldn't keep his hand out of the cookie jar," he claimed with casual disrespect. He was referring to the University's provost, its second-in-command, who had just authorized far higher raises for executive-level administrators than he had for the faculty (and, for the record, completely legally).[1]

The Blogger was a tenured full professor with a yen for transparency, a deep commitment to shared governance, and a compulsive need to test the limits of academic freedom and the First Amendment. A successful teacher and a well-published scholar, he was as unassuming in real life as he was wittily caustic in his online persona. He had been a harsh critic of The Hat's predecessor for presiding over a period of decline; a measured skeptic of The Hat himself, but one who rallied to his cause upon his defenestration; and a long-standing University Senate activist and union opponent who, in a dramatic U-turn, joined the union organizing committee when it became clear that the card-check campaign would succeed.[2] In later years, The Blogger alternated between union leadership positions and the presidency of the Senate itself. He thus personally embodied the structural conflict that pitted both of the University's organs of faculty representation against its own executive leadership. During an era of leadership crisis, when a string of short-term presidents and provosts rotated through the central administration building, top administrators presented an easy target for all the frustrations, resentments, and anxieties that marred the decade.

The University's woes were by no means unusual, nor were The Blogger's complaints merely the cranky eruptions of a disgruntled gadfly. Faculty everywhere refer to administrators only half-jokingly as "the dark side." In 2011, the Johns Hopkins University professor Benjamin Ginsberg drew up a sweeping bill of indictment in *The Fall of the Faculty: The Rise of the All-Administrative University and Why It Matters*.[3] Ginsberg cited the undisputed fact that in the last quarter of the twentieth century the number of full-time faculty increased by only 51 percent nationwide, whereas the ranks of administrators grew 85 percent, and other nonacademic professionals grew by a whopping 240 percent. He set aside the usual explanations, including the escalating need for nonacademic services (such as information technology, student support, and fund-raising); the onerous new mandates, regulations, and accountability regimes imposed by federal and state governments and accrediting and licensure agencies; and the faculty's own eagerness to shift irksome administrative chores onto staff to gain more time for their own research.

For Ginsberg, the real culprit was "administrative imperialists." Like bureaucrats everywhere, these creatures allegedly expand their fiefdoms simply because they can. Dipping into pots of gold filled by tuition dollars, they love to multiply the ranks of "deanlets," "deanlings," and associate and assistant vice provosts and vice presidents of all sorts, whose principal function ostensibly consists purely in giving their superiors a larger number of direct reports to boss around. Among other dastardly techniques are what Ginsberg labeled "corruption," "theft," and "fraud." At the root of the problem was the collapse of the tenure system and the rise of adjunct faculty, a trend Ginsberg conceded had many complex causes in addition to the opportunism of power-hungry administrators. In Ginsberg's view, "there is no academic freedom without tenure," and the university and its academic ideals could only be redeemed by a return to a happier era when professors sat at the commanding heights and administrators knew their place.

Of all the debates and controversies narrated in this book, this one is the most stagnant and persistently unenlightening. A decade later, critics of administrative bloat, even and especially at the most prestigious institutions, were still making much the same arguments.[4] Contributors are often proudly ignorant of how administration works, prone to Golden Age thinking about bygone eras of muscular shared governance, and strangely unreflective about the hard work required to maintain the delicate, increasingly endangered academic ecosystem that protects their own freedom to teach and research—and criticize their own leaders.[5]

In this chapter I lift the lid on what administrators do. I show how a bevy of skilled (and, yes, often well-paid) administrators are needed to ensure that their employers remain competitive with their peers over a broad domain of distinct functions and portfolios. Just as in the treatment of tuition in chapter 2, I follow the money to ask what the allocation of resources reveals about the distribution of power among different roles. The analysis begins with a coarse reckoning of administrative spending and personnel hiring trends at the University relative to its peers. This opens up a series of hypotheses about the causes, scale, and shape of administrative growth during the 2010s. A more granular analysis follows focused on student recruitment and retention, plus management of the institution's public image, political relationships, and donor base. These are the areas that were of central, even existential, importance to the University as it navigated public disinvestment, emancipation from the State Board, the need to recruit tuition-paying students, faculty unionization, and its own ambitions to keep pace with its peers.

Near the end, I take stock of two areas—college sports and executive compensation—in which the hazards of corruption are greater and public criticisms of runaway costs are more legitimate. Assessing not just the quantity but also the quality of new administration, I scan for signs of a new corporate, managerial, market-driven ethos in an institution ostensibly governed by purer academic and intellectual norms. Corporate practices are indeed spreading, but mainly to thicken universities' administrative shells to better protect their academic cores, and thereby to compensate for the ongoing withdrawal of states' financial, political, and administrative support.

ADMINISTRATIVE BLOAT?

Each year, the federal government collects a raft of statistics on each U.S. college and university, providing breakdowns on how much they spend on different categories of activity. This enables the public not only to track increases (or more rarely decreases) in expenditures within a single institution but also to compare that institution with others of a similar type. Obviously, the most essential activity is instruction (which, importantly, includes the full salaries of tenure-track faculty who also do research). Federal statistics also tabulate other research expenditures (such as stand-alone research institutes, grant-funded projects, and infrastructure), noninstructional student services (e.g., the admissions and registrar's offices and student clubs and organizations), and two categories called "academic support" and "institutional support." Academic support includes things like libraries, museums, and computing centers, plus deans and other central academic administrators who oversee the core missions of teaching and research. Student advisors, whose ranks have been expanding along with the escalating complexity of college life and of the undergraduate curriculum, are variously counted under academic support or student services, and sometimes under instruction.

Institutional support is the catch-all category that often attracts controversy. In addition to routine functions such as payroll, human resources, IT, and campus maintenance, it includes high-paid executives and offices for fund-raising, public relations, brand management, and lobbying, which are often derided as wasteful, excessive, dishonest, or sordid. As noted in chapter 2, "auxiliary enterprises" financed by student fees or other revenue streams are generally not included in the tabulations of core expenses. Auxiliaries include residence and dining halls, student health services, and intercollegiate athletics—the last of which attracts its own share of criticism.[6]

If organizational budgets reflect organizational priorities, figure 4.1 offers clear insights into the University's focus on students during the 2010s. In every category except research, which declined in real terms, spending increased far more than the cumulative rate of inflation. This should come as no surprise given the analysis of tuition increases and the "cost disease" (see chapter 2),

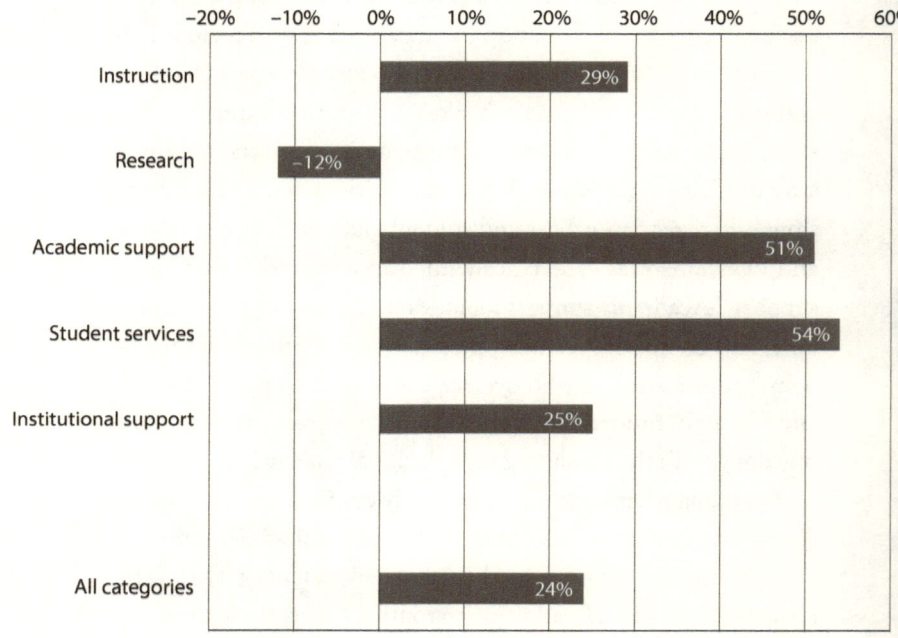

FIGURE 4.1 Increases in selected core expenditures, by category, 2010–2020.

Source: Office of Institutional Research. Expenditures for 2010 are adjusted to 2020 constant dollars based on 19 percent overall inflation. "Revenue and Expenditures," https://perma.cc/T4TR-B4U5, three-year averages (FY09–11 and FY19–21). Public service and other core expenses are omitted.

not to mention the faculty union's success in bargaining significant raises. Corresponding to real increases of 2.2 percent to 2.6 percent each year for ten years, the figures for instruction, institutional support, and all categories combined still fall comfortably below the 3 percent gap between consumer inflation and annual cost rises that experts regard as the maximum sustainable level. In contrast, the most remarkable change, with real increases of over 50 percent, came in the two noninstructional but still student-centered categories of academic support and student services. These expenses pay for all manner of university staff, activities, materials, and services to enhance students' academic experience and to tend to their psychological, social, physical, and financial well-being.

Comparing the University's record of growth with that of similar institutions tells a complementary story: one in which it decisively closed the gap that had separated it from its peers. Figure 4.2 switches the dimension of analysis from total expenditures to expenditures per student to place the University alongside other institutions of varying enrollment size. Compared with all other public four-year universities, the University repositioned itself from laggard to leader by devoting its resources to both instruction and other student-oriented functions. Strikingly, it moved up by more than 30 percentage points in both instruction and student services relative to that benchmark. Only in academic support, where it began far behind, did it still slightly trail the national average by the end of the decade. In institutional support and overall totals, it likewise closed the gap and even overshot it by a modest amount. An alternative set of peers is offered by *private* research universities, specifically those categorized as having "high research activity." Although the University pulled within striking distance of these comparators in instruction and research (another reassuring sign that it prioritized teaching and knowledge creation), figure 4.2 reveals that private research universities still spend almost twice as much in all other categories, whether focused on students or not.[7]

What I call the para-academic side of the University—academic advisors of all sorts, plus financial aid specialists, career placement counselors, student life professionals, and other occupations who support students but do not deliver academic instruction—grew more than any other component of

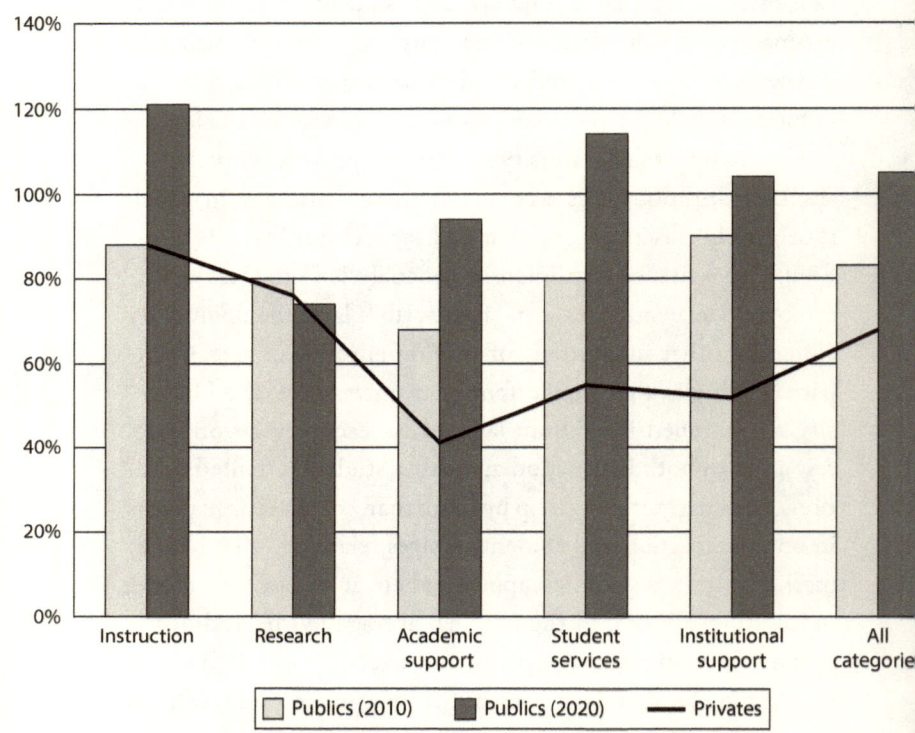

FIGURE 4.2 Per-student expenditures at the University as a percentage of national averages, by category.

Source: National Center for Education Statistics. Expenditures for 2010 are adjusted to 2020 constant dollars based on 19 percent overall inflation. IPEDS Data Feedback reports for the University (2011, 2021, and 2019, each reporting on the prior year) and Digest of Education Statistics tables 334.10 (four-year publics in 2010 and 2020, at https://perma.cc/9FK3-DMVB) and 334.40 (privates with high research activity in 2018, at https://perma.cc/6SR3-JXKB). Public service and other core expenses are omitted.

its workforce during the 2010s, at least in proportional terms. During the middle years of the decade, the University enlarged the category of "instructional support occupations" by fully 230 employees in only five years, an enormous 134 percent leap. In contrast, it grew the faculty by only 15 percent, shrank the proportion of managers, and held relatively flat, at 7 percent, the increase in the number of other employees, ranging from clerical and maintenance staff to IT, finance, legal, medical, and other nonacademic professionals.[8]

In growing its nonfaculty, nonmanagerial academic administrative staff, and at a far higher rate than the full-time faculty itself, the University participated in a long-standing national trend. The Delta Cost Project, which in recent years has been the most cited objective study of administrative expansion, found exactly the same pattern in analyzing the prior decade, from 2000 to 2012.[9] That report confirmed, on one hand, the overall shift toward administration bemoaned by Ginsberg, The Blogger, and many others. It underscored that the faculty now constitute only about 25 to 30 percent of all jobs at research universities, and that the ratio of faculty to administrators declined precipitously, from 3.5 to 2.2 between 1990 and 2012, at these institutions.[10] But the Delta study also showed that recent growth in the administrative ranks has been concentrated, not in the highest-paid executive and managerial positions but in more middle-class professional occupations. Among these, noninstructional student services, such as student advising and counseling, predominated. Upward pressures on tuition spring in large part from universities' need to recruit and retain highly educated professionals by paying them competitive market rates. But faculty salaries are not entirely to blame for this trend. The study found an even greater effect from the growing share of nonfaculty professionals being added to university payrolls. Even when these employees' individual salaries are comparatively modest, their collective numbers—again, 230 of them at the University—generate significant added expense. As a nationwide phenomenon, such growth has been going on since the 1990s, far longer than the growth of upper executive and managerial personnel, which only gained steam a decade later.[11]

Inherent structural differences between the labor markets for faculty and administrative staff help explain this pattern. As a group, nonfaculty professionals are hired in a far more fluid job market than faculty members. On several national clearinghouses, such as the *Chronicle of Higher Education*, both position descriptions and salaries are constantly and publicly available to administrators looking to change employers. Not only at the executive but also at the upper-middle level, an army of headhunting firms assists in moving these professionals from place to place, advising them along the way about compensation expectations. But at all levels, from frontline academic advisors and admissions recruiters to middle level fund-raisers and IT experts to managerial level vice presidents and vice provosts of all sorts, university administrators have year-round opportunities to bounce across the country and bargain for higher salaries in the process. For an industry in which employee compensation accounts for 80 percent of all expenses, the rising overall cost associated with these nonfaculty professionals derives from a highly competitive labor market in which those with skills and geographic mobility can command ever-higher salaries.

Faculty job markets are even more competitive, often ridiculously so, sometimes with hundreds of applicants for each available tenure-track faculty position. But they are far less fluid than administrator job markets. It takes a year or more to hire a tenure-track professor, and sometimes two or three years to recruit a top scientist whose laboratory and research staff may be hard to relocate. Even full-time non-tenure-track instructors are now typically hired through national job searches lasting many months. In contrast, nonfaculty professionals can and do pick up stakes within a matter of weeks, just as educated professionals do in nonacademic occupations. And whereas faculty are like Galápagos finches, highly evolved subspecialists in esoteric academic niches, administrators are, if not complete generalists, at least routinely able to parlay skill sets acquired in one sector into job opportunities in another. As a telling recent trend, trained PhDs who once hoped to become professors have instead begun to embark on "alt-ac" (alternative to academic) careers by redescribing their skills in dissertation research and classroom management in terms that win them nonacademic positions in middle level university administration. In short, if the faculty job hunt remains a buyer's market in most fields, a circumstance that helps fuel adjunctification, the opposite is true for administrators, who thrive in a seller's market.

This broad picture of administrative growth, centered on middle level para-academic professionals rather than on the headline-grabbing salaries of the topmost executive administrators, leads to a series of provisional conclusions that are explored further in the following sections. Among these are that, in the 2010s, the University

- continued to prioritize its core academic mission.
- found that students' needs for noninstructional academic support and especially nonacademic student services warranted even greater proportional increases.
- refrained from harvesting extra tuition revenue to subsidize research, and even shrank its real expenditures on research infrastructure.
- moderately restrained the growth of institutional support even though it still far outpaced inflation.
- likewise reined in the growth of executive and managerial positions, at least in numbers if not necessarily in their aggregate compensation.

With these hypotheses derived from crude aggregate data, I now turn to a more granular look at how the University reformed and revamped the structure of its managerial, noninstructional, nonacademic functions in the 2010s. A series of top-level reorganizations at the University offers revealing insights into internal administrative politics, as executive leaders responded to and implemented changes to institution-wide values and goals.

RECRUITING AND RETAINING STUDENTS

I begin with students. Delving into the broad expense categories of "student services" and "academic support" reveals how the University prioritized the recruitment and retention of undergraduates during the 2010s. Any institution as dependent as the University is on undergraduate tuition, specifically out-of-state tuition, must put a premium on identifying, contacting, courting, and marketing the college experience to prospective students so they will enroll in sufficient numbers to balance the books. Initiatives to promote degree completion pay real dividends by reducing enrollment attrition and the attendant loss in tuition revenue. Added to this financial necessity is the ethical obligation to help students, once they enroll, graduate in a timely fashion, as well to provide extra support to those who might otherwise drop out for academic, financial, social, medical, or psychological reasons. These twin imperatives—recruiting and retaining undergraduates—helped define the University's enrollment management strategy as it strained to reconcile public disinvestment with an ongoing commitment to its public mission. The monies invested in specific initiatives to further these goals explain the disproportionate increases in noninstructional academic support and student services noted previously.

In Fall 2012, the University's highly successful vice provost of enrollment management was promoted to a vice presidency. What might seem to be an inconsequential change in title for a job well done turned out to be the first step in building what can deservedly be labeled an internal institutional empire, and a high-performing one at that. Enrollment management includes the admissions office, the registrar, the financial aid office, and other routine student-facing services. Many public flagship institutions keep these functions under the jurisdiction of the provost. Such universities typically enjoy a captive pool of well-qualified in-state students who reliably apply in sufficient numbers, supplemented by a steady stream of out-of-staters, and therefore they do not have to worry much about filling their freshman classes. This allows enrollment management offices to focus on properly academic issues—screening the qualifications of high-school applicants, and applying various academic policies to them after they matriculate—that properly belong under provost oversight.

But it was clear by the early 2010s that the University's solvency depended on a highly aggressive admissions, marketing, and communications operation. Enrollment management became a sophisticated and highly professionalized function that came complete with savvy media experts, algorithmically driven "customer relations management" software to initiate and maintain electronic contact with prospective students, and a small army of recruiters who fanned out to other states, near and far, to press the flesh at high school college fairs.[12] At the University, growing annual budgets for the Admissions Office and Strategic Communications (a new $1.9 million organization) reflected these priorities.[13] Overall, Enrollment Management's (EM's) total administrative budget (excluding financial aid scholarships given out to students, which are monies not tied to paying for administrative staff and services) grew by 78 percent over the decade.[14] EM clearly merited a vice presidential portfolio and a seat on the president's Cabinet at an institution that now walked, talked, and looked much like a private university.

A second and even bigger power shift occurred in October 2016 when the Vice President for Student Life, who had rebuilt both the student union and the recreation center, departed for a higher position in another state. Four months later, amid the vacuum in power, large chunks of her portfolio were transferred to EM, which was duly rechristened Student Services and Enrollment Management (SSEM). This reorganization affected two enormous auxiliary enterprises—Housing (including dormitories and dining halls) and the Student Health Center (including mental health counseling)—with a combined budget of nearly $80 million in 2020. Although rising costs for auxiliaries are driven mainly by market prices for, in this case, rental housing and health care, they do generate enough discretionary resources, enough legitimate "slush," to finance worthy special initiatives that SSEM leadership might favor—academic programming in the dormitories, for example, where over the years Housing proved far more able to contribute resources for collaborative ventures than its poorer cousins in the academic schools and colleges.

Student Life, which had previously housed these auxiliaries, commanded their resources, and enjoyed the political heft that came with their eight-figure budgets, was verily gutted by their removal. It was instead left with a hodgepodge of essential and important but strategically marginal, administratively unappealing, and financially constrained functions and services. These included the Dean of Students office (overseeing student misconduct and crisis issues), the student union, the career center, student government, and the physical education and student recreation programs. The vice presidency for Student Life was filled by two interims promoted internally from more junior positions, but a proper national search for a permanent incumbent had not been undertaken even by the early 2020s. No public rationale was ever given for scrambling these functions between SSEM and Student Life. In retrospect it is difficult to deduce any strategy other than the desire to amalgamate the most vitally important nonacademic, undergraduate-centered functions into a single large, integrated organization. Whereas Student Life's headline budget fell a whopping 82 percent in real terms in the 2010s, SSEM's stood at $118 million in 2020. This made SSEM the third largest organization in the entire University, trailing only the College of Arts and Sciences ($163 million) and the Division of Athletics ($133 million).

Hefty and gregarious, optimistic and blunt, the now Vice President for Student Services and Enrollment Management rose through the ranks as a natural salesperson who, like all good salespeople, believed in his own product: the University's world-famous brand. Under his stewardship, the University set enrollment records, managed the politically tricky balance of enrolling enough in-state students to appease watchful legislators while also recruiting enough out-of-state and international students to pay full tuition, and steadily increased the average standardized test scores and GPAs of each new entering class. SSEM's vice president also created a highly professional organization distinguished by high staff morale and shared purpose at a time when leadership turnover elsewhere in the central administration, not to mention the faculty grievances that had fueled unionization, made other quarters of the institution seem perennially unhappy. As a sign of organizational pride and loyalty to the university brand, SSEM staffers began to sport knit cotton polo shirts or the collarless shiny synthetics favored by the more athletically inclined, but always with SSEM logos. Unlike many other campus entities, notably the academic departments, SSEM's value to the institution could be straightforwardly judged using quantified performance metrics: admission yield rates, measures of academic degree progress, even the number of transactions per day processed by the Registrar's Office. To manage it all, a staff of associate vice presidents was augmented by various data wranglers, strategic communications specialists, and a chief of staff who coordinated the top leadership group.

SSEM now became perhaps the most thoroughly corporatized organization within the University. Its detailed 2022 strategic plan ran to fifty-five pages, in a stark contrast with Student Life's paltry two-page infographic.[15] It enumerated hundreds of bullet points, metrics, and deliverables, all clearly aligned with critical institutional needs. With invocations of "utilization targets" and "best practices," it resembled corporate strategic plans everywhere. The plan boasted a range of substantive, actionable goals, such as identifying "risk points" during students' progress toward degree completion, hybrid virtual and in-person advising to "meet students and families where they are," and programs to enhance food security, body acceptance, uptake of STD screening services, teletherapy, career pathway mapping, and social connectedness—all with a special accent on underserved populations. The document is just as noteworthy for the attention it gives to the professional development, onboarding, on-the-job training, and morale of the SSEM staff itself, as well as to the importance of knitting SSEM's numerous subunits together into a cohesive whole. Identical goal-oriented phrases crop up in widely different functions, from health care to registrar services, newly fused together in what otherwise could have felt like a forced bureaucratic merger. SSEM took pains to stress the importance of collaborative relationships with outside partners—including Student Life and the academic schools and colleges—but the real emphasis was on community-building and esprit de corps across its own organization chart. Implicitly, the unit argued that the best way to serve students is to support the employees who serve them.

FUND-RAISING AND FRIEND-RAISING

Peeking under the hood of "institutional support" reveals the fascinating swirl of activity that followed the dissolution of the State Board of Higher Education. Top administrators were suddenly flying without a net, facing the same challenges as their private-university counterparts. The ensuing reconfiguration of vice presidential portfolios dramatically depicts how the University pivoted from its prior role as a unit of the now-defunct state university system to one that now had to manage its own revenues, political connections, public image, collective ambitions, and risk. A set of functions that one might call "fund-raising and friend-raising" expanded to convince both public advocates and private donors to support its new, hybrid, privately funded, publicly oriented mission. These functions had assumed existential importance for a newly emancipated university, so it is worth tracking expenditure growth in this area and comparing it with more routine functions also gathered under the broad rubric of institutional support.

Two large administrative reorganizations were undertaken midway through the decade to cultivate financial and political support and a general sense of public goodwill toward the University. First, in 2013–14, the vice presidencies for "development" and "university relations" were combined into a single unit called "advancement."[16] "Development," in this context, refers to fund-raising from individual donors and other private entities. These range from prospective big fish who receive special attention to the small to midsized contributors who typically either donate annually or designate portions of their estates to their alma mater. Most earmark their philanthropy for a particular academic program or student scholarship. Corporate and foundation philanthropy, which is a significant source of revenue at some peer institutions, did not figure prominently in the University's fund-raising profile. And athletics had its own, separate development operation because relatively few sports donors, with the notable exception of the Big Donor, show an interest in academics, or vice versa. Fund-raisers in the Development Office stewarded everyone else. As seen in chapter 1, the University's fund-raising haul reached unprecedented levels by the end of the 2010s. This remained true even after setting aside the blockbuster donations for two new satellite campuses: the *non*-marquee-level donations raised by staff were also setting records by the early 2020s.[17]

The other advancement offices, those inherited from University Relations, included the alumni association, which stimulates warm sentiments about the alma mater to seed the ground for future donations and political advocacy, and a set of three government and community relations offices focused on the federal, state, and local levels.[18] The state-level office was particularly successful in lobbying state legislators and the statewide Higher Education Coordinating Commission. Despite a traumatic rupture with the former state university system, it acted in remarkable concert with the other newly independent public universities. Because of its newfound freedom to advocate for its own interests, the University reaped significant increases in state appropriations after the Recession dip bottomed out in 2012. This uptick largely tracked the overall rebound of the state economy, but it also reflected a sustained political damage-control effort that, by 2021, had increased state appropriations by an impressive 56 percent in real terms relative to that nadir.[19]

In the second major reorganization of 2016, a new vice presidency was hived off of advancement to focus exclusively on strategic communications. The spur to this reorganization was the curation of the University's public brand. That effort began with a $5 million private donation earmarked for a campuswide "rebranding" via an upgrade of the University's web presence, print promotions, and other media products and strategies. A nationally respected creative consulting firm named 160 over 90 was hired to kick-start the job. (The firm's name referred to its ability to get consumers' blood pumping even if, in a lapse of self-branding, it suggested a worrisome level of clinical hypertension.) The consultants' charge was to bring greater prominence to the academic side of a university whose public image had for long been tied to its sports teams and party-school reputation. A public relations team consisting largely of young men, some sporting fade haircuts or stylishly untucked dress shirts, descended on campus to interview administrators, deans, and a handpicked selection of faculty. A new brand template was duly launched, consisting of a new set of fonts, colors, icons, images, and taglines for use on university websites and promotional materials of all sorts. The University also benefited from the near-collapse of the venerable local newspaper—nationwide, local journalism nearly died in the 2010s thanks to the rise of online media—by adding to its staff several knowledgeable ex-reporters who had once exposed the institution's foibles but who were now employed to sing its praises.

Branding and corporate public relations activities have attracted deserved criticism in recent years. Hype, clichés, conformism, and a fast and loose attitude toward anecdotes and statistics that ostensibly demonstrate universities' unparalleled greatness are among the dangers of the new regime in strategic communications.[20] One wonders, too, whether students' mental health anxieties are exacerbated by the glossy marketing brochures that depict their peers as uniformly ecstatic and diverse, lolling about on evergreen campus quads. But public relations, despite being inevitably at odds with honest truth-telling, is universally seen as the cost of doing business at virtually all higher education institutions, private and public.

It was thus a surprising reversal when President Five abruptly pulled the plug on the new branding initiative. A major national higher education trade publication credited the University with avoiding the "ridiculously expensive" and "time-intensive enterprise" of overinvesting in the curation its public brand. It was also praised for trying to curtail the inefficient redundancies that occur when schools, colleges, and administrative units create their own rival communications offices.[21] However, despite these plaudits, different subunits of the University continued to engage in precisely that activity. In 2021, Schools and Colleges still spent $1.9 million on their own in-house public relations shops.[22] Most of that money went to magazines, websites, and other outreach to advertise local points of pride overlooked by central and SSEM communications staffs. But part of the point was to gain notoriety within the university administration itself. Rather than vying for the attention of outside constituencies, intra-institutional strategic communications help to attract the notice and secure the patronage of senior leaders. This follows as a natural consequence of the need to compete for resources within any complex organization. Wherever one looks, inside or out, public relations lubricates the gears of the unfettered university.

The financial impact of all of these changes is shown in table 4.1. Taken together, expenditures for fund-raising and

Table 4.1 Institutional support (selected functions)

Administrative function	2010	2020	% change
Fund-raising and friend-raising	$17,664,164	$25,285,322	+43
General administration	$67,700,149	$89,152,221	+32
Information services	$19,552,196	$28,032,148	+43

Source: Budget and Resource Planning (BRP), "Level 4 Expenditure Report FY08–11," https://perma.cc/K6QP-MZKY; BRP, "Level 5 Expenditure Report for FY19," https://perma.cc/NNV4-6VFF; BRP, "Level 5 Expenditure Report for FY20," https://perma.cc/3U7V-XEZL; and BRP, "Level 5 Expenditure Report for FY21," https://perma.cc/3ZWR-DTDU. Figures are three-year averages (FY09–11 and FY19–21). Dollar figures for 2010 are adjusted to 2020 constant dollars based on 19 percent overall inflation. "Fund-raising and friend-raising" includes development, alumni relations, government and community relations (federal, state, and local), strategic communications, and related smaller offices.

friend-raising increased by 43 percent in real terms over the decade. This is notably greater than the 32 percent increase in that component of institutional support attributable to routine financial and administrative functions, such as human resources, budget and payroll, public safety, and campus services and facilities maintenance. It also happens to match the 43 percent real rise in information services (read: information technology) expenditures, which are also roughly the same in absolute terms ($25 million versus $28 million). This last is an especially revealing comparison; few would deny that universities' need for improved computing equipment and information technology services skyrocketed over the decade, or that the cost for skilled IT labor rose commensurately.[23] This juxtaposition shows that, whether by design or more likely by accident, the University treated fund-raising and friend-raising as a mission-critical function on the same priority level as IT equipment and services. Both are inescapable cost drivers in a competitive climate.

ATHLETICS

Here is as good a place as any to say a few words about intercollegiate athletics. This is an enterprise that can straightforwardly be grouped under the rubric of fund-raising and friend-raising. Notionally, college sports once served to integrate the mental and physical development of scholar-athletes. But today they amount to a lucrative entertainment business appended by historical accident to the real university. There are plenty of good reasons to criticize college sports for the ways they overshadow education and taint institutional reputations.[24] Certainly the University courted its fair share of notoriety during the 2010s. A translucent glass advising building for student-athletes—wags dubbed it the "jock box"—pointed up the decrepitude of the nearby residence halls and science labs, and thus the gulf separating the athletic haves from the academic have-nots. A shiny aluminum-clad basketball arena, despite also being funded by the Big Donor, in fact saddled the University with risky long-term debt. As for coaches' salaries, the less said about that the better.

Sports-related scandals also helped topple two presidents. Early in his tenure, The Hat fired the athletic director for underperformance, but not before approving a $2.3 million golden parachute that easily exceeded what a typical University graduate could expect to earn in a lifetime—by actually holding down a job. That debacle grievously undermined The Hat's political stature, perhaps fatally, at the very moment he desperately needed gubernatorial and legislative support for his New Partnership proposal. Later, an alleged gang rape, which involved three Black basketball players and a white female undergraduate, ensnared the basketball coach, multiple administrators, and a different president in allegations—ultimately disproven—of covering up the crime. Multiple campus protests erupted at the intersection of race, sex, and sports, all but destroying the possibility of reasoned discourse on such a vexed trio of controversial topics. In a damning indictment of campus culture, a University Senate task force later reported that "despite the relatively small number of students directly involved in their activities, Athletics and Fraternity and Sorority Life (FSL) play disproportionately powerful roles in facilitating or tolerating conditions in which sexual violence occurs on campus."[25] The short-lived President Three's clumsy public handling of the rape crisis culminated in his sudden resignation at what was easily the low point of the entire decade.

Even at the best of times, university presidents must routinely engage in well-intentioned but transparent hypocrisy to reconcile academic values with those of college sports. More so even than their souls, presidents' time is at risk: perhaps the biggest objective downside to big-time college athletics is that it robs them of the bandwidth needed to tend to all the other academic and institutional priorities of the universities they manage. The only viable solution—which is the lesson of this chapter over all—is to delegate as much as possible to a cadre of well-paid administrators who are consummate experts in their fields, whether finance, NCAA compliance, Title IX policies, risk management, TV contracts, conference dealmaking, branding, booster relations, the hiring and firing of coaching staff, and, not least, the well-being of student-athletes themselves. The belated professionalization of the University's Athletic Department, which went on to enjoy stable and effective leadership throughout the rest of the 2010s, revealed the wisdom of that strategy, arrived at after a painful learning process.

For all the inequities—and iniquities—attending intercollegiate athletics, the devil's bargain is worth making. The end goal is to cultivate goodwill among supporters, whether donors who loosen their wallets at a boozy tailgate or in an exclusive skybox, taxpayers who may otherwise be indifferent to the intellectual missions of their own public universities, or families who passively learn about academic offerings during halftime infomercials. At the University, that bargain was all but free of charge. Unusually among peer universities, *no* general fund dollars went to the support of athletics, which was financed solely through ticket sales, private donations, merchandising, and NCAA and conference revenues from lucrative television broadcast deals.[26] To this one can also add the unique ability of college sports to attract high-paying students from both in and out of state. Reckoning Facebook "likes" by ZIP code, the University's college football team was more popular in large swaths of neighboring states than those states' own flagship teams.[27] For tuition-dependent institutions, that kind of brand appeal can spell the difference between prosperity and insolvency.

Crucially, for all the baleful influence athletics is claimed to exert over universities, for all the genuine scandals that do rock college sports, and for all the sins the University itself may have committed, there is no evidence that decision-making in the University's academic core was corrupted or manipulated through undue influence by intercollegiate athletics in the 2010s.[28] Quite the contrary: athletic departments and academic departments simply compete against their peers within two separate cultural and administrative universes. However jarring the juxtaposition of sports and scholarship, the physical and the intellectual, over-the-top bluster and truth-seeking sobriety, aggression and pacifism, team spirit and individual merit—all dualities marking the cohabitation of athletics and academics within higher education—the former demonstrably benefits the latter on any dispassionate view. Sports are a magnet for funds and friends who benefit the university's core missions.

EXECUTIVES AND MANAGERS

I conclude with the large group of executive and managerial professionals whose high compensation attracts the most scrutiny from critics of administrative bloat. As of mid-2021, 103 administrators at the University earned higher salaries than the average full professor, who made $145,026, which was itself a hefty upper-middle-class income.[29] This group of administrators included the twenty-eight uppermost employees designated "executive leadership," a category that includes the president, provost, vice presidents, vice provosts, academic deans, and a handful of others.[30] Among the remaining seventy-five were a sprinkling of doctors, lawyers, and other high-paid professionals from the realms of finance, construction, technology, public relations, and other fields with ready counterparts outside of higher education, and whose salaries could therefore be expected to track those in other sectors of the economy.[31] But the majority of these senior managers held positions that are indigenous to university administration, quite often having been spawned within the last decade or two. These include many of the associate and assistant vice presidents; associate and assistant vice provosts; associate deans and senior associate deans; and executive directors, plain-vanilla directors, and senior associate directors whose proliferation has been bemoaned by Ginsberg and satirized by The Blogger. Some of these are administrators drawn from the faculty, but most are not.

The collective influence of these managers altered not just the quantity but the quality of administration. Setting aside the motley corporate borrowings from strategic planning to brand management whose tangible impact is difficult to pin down, one concrete and revealing indicator is the number of "chiefs of staff" employed by the University. Chiefs of staff are high-paid managers who typically report to vice presidents, executive directors, or other senior leaders, unburdening those leaders of the prior duty of managing their own staff. Another of their key functions is to interact with their counterparts in other leadership offices. The number of chiefs of staff grew from only two in 2010 to eleven in 2021, thereby interposing a new stratum of gatekeepers between management and frontline staff and faculty and widening the hierarchy of status and power that separates the two groups.[32]

The total cost of executives and managers grew just as inexorably as faculty salaries and, in strategically important quarters of the university, far more rapidly. Taken together, the aggregate compensation of the top one hundred administrators, including salary and benefits, totaled well over $30 million a year.[33] Skyrocketing salaries were a perverse side effect of unstable leadership. Early in the 2010s, with a succession of five presidents and a rotating cast of ambitious nonacademic vice presidents, successful candidates for administrative jobs could often bargain for high salaries as a form of hazard pay for stepping into a tenuous position. Only when the waters calmed was the University able to introduce greater rationality to a system that had grown in unmonitored fashion. Late in the decade, the University mounted a from top to bottom "banding" exercise to nudge salaries of all administrators toward greater equity and transparency.[34] A newly introduced compensation scheme comprised fifteen distinct ranges of pay corresponding to ever-higher levels of responsibility and required skill. New protocols were introduced to ensure that individual administrators were recruited in open and competitive national searches. That said, even a concerted initiative could only do so much to bring order and system to the administration of a large, complex, multipurpose institution. In the new semiprivatized university, as has long been the case at its fully private counterparts, the law of the labor market reigns supreme.

Faculty understandably resist the imposition of a new stratum of high-paid managers, executives, and gatekeepers. Class resentment and status anxiety—"These people don't even have PhDs!"—undeniably play a role. Certainly, universities have lost, probably irretrievably, the flatter, simpler, more collegial, and more consultative governance that used to suffice when they were much less complex and much more dependent on whatever funding the state legislature did or did not supply. In this age, university administrations confront new challenges and new opportunities: to raise their own revenues; to manage their public image and reputation; to augment core academic functions with an expanding array of student services and amenities; to balance teaching and research within the academic core; and to anticipate risks and neutralize threats of all kinds, from scandals around race, gender, and athletics (or all three at once) to unionized labor actions to financial meltdowns to global pandemics.

As scholars have long pointed out, the governance of large research universities is anarchic, opportunistic, and uncoordinated by design. Within the academic core, this design feature has the salutary effect of protecting academic creativity, spontaneity, and intellectual freedom.[35] But outside of it, a thick administrative shell is required to protect this fragile ecosystem from all the challenges and threats that might harm its chaotically utopian functioning.[36] As those external pressures, whether hostile or well-intentioned, have become greater, it is no surprise that the shell has grown faster than the core.

The irony is that the emancipation of public universities from public oversight begets more bureaucracy, not less. The increased autonomy, independence, devolution, and local control granted to public universities forces them to sink a greater share of their own resources into charting their own course, leading them to replicate and duplicate functions that previously were handled by higher public authorities such as state university systems and governmental compliance agencies. The unfettered university is more intensively managed and administered than the classic public university of the twentieth century. The shifts in administrative resources and strategic priorities narrated in this chapter all required a cadre of managerial leaders to first formulate strategic decisions and then carry them out. Whether that set of functions is worth more than $30 million a year is beside the point. The kind of market discipline imposed in the corporate world, where profits and losses can be tracked against measurable indicators of employee performance, simply does not exist in higher education, nor is it clear that it ever should. But the need to compete for students, for faculty, and for public favor has a powerful disciplining effect of its own. As with so many of the other questions of money and power tackled in the chapters so far, institutional survival and legitimacy depend on pleasing these various groups. In the next group of chapters, I turn to the far trickier question of whether public universities do as well by their multiple missions as they do by their multiple stakeholders.

II

MISSIONS

The real problems that beset today's public universities lurk in areas that do not make the headlines. When we turn from stakeholders to missions, it is clear that universities are producing solid but decidedly suboptimal outcomes. The root causes of underperformance are often public policies and public pressures that are misaligned with universities' internal organization and culture. Unintended consequences result when well-intentioned outsiders—be they politicians, accreditors, government entities, or nongovernmental advocacy groups—try to steer, nudge, regulate, or override universities' own incentives and behaviors with counterproductive mandates.

This is true for each of the four principal missions that the public university fulfills. In *research*, a STEM-driven quest for higher rankings focuses institutions on boosting metrics of research productivity rather than on nurturing authentic creativity. The result is troubling evidence of scientific and scholarly stagnation. In *teaching*, the national college completion agenda focuses universities on bureaucratic assessments of learning and teaching rather than on pedagogical innovations that might actually improve student success. The result is an epidemic of stress and anxiety among students bearing the strain of that disconnect. As for *diversity*, the Supreme Court has spent generations moving the goalposts on constitutionally permissible uses of race in college admissions. The result is a right-wing populist backlash that robs energy and resources from shoring up the declining K–12 school systems that feed into higher education. And the university's public *impact* mission is the exception that proves the rule. Today's innovation and entrepreneurship initiatives flourish in a competitive arena carved out by an enlightened public policy and populated by a range of public-private partnerships.

5

RESEARCH

Do rankings of research universities distort their priorities and distract from their missions?

The Association of American Universities (AAU) exerts a remarkably seductive pull for what amounts to a mid-sized lobbying shop. Its headquarters are at One Dupont Circle in Washington, D.C., the nationwide nerve center for higher education advocacy groups. But to members and aspiring members, this suite of fifth floor offices is the nation's single most exclusive and coveted club. Founded in 1900 by a handful of elite universities, the AAU includes the seventy-one most prestigious research institutions in North America, thirty-one of them private and forty public. What the *U.S. News and World Report* and similar college rankings are to students and parents, the AAU is to faculty and administrators—especially those at public institutions.

For public research universities, AAU status is a designation elite enough to be worth striving for, but not so elite as to be unattainable. The top private schools owe their high *U.S. News and World Report* rankings to a combination of selective admissions and research excellence. But large public institutions simply cannot be exclusive enough in their undergraduate admissions policies—they cannot manage to reject enough worthy applicants—to move up in rank. Only a handful of public AAUs, such as Berkeley, UCLA, Michigan, North Carolina, and Virginia, routinely make the *U.S. News and World Report* top twenty-five national research universities, a list that otherwise includes only private AAUs.[1] However, because of their large scale, public universities most certainly can compete on the basis of their research, which is what the AAU prizes above all else. Research is the coin of the realm in worldwide university rankings as well.

Measured by research grant dollars and PhD production, the United States has 146 "Research 1" (R1) universities and another 133 classified as "Research 2" (R2). These two classifications and a handful of others were created in the 1970s to *discourage* America's vast diversity of higher education institutions from competing on a single scale that runs from the Ivy League down to lowly commuter schools.[2] But in practice these labels only opened the door for even more intense competitions within and among the various subgroups by giving them specific targets to shoot for. Just as every ambitious R2 girds its resources to vault into R1 territory, so too do the top R1s pine to be asked to join the AAU. For the University, staying afloat in that competition became a big problem in the 2010s.

The AAU's eligibility criteria are publicly posted, but membership is by invitation only. The University had been inducted in 1969, largely on the strength of molecular biology and a few other marquee science programs. But it was a middling research player at the time and had lost a lot of ground in the decades since then. Lacking medical and engineering schools, which win the lion's share of research grants, it had been lapped many times over by rivals. By 2010, an intimidating roster of twenty-eight *non*-AAU institutions surpassed the University in research dollars.³ Up-and-coming RIs reverse-engineered the eligibility criteria to argue that by the AAU's own standards, they had a better claim to membership than the ones seemingly grandfathered in at the bottom of the list—like the University.

In 2010, the president of the AAU announced that in the future, existing members would be periodically compared with their non-AAU competitors to assess their ongoing eligibility. In 2011, shockwaves rippled across higher education when the AAU expelled a midwestern public flagship after 102 years of membership. This led another (private) university to resign before it too could be asked to leave. Seeing the writing on the wall, the University grasped its best hope to hang on after the firing of The Hat: it recruited that same AAU president, now retired, to serve as interim president in 2012.⁴

Maintaining the University's AAU membership went on to become the second most important institutional priority of the 2010s, after the prime imperative of recruiting tuition-paying students. This was not just a prestige marker; AAU status provided the dominant substantive intellectual value that knit the campus together for much of the decade. The University's official 2009 Academic Plan stated that "Goal 1 [is] To Achieve and Sustain AAU Excellence *on a Human Scale*"—a clever turn of phrase that parlayed its modest size into an advantage.⁵ Acting as a lodestar for its newfound independence, that goal was used to orient the new Board of Trustees, made a de facto job qualification for new presidents, touted to visitors as a badge of quality, and broken down into specific action items in obligatory reports to the University's official accrediting agency.⁶

Invoking AAU standards of excellence also structured the conflict between faculty and administration during unionization and its aftermath. Whatever disagreements and opportunity costs came with the arduous processes of collective bargaining, leaders on both sides converged in citing fellow AAU institutions as "aspirational peers" to wage arguments over principles, processes, and resources.[7] The rhetoric of AAU excellence proved capacious enough to anchor the University in its historic liberal arts identity while also guiding it into a science-dominated future. It would later mediate the University's embrace of applied science, commercialized discovery, and real-world economic and social impact. Manifest in a brand new applied science campus (see chapter 8), this would give it a modest foothold in a world otherwise dominated by juggernauts in biomedical, physical, and engineering sciences.

Practically no one questioned whether the drive to stay in the AAU was a worthy goal. Perhaps this reflected the captivating appeal of a Little Engine That Could narrative, or perhaps a collective aversion to staring into an abyss of mediocrity that would supposedly open up if the University were kicked out. In any event, it prescribed a series of concrete action steps to guide the University through a period of uncertainty and instability. The struggle to maintain AAU membership turned a gnawing fear of institutional decline into a set of practical questions about how best to organize the University around a single-minded pursuit to catch up with the competition. Adopting the mission and values of the AAU's then sixty-odd research powerhouses, and adapting them to the resources and culture of one of its smallest members, gave University leaders a script to follow. Lending specificity to platitudes about "research excellence," that script dictated the development of benchmarking studies, strategic planning and visioning exercises, processes to identify and grow areas of intellectual promise, fund-raising pitches, and a revolution in academic budgeting. Most controversially, it spurred the creation of quantitative metrics that could be used to measure, visualize, adjust, and incentivize the production of new knowledge by academic departments. A move redolent of corporate managerialism and part of a galloping global trend, the use of numerical productivity indicators was scaled back almost as soon as it was introduced, but not before forcing tough trade-offs between research and the University's other core mission, teaching.

"EXCELLENCE" AND THE RISE OF STEM

For a long time, the story of research excellence in the modern United States was a story of farsighted government largesse. As early as the late 1940s, federal policy makers made a critical decision to fund basic and not just applied research: to support the investigation of fundamental scientific processes such as the structure of the atom or the workings of the cell rather than favoring projects with immediate practical or commercial payoff. Generous grants for the physical and biological sciences flowed through the National Science Foundation (NSF), the National Institutes of Health (NIH), and various cabinet-level departments. To hold these agencies true to intellectual rather than political aims, rigorous peer review protocols were adopted to ensure that faculty evaluated other faculty in determining the quality and viability of research proposals. Politicians and bureaucrats merely set the budgets and wrote the checks—including for both "direct costs" (salaries for laboratory workers or the costs of scientific equipment and materials) and "indirect costs" (buildings, utilities, support staff, and other overhead expenses not directly attributable to any given project). A single institution-wide "facilities and administration" (F&A) percentage was tacked on to each successful NSF or NIH grant to avoid tediously computing indirect costs on individual proposals.

Generous F&A rates during higher education's twentieth-century Golden Age had allowed universities to make long-term capital investments in laboratory space and equipment without having to raise all the needed funds from other sources such as state legislatures, private philanthropists, or corporate sponsors.

Although it remains by far the largest supporter of university research, the federal government has proven to be a more fickle patron since the Cold War ended in 1989. Deficit reduction soon edged out defense spending as a federal policy priority. The 1993 cancellation of the Superconducting Super Collider particle accelerator marked an end to blank checks for blue-sky big science. The 1990s were a low point for the public reputation of higher education in general. This was when the concept of "political correctness" entered mainstream usage as an attack on colleges for being at odds with mainstream cultural values. Research universities were singled out as neglecting both undergraduate education and national economic needs in the pursuit of Ivory Tower research and its associated prestige.[8]

Ever since then, federal support for university research has oscillated unreliably for political and fiscal reasons. Thus, when the Great Recession came along, Congress juiced the system once more through the massive 2009 stimulus bill, only to sequester billions of federal grant dollars during the debt ceiling standoff two years later. It was all up and down: the vagaries of federal research funding paralleled the volatility of state higher education funding during these same decades.[9] For universities with long time horizons, especially for expensive capital investments such as scientific laboratories, the frustrating combination of austerity and uncertainty imposed by government patrons had become a chronic fact of life.

America's politically savvy science establishment reacted to this uncertainty by latching on to widespread fears that the United

States was losing its edge in the world. At the dawn of a new millennium marked by the trauma of 9/11, the invention of the internet, and the rise of China as a manufacturing superpower, scientific research clearly held direct relevance to pressing problems of national security, economic prosperity, and global competitiveness. Advocates for research universities rallied around a four-letter solution for all of these challenges: STEM (science, technology, engineering, and mathematics), an acronym coined (or at least popularized) circa 2001 by an NSF staffer, and an alternative to the uglier-sounding "SMET."[10] Bolstering STEM emerged as the central focus of a clarion 2007 report authored by a blue-ribbon commission sponsored by the National Academies of Science, Engineering, and Medicine. Ominously titled *Rising Above the Gathering Storm*, its authors included research university presidents, major corporate CEOs, and some of the country's top practicing scientists. Leading with K–12 education, the report called for training "10,000 teachers for 10 million minds" before building a pipeline into universities through undergraduate scholarships and graduate student fellowships.[11]

Rising Above the Gathering Storm and a flurry of editorials tied America's competition with rival world powers to research universities' competition among each other. Congress's aptly named America COMPETES Act, passed in 2007 and renewed in 2010 and 2022, put federal money and policy muscle behind its recommendations. In 2012, the National Research Council (NRC), an arm of the National Academies, issued its own report on the problems besetting research universities: federal and state funding had fallen; corporations had slashed their own R&D operations because they now relied on universities to produce marketable breakthroughs; and the ratcheting back of F&A rates since the 1990s had created unsustainable shortfalls requiring universities to subsidize federal grants out of their own pockets.[12] The AAU chimed in on the need to "ensure national competitiveness" by investing in "basic research across all scientific disciplines," even including the social and behavioral sciences (albeit still leaving arts and humanities unmentioned). It too stressed "our STEM literacy and talent base" as being critical to America's global leadership.[13] A few years later, the AAU launched a major undergraduate STEM initiative—to date, its only major programmatic engagement with the university's core function of teaching.[14]

Thanks to political mobilization by American scientists a decade after the disorienting end of the Cold War, the 2000s and 2010s turbocharged STEM discourse in a way not seen since the panic over the Soviet Sputnik satellites in the 1950s and 1960s. Although there was nothing remotely novel about the federal government's privileging of science and technology research, the new acronym brilliantly recombined values and interests that had drifted out of coordination with one another: from the curiosity and creativity that K–12 teachers could instill by inducting children into the wonders of science, through the practical financial and institutional difficulties being faced by U.S. research universities navigating an uncertain funding landscape, through the most important geopolitical challenges of a new millennium.[15] Fighting for STEM gave the scientific research establishment new grounds on which to compete after America's Soviet archrivals had been consigned to history. STEM artfully transmuted anxieties about global competitiveness into a national campaign that the science establishment could lead. Such an innocuous word identified a set of priorities seemingly everyone could agree upon, even as it subtly excluded other intellectual pursuits—the arts, humanities, and social sciences—as having secondary value (notwithstanding the recent "STEAM" neologism, adding a letter for "arts," which reeks of desperation). Achievements in STEM provided a substantive yardstick for exhortations about "research excellence" that first became a staple of administrator discourse in the 1990s but had otherwise remained maddeningly underspecified.[16] Allowing individual institutions to pursue these goals on their own terms was part of the understated genius of the new policy push and its architects in national advocacy organizations.

RANKING AND BENCHMARKING

Individual universities labor under no intrinsic obligation to serve the nation's goals or fortify it for global competition with rivals on the world stage. The social contract that affords them autonomy in exchange for public service is instead nebulous and implicit. Universities' reasons for pursuing research excellence are driven far more by their own local missions, aspirations, and capacities. But because the U.S. federal government funds the vast majority of external research grants—over 75 percent at the University, which is not atypical—both public and private research universities take their cues from national scientific research priorities.[17] At the onset of the 2010s, they were receiving decidedly mixed signals from the federal government, however. On one hand, universities confronted an orchestrated push for more STEM research to serve the national goals of prosperity, security, and global competitiveness. On the other hand, they confronted a gridlocked political climate that created zig-zagging federal budgets and irresolute policy commitments. This dilemma ensured that even as competition for federal research dollars was becoming more strategically focused, it was also becoming more cutthroat and capricious.

For the University, the intensified competition for federal grant dollars intersected alarmingly with the AAU's threat to cull the herd at the very moment when presidents were coming and going and its in-house research administration was in disarray. In this flurry of overlapping crises, there was only one clear thing to do: try to stay in the AAU.

Acting in the University's favor was the very real advantage that the AAU had never been crudely dedicated to only the richest institutions or just to STEM research. Having a small but ambitious liberal arts–based public research university even burnished the AAU's claim to be inclusive, diverse, broad-minded, and concerned as much with quality as with quantity. To be sure, its membership criteria did emphasize quantified measures with an overwhelming priority on STEM fields: federal research grant dollars; the number of faculty with membership in the prestigious National Academies for Science, Engineering, and Medicine; and citation indices to measure how often faculty-authored research articles (but typically not books—the staple of liberal arts professors) are cited by peers. Tabulations of faculty honors and awards in *all* fields designated as "highly prestigious" by the NRC were the one important concession to nonscience faculty such as Fulbright or Guggenheim winners in the humanities and social sciences. And all these were in any case only "first stage" factors; a second stage depended on "a more qualitative set of judgments"—in effect, what other members of the AAU club thought.[18]

Education is distinctly secondary to research for the AAU. Wisely, with respect to graduate education, it warns that although the production of PhDs is part and parcel of any major research university's mission, schools should not game the metrics by needlessly expanding their graduate programs in a terrible academic job market, which is a key driver of adjunctification. As for undergraduate education, the AAU remains agnostic but not uninterested. Responding to 1990s-era criticisms that research universities neglected their student constituency, the AAU expects each member to be "meeting its commitment" to undergraduates but stresses that its membership committee will be "flexible in this assessment."

No one knew exactly where things stood until 2013, when the University undertook a comprehensive benchmarking exercise to compare itself against the entire set of what were then thirty-four public AAU institutions. University leaders presented the results at one of the very first new Board of Trustees meetings.[19] No one suggested that the effort to stay in the AAU was being undertaken to preserve an empty status marker, or to salve the egos of bruised and disgruntled faculty. Rather, AAU benchmarking was framed as a logical imperative flowing from the competitive situation in which every research university now operated, yet one still tied to the University's noblest proclaimed mission of advancing human knowledge: "We *compete* every day for the intellectual and financial *resources* that allow us to achieve our basic *mission*: advancement of *knowledge*."[20] The newly emancipated University had lifted its gaze above the State to the national arena and beyond.

The benchmarking exercise required crafting a set of metrics to track how well the institution was doing. Measures valued by external ranking organizations were combined with ones that were primarily of interest to internal stakeholders. Wherever one looked, the report's findings were sobering. On all of the most important metrics, the University either ranked near the top or near the bottom of the list, whichever was worse. Often it came in dead last in the AAU. Overall, the University's position could be summed up in two sentences. Its tenure-track faculty taught far fewer graduate students and far more undergraduate students—and in larger classes, on average—than national AAU peers. And its teaching-heavy composition translated into a lagging record of research accomplishments.[21] On the research metrics that mattered most, those focused on the sciences—federal grant dollars, articles published, and (article) citations earned—the University fell in the bottom quartile, if not at the very bottom of the list. The conclusion for administrators was inescapable: putting a meaningful dent in any of these high-stakes indicators of research productivity necessitated massive new investments in STEM.

To bolster its STEM profile, however, the University would have to dig itself into an even deeper hole financially. Like most of its peers, it had long had to add significant subsidies to federal indirect cost reimbursements to cover the actual expense of research—a figure on the order of $1,000 per student.[22] Even this was far less than what peer universities paid.[23] Federal research grants have been a money-losing enterprise since the cutbacks of the 1990s. State, corporate, and philanthropic foundation grants are typically even more so because of lower indirect cost reimbursements.[24] The typical public research university now pays about one-fifth of all research expenditures out of its own pockets.[25] In addition to the mounting costs of scientific equipment and regulatory compliance, one of the most acute cost drivers is the escalating expense of recruiting and retaining science faculty in a competitive job market. It is not simply that tenure-track scientists earn more and teach less than their liberal arts counterparts (see chapter 2). In addition, there is the problem of financing the six- or seven-digit startup packages needed to woo star faculty from other institutions so they can (re)establish costly laboratories upon relocating. Whereas F&A returns used to provide enough surplus revenue that some of it could be recycled into startup packages, that money now had to come from somewhere else, including state appropriations, student tuition, and other sources.

An influential strain of thought in the scholarship on higher education stresses "resource dependency" as an explanation for the strategies institutions pursue. In essence, the theory holds, universities adapt themselves to follow the sources of their income and maximize outside resources. One might attempt to apply that theory to the University by claiming that after securing a reliable stream of tuition-paying student customers in the early 2010s, it shifted in the mid-2010s to wooing other patrons, in the form of federal funding agencies such as the NIH and the NSF. It is clear now, however, that that would have been a money-losing strategy. Alternatively, one might claim that the University had to visibly support STEM disciplines to recruit enough *students* interested in those fields. But if this is true, it chose one of the most expensive ways of achieving that goal: by sinking its resources into laboratories and equipment that most students would never encounter during their four years on campus.

Research is a loss leader that universities tolerate for a complex blend of motivations ranging from serving their core academic mission to signaling robustness and quality to rankings-conscious consumers and policy makers. The benchmarking exercise offers a clue to why the University pursued research excellence despite it all: not necessarily to ascend the rankings, which had now been revealed as a Sisyphean task, but to better harness its latent competitive potentials. The next step, an engagement with quantitative metrics, would take it much deeper into the question of how best to accomplish this goal.

METRICS AND PRODUCTIVITY INDICATORS

For what it was worth, the University's overall ranking was relegated to an appendix in the 2013 benchmarking report. It came in at a lackluster number 115 among national universities, according to *U.S. News and World Report*.[26] To their credit, no university leaders ever cited rankings as reasons for or against any particular course of action. Rankings convey a false sense of precision because they are based on arbitrary and continually readjusted weightings of different factors cobbled together into one number. They rely more on academic reputation (as measured by surveys of university presidents) than on direct indicators of research prowess (which are themselves controversial). In addition to amalgamating different things, they include factors that cannot be directly influenced, derive from opaque and unscientific formulas, depend on inconsistently reported and sometimes falsified data, and serve the commercial interests of their producers rather than the goals of universities and policy makers.

Rankings are simply too crude an instrument to plot a coherent institutional strategy for the broad middle tier of large research universities. In contrast, *metrics* provide a degree of granular detail, defensible objectivity, and actionable incentives that one-dimensional university-level rankings lack. Metrics track multiple quantifiable factors at multiple levels within an institutional hierarchy, and they blend a variety of strategies, graphic and numerical, comparative and absolute. In short, they pick up where rankings leave off, by surfacing areas where administrative intervention can make a difference at the local and institutional levels.[27] To pursue its plan for AAU excellence, the University thus embarked on a multiyear effort to use quantitative metrics to visualize and improve the research productivity of its own departments.

In an era of big data, there has been a worldwide move to adopt quantifiable measures of research output to incentivize faculty and departments to produce more scholarship. Many of the "bibliometrics" on which such performance indicators are based were created decades ago by librarians to guide purchasing decisions on individual scientific journals, but they have since been repurposed out of all proportion to their original limited uses.[28] What used to be simple article citation indices have graduated into speciously precise "impact factors" and other measures tailor-made to stoke competition among individuals, departments, and whole universities. A private firm called Academic Analytics exemplifies the culture of research productivity that has taken hold around that quest. The firm was founded in 2005 by an ex-administrator who perceived a growing market for actionable information that could be used in making strategic decisions about over- and underperforming departments. Employed by the AAU, which relies on its Faculty Scholarly Productivity database to track faculty awards and memberships in prestigious honor societies, Academic Analytics was also contracted by the University in the mid-2010s to inform its own quest for research excellence. Among the firm's most visually attractive products is the flower chart shown in figure 5.1, which compellingly illustrates both the seductions and the dangers of cutting-edge research metrics.

Any provost, dean, or department head is supposed to be able to scan a flower chart like this to gain a rapid overview of a given department's aggregate productivity. Different petals signify the key indicators of research productivity measured by the AAU and other gatekeeping and grant-making agencies: articles, books, citations, faculty awards, and grant dollars. Within each petal, individual criteria are broken down further, affording different takes on the same underlying measure. For example, an otherwise mediocre department with a few superstars might show a high measure of articles per faculty member but a low number of faculty members who had published any articles at all. A jagged swatch illustrates unevenness across variables, whereas a clean pie slice indicates consistency across submeasures. All

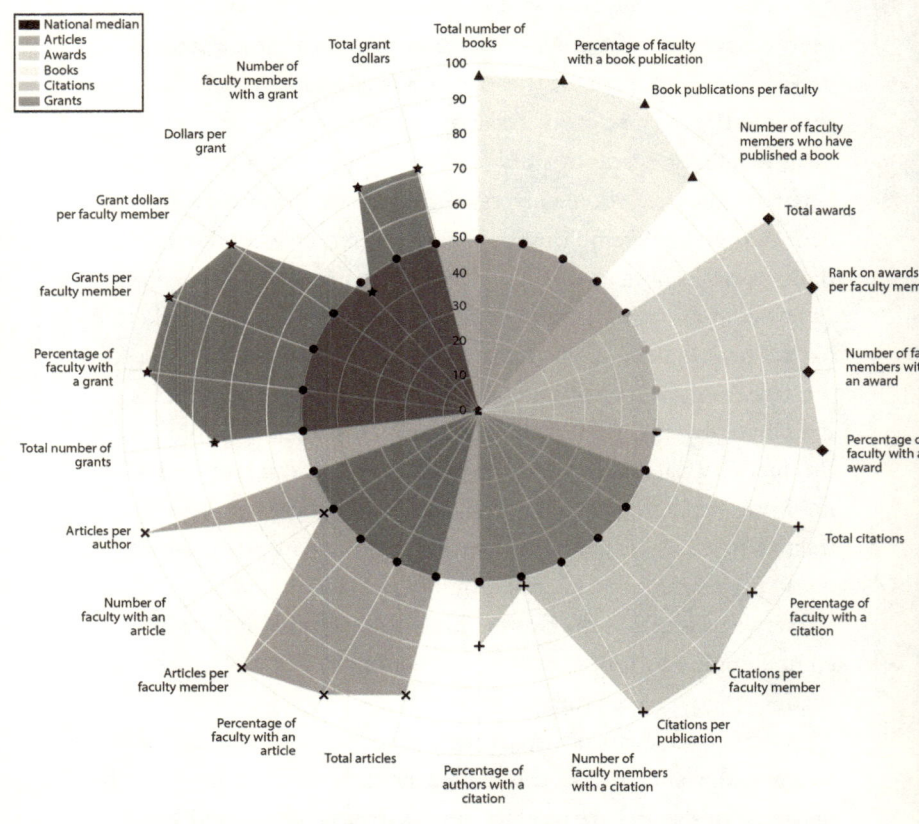

FIGURE 5.1 Academic Analytics flower chart.

Source: Redrawn with permission from Academic Analytics.

of these metrics are benchmarked against the national median, shown as a perfect circle in shadow at the center.

Ostensibly, the flower chart format allows any viewer to assess, in an instant, where a department either lags or surpasses its peers on any particular criterion. Rather than subjecting an academic unit to a crude one-dimensional ranking, the circular presentation allows twenty-six distinct variables to plotted at once. This facilitates a more strategic, targeted, nuanced approach to departmental management than, say, a blunt dictate from the dean to move up the ranks by mindlessly imitating what higher-ranked departments seem to be doing. For example, a chemistry department with a strong track record of winning research grants but comparatively few faculty awards might be given administrative support to help high performers apply for and receive national prizes and recognitions. Departments themselves can refer to these measures in conversations with deans and provosts who may not know anything about their fields but who can at least see how well they stack up against relevant peers and argue for exceptions on that basis. Thus a sociology department whose faculty happen to excel at writing books might point out that it occupies a valuable intellectual niche in a field that in general values articles more highly—and it can concretize that claim with reference to award metrics shown on the flower chart.

Despite or perhaps because of their immediate appeal, metrics and analytics are fraught with as many methodological and political problems as rankings. Rankings at least rest on avowedly subjective factors such as reputation, whereas metrics convey a deceptive objectivity that can short-circuit thoughtful decisions. Systematic weaknesses underlying the data, such as the omission of book citations or, to cite another flaw, the frequent exclusion of publications in languages other than English or in media that are more than a few decades old, disappear when they are rendered as attractively simplified infographics. On a philosophical level, there is the danger that by measuring what one values one comes to value that which happens to be measurable. Just because it is convenient to tabulate a particular productivity measure does not mean it should guide actual decision-making. Just because each measure occupies the same graphical area on a flower chart does not mean that all such measures are equal to one another. Perverse outcomes can result when, for example, faculty are incentivized to break long articles into several publishable pieces, boost article citation impact measures by citing friends as a quid pro quo for being cited by them in turn, or to forego ambitious projects entirely for fear that they will not result in a quantifiably prestigious end product. The research rankings community has itself codified these caveats and concerns, notably in the Leiden Manifesto of 2015.[29]

In the face of such criticisms, the University in 2018 conducted a searching discussion about whether Academic Analytics and other such metrics should be used at all in faculty management and institution-wide strategic planning. A number of safeguards were put in place. Administrators disavowed apples-to-oranges comparisons of departments in different fields within the University, recognizing that each discipline had its own peculiar standards of productivity and quality. Articles, grants, and citations were by no means universal benchmarks, especially outside the sciences, and even within the sciences different fields had different rhythms of publication and different conventions of citation. So, too, *outside* the sciences some fields had wildly divergent access to high-dollar grants and prestigious honors. Individual departments were therefore invited to suggest the criteria they themselves would prefer to be measured by, and in limited cases were even allowed to vet and verify the data that were furnished to the University. Administrators nonetheless defended the use of metrics as an essential component of communication with both external and internal stakeholders as well as the high-stakes task of allocating limited resources.[30]

The logical endpoint of a process that began with national rankings and proceeded from institutional metrics down to department-level readouts was one that measured individual faculty members' research productivity. Here the University's faculty union proved especially vigilant. Under the collective bargaining agreement, the introduction of rigorous post-tenure reviews where none had existed before intensified the level of scrutiny across a faculty member's research career. Union leaders therefore wanted to ensure that metrics crafted for entire departments would not be inappropriately repurposed for the evaluation of individual professors, and that raw numbers should never be allowed to substitute for holistic, qualitative peer review by faculty in one's own discipline. A memorandum of understanding with the union set out the guardrails. In it, the administration committed to both qualitative and quantitative measures of faculty work; to rely on metrics only to evaluate departments in aggregate, not for assessing individual scholars; and to refrain from compelling departments to use Academic Analytics products unless they elected to do so for their own reasons.[31]

The *reductio ad absurdum* of individualized performance metrics is the so-called h-index. The h-index is defined for any given author as the highest number X such that X of that author's total number of peer-reviewed publications are cited at least X times in other peer-reviewed publications. It thus elegantly (or reductively) combines measures of both output and impact in a single number, which is the next best thing to an actual ranking of one's stature in a field. Accomplished scholars take all of this with a heavy grain of salt. The best of them disavow the validity of any such measure with the same vehemence that Harvard and Yale disavow *U.S. News and World Report* rankings. But in a culture as competitive and rankings-conscious as the United States, the voluntary uptake of compare-and-despair measures of all sorts, from the personal to the global levels, is such a powerful and pervasive phenomenon that it need not even be enforced by advocacy organizations, institutional policies, or union contracts. Instead it is simply a growing part of academics' professional socialization.

STRATEGIC PLANNING AND BUDGETING

The University's dalliance with Academic Analytics was largely fruitless in the end. But the chase for quantifiable productivity gains did trigger major institutional changes well beyond the constricted and constricting question of what it would take to catch up with AAU peers. The gaps it revealed between resources and priorities led to the demise of Responsibility Center Management (RCM) budgeting, and the gaps it revealed between local incentives and institution-level decisions led to a newly strategic approach to faculty hiring. Combined, these steps at long last put intellectual questions at the heart of the University's topmost discussions of its academic mission in general, and of its research direction in particular. When University leaders ceased talking about the AAU in the late 2010s, it was because that quest had reverted from being a proxy for substantive intellectual values to the vanity project that, at root, it always had been.

For all of their limitations, research metrics could at least be used to push back on decisions driven by the other major metrics-driven enterprise at the University: the RCM-style New Budget Model that since 2010 had determined school and college budgets based on undergraduate enrollments. Academic budgeting was already being reevaluated amid concerns that the scramble to accommodate new students had engulfed any rival conceptions of the value of faculty research and the intellectual composition of the academic departments. Not only had the formulaic routing of tuition dollars based on student demand neglected to identify areas of genuine intellectual importance and research-dollar potential, but the budget model was also floundering on its own terms, creating unsustainable deficits in some of the schools and colleges and failing to account for the ever-expanding needs of central administration. Various patches and fixes were needed to bail out critical units, and overall budget volatility disrupted coherent planning despite the administration's best efforts to smooth out fluctuations year over year.[32]

The Academic Allocation Model that replaced the New Budget Model in 2018 both tackled these technical issues and marked a quantum leap toward centralizing the University's research strategy. Its key feature was to relocate budgetary authority for hiring tenure-track professors to the Provost's Office, taking it away from deans in the schools and colleges. The new 2018 model also centralized funding for graduate student instructors because PhD programs are likewise essential to research. Most other expenditures—including for the very large cadre of non-tenure-track instructors who did half of the University's teaching—were now funded out of deans' "general operations allocations." Any new expenses associated with promotions and raises for instructors were explicitly made the decentralized burden of the various schools and colleges. Henceforth deans and department heads would take point on the management of teaching, thus freeing the provost and other central administrators to focus on beefing up the University's research profile—using whatever blend of quantifiable measures and subjective arguments could be marshaled for determining its priorities. Monitoring and maintaining the all-important metrics of tenure-track faculty and PhD production critical to any research university had migrated fully to the central administration.[33] The net effect was to decouple tenure-track faculty hiring, and thus research priorities, from student demand for teaching.

The new balance of power was baked into the next significant change of the late decade, a revolution in strategic planning to augment the revolution in academic budgeting. The Institutional Hiring Plan (IHP) piloted in 2017, and refined every year thereafter, marked the culmination of the entire effort begun four years earlier to benchmark the University. It followed several false starts. For example, a call in 2009 for "Big Ideas" attempted to put intellectually compelling initiatives at the top of the provost's to-do list but ended abortively because of low funding and poor administrative follow-through.[34] Later, under the New Budget Model, calls for cross-college collaborations fared poorly because deans had budgetary incentives to compete with one another instead of joining forces in areas of shared intellectual interest. So-called cluster hiring, whereby faculty sharing a common thematic interest are simultaneously hired across multiple academic disciplines, is difficult even in the best of circumstances owing to the need to relocate multiple new faculty members all at once. For these and other reasons, a master plan for building the tenure-track faculty was needed to make bold bets on fields of promise and painful choices in areas of decline. Any institution making a concerted effort to boost its research output, reputational recognition, and quantifiable productivity simply had to centralize tenure-track hiring to build the very faculty whose job it is to produce research.

The IHP was framed as a holistic process encompassing teaching, research, and diversity, all measured using both quantitative metrics and qualitative arguments. That said, achieving or maintaining "national or international leadership" in high-profile research fields was its overarching goal. The aim was to double down on the University's competitive advantages while also identifying new areas where it could move from good to great with a few smart hires. Student demand was inevitably still important but now became distinctly secondary as departments fought for new faculty positions. Rising enrollments were no guarantee of success in this competition, and conversely, a department with genuine research distinction could still win out despite declining student interest.[35]

Wrestling with metrics had succeeded in cracking open an old system and facilitated a newly strategic approach to research and academic mission. The University had long since broken with the default assumption, pervasive in academia, that when, say, a French Enlightenment historian retires, that person is replaced by another one in the same subspecialty. Already under the New Budget Model, every vacant tenure-track faculty line had to be justified anew because that model broke so decisively with the previous way of doing things. The IHP simply pushed that logic in a new direction by subjecting all such hiring to a triad of criteria centered on research excellence, student success, and demographic diversity.

In its first five years of operation (it was suspended in 2020–21 due to the COVID-19 pandemic), the IHP accumulated enough of a record to venture some tentative conclusions. Restocking vacated faculty positions in plain-vanilla subspecialties continued in fields from taxation to trumpet, but it was dramatically curtailed. Novel areas were distinctly privileged instead. Although it is impossible to fully distinguish genuinely new fields from old ones that had been opportunistically relabeled, perhaps 50 percent of tenure-track searches in the early 2020s were in specialties of novel intellectual interest—from computational neuroscience to comic and cartoon studies, and from green development to Pacific Islander studies.[36]

Most notably, the University had reverted to identifying "big ideas" with intellectual excitement and distinction as it had done before, but now with more resources and better execution.

Trustee presentations were often plucked from the most exciting IHP cluster proposals to give outsiders a taste of what top faculty researchers were keen on investigating. Roughly a fifth of all new tenure-track hires belonged to an identified strategic cluster or central initiative, whether at the multicollege, provost, or presidential level. Especially at the highest levels, the University's STEM focus became predominant.[37] Faculty in other disciplines quibbled that these were not the right priorities, or even that they took their cues from what seemed popular or fashionable at a given moment, but there is no doubt that the institution's faculty hiring priorities had graduated beyond a simple chase for better numbers.

A CRISIS IN CREATIVITY?

The issue of AAU status was quietly dropped in the late 2010s. By then it had dramatically reshaped the ways the University pursued research and the reasons it gave for doing so. Nationwide, the entire rationale for university research had undergone a sea change. Idealists had once argued that research and teaching are two sides of the same coin: that the search for new knowledge is inseparable from the act of passing it along to others. That alternative conception of curiosity, creativity, and exploration had now been marginalized. Institutionally, the nation's universities have long since abandoned that ideal by starkly reducing the proportion of tenure-track faculty who wear both hats, and arguably suffering little loss in educational quality as a result (a question taken up in chapter 6). Other rationales for research have proven more potent. "Excellence" and "impact" have now replaced curiosity and creativity as the prime public justifications for research across all of higher education, and a catchy new acronym, "STEM," has been coined to lend intellectual flair to these banalities. Yet this has come at a time when the tensions between research and other priorities are greater than ever before. Skeptics, including those who call for a "new AAU" founded on nobler goals, have good reason to raise objections to university rankings and the fetishization of research dollars on which they rest.[38] These quests require investments of time and resources that increasingly crowd out other values—not only teaching but even the creation of knowledge itself.

Where had the whole AAU push left the University? Leaders in the early 2010s had mounted a metrics-driven effort to meet national benchmarks of research excellence. But only a few years later, they backed away from that same effort to pursue a more qualitatively and locally defined strategy. Questions abounded. Was the pursuit of research excellence a dead end, a period wasted on a chimerical quest? Was it a dose of necessary medicine to get the University from point A to point B—sunsetting a budget model that had outlived its usefulness, ending business as usual in faculty hiring, substituting substantive strategic planning in place of one-off calls for Big Ideas, and reconciling faculty and administration after a period of conflict? Or was this perhaps a cyclical story rather than a linear one, in which the decentralization and recentralization of decision-making merely reflected a periodic swing of the pendulum? Did the AAU push provide a collective learning experience to fortify the University for a new century? Did it create a new faculty persona animated by metrics, productivity incentives, and review protocols? Or did it leave an older ethos of curiosity- and creativity-driven exploration intact after an interlude of institutional heartburn? What was the effect on the culture of inquiry and the free play of ideas?

It is still too early to offer long-term answers to these questions, but that is precisely the point. If the role of the 2010s in the

University's long-term saga is a story that cannot yet be written, it is in the pressure to engage in short-term calculations that the heart of *this* story lies. Short-term calculations cascade into long-term outcomes, as is always the case. But in the competitive climate of the new millennium, these are practically the *only* types of calculations that the leaders of middle-tier institutions have the luxury of making. With respect to research excellence, as with every other issue confronted in this book—public disinvestment, rising tuition, faculty discontent, administrative bloat—the University responded rationally to the challenges it faced in the moment. It navigated demands from stakeholders by amalgamating their motives and wishes into a determined course of action, and it made what it could of its newfound local freedoms to contend with various national and global pressures that their peers and competitors also experienced.

What University leaders could not so easily do was question the underlying premises of the enterprise on which nearly all research universities have now embarked the world over. These include questions about whether STEM research is the most valuable research, whether budgetary dollar amounts are the best way to measure that value, and whether other numerical indicators, such as citation indices and impact factors, are superior to traditional, subjective peer review in assessing the merits of individual research projects. Then there is the unexamined belief that competition is everywhere and always a good thing, whether on the global, institutional, or personal levels. If competition produces creativity, the thinking goes, more competition must produce more creativity—even when productivity incentives have demonstrably perverse effects on institutional behavior and individual morale. That assumption neglects what really produces innovation, which is community: webs of scholars and scientists clustered in local university departments but ramifying across subspecialist networks spanning the world. These global networks of colleagues, what are called "disciplines," organize individual scholars who vie both *with* and *against* one another to make breakthroughs. Metrics of productivity and influence only register the effects of those competitions and cannot capture what animates disciplines internally, which is the set of ideas and problems, questions and quests, that drive any given field. By substituting an artificial competition in place of a natural collegiality encompassing both rivalry and cooperation, productivity mandates can even do damage to the very spirit that enlivens the research enterprise.

Fortunately, the American system of higher education is distinguished by its loose coupling at every level. The country is both wealthy and decentralized enough to tolerate an often chaotic variety of rival ideals and values, and too predisposed toward individualism and against regulatory state power to do otherwise. In many European and Asian systems, preeminently Great Britain, research productivity is much more intrusively orchestrated by technocrats and policy makers, and concerted excellence quests are routinely launched with the avowed purpose of beating rivals—not least the United States itself, still the world's leader in scientific research.[39] We can be glad that similar efforts have gained little traction in this country. Yet it bears remembering that America invented the rankings culture in higher education, and that culture is all the more powerful for being informally ascendant rather than bureaucratically enforced. One should therefore look to the United States, and especially its AAU trendsetters, for clues about how well the research enterprise is succeeding. Alas, there are ample signs that it has reached a point of diminishing returns.

A growing scholarly literature points to worrisome indicators of "scientific stagnation" even in the most productive, prestigious, quantitatively dominant sectors of the modern academy and the wider economy. For research productivity is not just declining in universities; in technology, agriculture, biomedicine, and other economic sectors, research *effort* is rising markedly even as research *outcomes* have plateaued or sunk.[40]

Within universities, the pressure exerted by metrics exacerbates this challenge. Some claim that perceptions of decline merely reflect the low-hanging fruit having already been plucked, but instead it may be the case that institutions have inadvertently undermined faculty creativity through changes to the incentives and reward structures that productivity indicators bring about. A "citation revolution" has reoriented scientists toward incremental me-too research projects rather than forays into fundamental questions on unproven tracks of inquiry. Search engines such as Google Scholar and Web of Science stoke an "impact factor mania" that, like any social media, grips the attention of faculty and administrators despite their best efforts to resist. STEM researchers who are disenchanted with these changes react with a mix of strategies ranging from passive resistance to creative ways of working outside the system.[41]

The cardinal value of play—the free play of ideas, the ability to indulge pure curiosity, the luxury to take time and even to waste time and resources—has been neglected despite mountains of evidence from the history of science that it is precisely under conditions of unpressured, unbounded exploration that the most revolutionary ideas tend to germinate.[42] The hunger games that began in the 1990s with the ratcheting back of federal largesse and continued into the 2010s with the capriciousness of scientific grant funding now intersect, perversely, with the opposite problem: a deceptive embarrassment of scholarly riches. The deluge of new papers that arrive every year increasingly deprives even the most diligent readers of the "cognitive slack" needed to digest novel ideas and mull their implications. Authentically novel contributions get crowded out in a flurry of publications that suggests a buzzing vitality, but only superficially. Looking deeper, what has instead resulted is a kind of Matthew effect whereby the most-cited papers accumulate even more recognition, rendering it that much harder for any new contribution to break into the top ranks.[43] Publication overload is a direct consequence of policies and incentives that push for more research irrespective of its value. That problem can only become worse at the international and global levels as the world at large becomes further knit together into one enormous scientific competition. Again, world university rankings are overwhelmingly determined by metrics of research prowess.

Research universities may now be facing what one scholar calls a "creativity crisis" that is not the result of any single cause, whether rankings, metrics, competition, or perverse incentives. The problem is rather an overall ecosystem imbalance. The power, influence, and wealth of America's science establishment has made it institutionally conservative. Creation and caution are out of balance, and risk aversion too often prevails over risk-taking and innovation.[44] While ensuring that scientific research serves the higher ends of ethics, sustainability, and social justice, that conservatism has undercut the buccaneer spirit that prevailed when luxury rather than austerity was the default setting for incubating scientific creativity. That spirit was much easier to keep alive when America's federally funded enterprise in research excellence was first established. Curiosity and free play still very much thrive in our research universities, but often in the many unmonitored interstices of faculty activity rather than in the now strategically hypermanaged centers of institutional decision-making.

6

TEACHING

How do universities ensure that students learn what they need for success in later life?

In the fall of 2019, the University opened a gleaming new Student Success Building in the dead center of campus, indeed on its most valuable piece of real estate: the administrator parking lot. Five stories tall and five years in the making, it held 64,000 square feet of new spaces to help incoming undergraduates forge a path through college. Its west-facing façade was an ultramodern glass box that, like an ant farm, revealed students busy at work with instructors and advisors. Pods of academic support staff, career counselors, and tutors were stationed throughout the building to greet wandering students and help them find their intellectual passions—or simply navigate the numerous academic requirements, financial and personal challenges, and rules and regulations that students confront when attending college.[1]

The Student Success Building sought to tackle, head-on, one of higher education's biggest challenges after the Great Recession. A widespread misconception held that only STEM and preprofessional degrees were worth the investment, because English and history majors would forever be condemned to work as baristas and live in their parents' basements. The worrisome amounts of debt that students were now carrying gave ample justification to such fears. Only that wasn't the problem. Careful job market analyses showed that when one sets physicians and engineers aside, science majors earned only slightly more over their careers than liberal arts majors. Although liberal arts majors initially earned less than business and other preprofessional majors, their cumulative earnings more than caught up by midcareer. A whopping 93 percent of employers, when surveyed, responded that a student's choice of major was of secondary importance in their hiring decisions. What they most prized were the soft skills—critical thinking, analytical reasoning, oral and written communication, and intellectual flexibility—that liberal arts students possess.[2]

The problem was not that students wound up in dead-end majors. It was that far too many were dropping out entirely, often just a few courses short of a degree. The failure to graduate condemned those students to decades of debt and underemployment because not having a bachelor's degree cripples one's job-hunting and income-earning prospects. For better or worse, a four-year degree (or higher) has become the price of admission to an economy-wide competition founded on knowledge-based credentials. President Five duly launched a multipronged "University Commitment" upon taking office in 2015. Driven by the measurable goal of increasing graduation rates by ten percentage points in five years, the plan put large dollar investments behind dozens of new academic advisors, increases in scholarship aid, and a comprehensive set of retention strategies.[3] A new "retention czar," not a faculty member but a professional administrator, was appointed to enact the needed organizational changes, and the office of undergraduate studies was renamed Undergraduate Education and Student Success (UESS). The symbolic and practical anchor for the whole college completion push would be the Student Success Building.

"Student success," like "research excellence," is a catchphrase that has become ubiquitous in higher education despite lacking a clear substantive meaning. What it signals—what changed over the 2010s—is that the burden for ensuring academic achievement has shifted from students themselves, where it used to lie, and onto institutions. "Will this investment pay off?" is the key question that any college or university must be prepared to answer in an era of skyrocketing tuition. Again, the answer remains yes, but only for students who finish their degrees. For that reason, today's universities bear an ethical responsibility to ensure that every student they admit has a decent chance of graduating and the support needed to get there.

This chapter shows how the University responded to the student success imperative both for its own reasons and because of external pressures from policy makers, advocacy organizations, and its accrediting agency. Nationwide, the student success movement and its public policy twin, the college completion agenda, have had major impacts on undergraduate education. Universities have been induced to assess student learning outcomes, evaluate teaching more rigorously, overhaul their advising practices, revamp financial aid processes, streamline their curricula, and unclutter academic policies that erect needless barriers to degree progress. Above all, they have been called upon to close persistent achievement gaps that disadvantage underrepresented minorities, first-generation college-goers, and other nontraditional learners. Higher education has taken on that mantle even though failures in K–12 education, in the social safety net, and in society at large are largely to blame for such inequities.

All of this is being done under the increasingly universal assumption that a bachelor's degree is the only viable path to a middle-class standard of living in twenty-first century America. Alas, the pressures produced by that policy consensus have had a distorting effect on undergraduate education. Just as the university's research mission has become preoccupied with productivity metrics as a proxy for real scientific and scholarly creativity, its teaching mission has become entangled in overly bureaucratic processes to document student success and increase degree production. The high stakes attached to these efforts consume campus energy and attention that might otherwise be devoted to authentic improvements to classroom teaching, curricular offerings, and student services. Only in the early 2020s, with the toll that COVID-19 took on student learning and mental health, did the price we pay for this flawed policy agenda become clear. Such is the fruit of a period that saw "college for all" become a national policy goal.[4]

THE COLLEGE COMPLETION AGENDA

The original impetus to the college completion agenda arose in business and policy circles from a desire in the early 2000s to improve the global competitiveness of the U.S. workforce. Although that economic goal has since expanded to remediating domestic racial and social injustice, the overarching imperatives and the underlying strategies have remained much the same. America's students, and *especially* the most disadvantaged among them, need to be better prepared to compete in a modern knowledge economy. Barack Obama, in his first address to a joint session of Congress in early 2009, made the case in purely instrumentalist terms: "In a global economy, where the most valuable skill you can sell is your knowledge, a good education is no longer just a pathway to opportunity. It is a prerequisite . . .

because we know the countries that out-teach us today will outcompete us tomorrow."[5]

The president of the United States exerts little influence over how universities teach. Nor does the federal government in general. States, too, enjoyed distinctly limited success in submitting universities to performance accountability regimes (see chapter 1). The college completion agenda was instead spearheaded by a coalition of philanthropic foundations, advocacy groups, policy entrepreneurs, education experts, and nongovernmental accrediting agencies who became all the more powerful for having set the terms of the debate from outside politics. Without anyone foisting that agenda upon them, universities adopted two of its key precepts by the end of the 2010s. First, they were now expected not just to offer wide *access* to students but to ensure their *success* as well. And second, to ensure that student success entailed actual learning, and did not simply produce graduates with empty credentials, a long-standing emphasis on student *engagement* as the mission of undergraduate education would give way to a new regime founded on the *assessment* of the actual outcomes of their learning.

The college completion agenda began as neither a Democratic nor a Republican but rather a bipartisan priority. Before Obama, it was the Bush administration, under Secretary of Education Margaret Spellings, that launched a blue-ribbon commission drawing widespread attention to academic underachievement. Its 2006 report, "A Test of Leadership," ominously observed that having pioneered the world's greatest system of higher education, the United States had fallen behind other countries who were educating larger proportions of their citizenries. "Not everyone needs to go to college"—that expectation was still some years in the future—"but everyone needs a postsecondary education."[6] America's colleges and universities were failing to meet that national need.

The Spellings Commission took special aim at America's historically unique, semiprivatized system of official accreditation. Since the early 1900s, most accredited colleges and universities in the United States have been subject to one of six regional accreditors. These nongovernmental, nonprofit voluntary organizations have two jobs: to certify institutions for federal financial aid (Title IV) eligibility and to discreetly recommend improvements to members through a process of peer visitation and self-study.[7] By delegating these tasks to independent accreditors, the U.S. federal government enabled a remarkably diverse and decentralized array of higher education institutions to flourish. But the Spellings Commission charged that this closed, clubbish, cartel-like system had failed to generate solid evidence that parents and students could use to determine whether college graduates were actually learning; nor did it provide enough rigorous data for policy makers to determine "whether the national investment in higher education is paying off." Not only did accreditors lack transparency, but they often impeded pedagogical and technological innovation. The commission stopped short of calling for federalizing accreditation, but it did insist that serious new accountability mechanisms be established to produce measurable, timely, actionable indicators of student learning. Such metrics must focus on "results and quality" and permit comparisons across the nation and across the world. Several sample tests including the Collegiate Learning Assessment (CLA) were held up as exemplars. Only five years since the No Child Left Behind Act (2001) had drastically reshaped K–12 education, higher education leaders feared that they too were about to be subjected to a regime of high-stakes standardized testing.

In a thriving free market of colleges and universities, the mere suggestion of a top-down regulatory bureaucracy (from a

Republican administration, no less) horrified academic leaders. Shirley Tilghman, the president of Princeton University, had even found her own institution in the crosshairs. Its regional accreditor, which oversees a swath of mid-Atlantic institutions as diverse as Adirondack Community College, Delaware State, and Holy Family University, threatened that Princeton needed to "document student learning assessment more quantitatively [or risk] losing [its] accreditation."[8] The sheer amount of paperwork that new assessment mandates required was insulting and wasteful. What was wrong, Tilghman asked, with conventional measures of quality—retention and graduation rates, job placement statistics, and alumni satisfaction surveys? Why reject old-fashioned grades for some newfangled scheme to assess learning? Universities should be freed from burdensome compliance regimes so they could focus on the real substance of education: research-based learning, senior theses, and interdisciplinary teaching. Those recipes for success had already been laid out, Tilghman noted, in a landmark 1998 Boyer Commission report that offered a blueprint for research universities after they were castigated for neglecting undergraduates in the 1990s.[9] There was no need to reinvent the wheel.

The universities' fears never came to pass. A short-lived "Voluntary System of Accountability" (VSA) was hastily launched and soon abandoned, and fitful attempts by the Department of Education to impose unprecedented new mandates on regional accreditors were stopped in their tracks by congressional action.[10] American higher education is simply too systemically resistant to governmental steering for such efforts to stand a chance. Into the breach, however, stepped a diverse set of nongovernmental organizations whose motives, from the altruistic to the self-interested, all aligned behind the college completion agenda. These included the Bill and Melinda Gates Foundation and the lesser-known Lumina Foundation, created from the proceeds of dissolving Sallie Mae, the former student loan marketing association. These two advocacy philanthropies collaborated with other organizations as diverse as the College Board, the American Association of Colleges and Universities (AAC&U), the National Governors' Association, the Education Advisory Board (EAB), and others.[11] Such were the types of groups that truly set the agenda for student success in the late 2000s.

Advocacy philanthropy works by leveraging private foundation grants to induce intermediary organizations to design, pilot, implement, publicize, and spread specific policy reforms. Typically, funders set simple, quantifiable headline targets—such as doubling the number of college degrees, or reaching 60 percent of the working-age population by 2025—as a means to focus energy and ensure accountability. The specific action items needed to move institutions toward these goals are then delegated via targeted grants to experts in the field, who then disseminate best practices through white papers, conferences, training sessions, customizable templates, checklists, and so-called rubrics, a gridlike tool to evaluate student work borrowed from K–12 education that has since become ubiquitous at the college level. Between the 2000s and the 2010s, foundations moved decisively in this new strategic direction, shifting their grant-making from traditional institution-building (for example, through capital projects or scholarships) to activist policy reform with a heavy accent on college completion. Reports appeared with catchy titles such as *Complete to Compete* and *Doubling the Numbers*.[12] Different foundations increasingly funded the same subset of grantees, creating coalitions of nongovernmental actors each committed to a distinct approach toward the same overall goal.[13] More than the tightly coordinated push for research excellence orchestrated by the U.S. scientific establishment in Washington,

D.C. (see chapter 5), the size, sophistication, and geographic range of what is now a vast student success network has produced a chorus of voices from different quarters all singing in harmony about the imperatives of college completion. Unlike individual donors, whose effect on universities remains localized, this new species of advocacy philanthropy exerts a decisive systemic influence on the national priorities of higher education, whether for good or ill.

As a result of the single-minded push for outcomes-based accountability, long-standing efforts to revitalize classroom teaching were subsumed under the assessment agenda. The guru of the entire student success movement, the Indiana University professor George Kuh, pivoted from "engagement" to "assessment" near the turn of the decade. Having pioneered the National Survey of Student Engagement (NSSE) in the 1990s, Kuh in 2008 founded the National Institute for Learning Outcomes Assessment (NILOA) with funds from Lumina, whose headquarters is just up the road in Indianapolis.[14] Kuh's influential list of "high-impact practices" to energize student learning, such as first-year seminars, undergraduate research opportunities, and community-based service learning, have proven particularly useful in widening access to students from diverse backgrounds unfamiliar with college life. Yet in the train of the student success movement, access was no longer enough: engagement must be proven to have taken effect through a subsequent exercise in assessment.

Embattled regional accrediting agencies smarting from political criticism naturally took up the assessment baton from ambitious advocacy organizations.[15] Under their influence, the term "learning outcomes" was all but mandated in lieu of milder formulations like "learning goals" or "learning objectives." This put a new onus on faculty members not just to articulate what their students are expected to learn but then to produce tangible evidence that their efforts in the classroom have yielded the prescribed results. The next section shows how learning outcomes assessment empowered regional accreditors to assert their ongoing relevance to the public oversight and regulation of colleges and universities.

WHAT STUDENTS SHOULD LEARN

What should every student be required to learn to assure public confidence in the degrees being bestowed upon them? For much of the 2010s, the University pursued one possible answer to this question by trying to improve its core curriculum, which is the set of courses that all undergraduates have to take, mostly in the first two years of college. Like most of its peers, it offered a vast cafeteria of options. Each student was obligated to assemble a balanced meal by choosing a certain number of proteins, starches, vegetables, and desserts in the form of designated "general education" courses in different areas—natural sciences, social sciences, humanities, and multiculturalism.

Fitful efforts to spice up these dishes were underway when a bomb dropped in 2011. That was the year that *Academically Adrift* was published. Based on nationwide results from the Collegiate Learning Assessment (CLA), the authors of that book argued that a staggering 45 percent of first- and second-year students showed "no significant gains in critical thinking, complex reasoning, and writing skills." These were the very years when most were focusing on core curriculum requirements. A large fraction of those students showed no demonstrable learning over all four years of college. One of the main reasons was how little time they spent studying, on average twelve hours a week—a disturbing lack of student engagement.[16] Debt-laden, a great many of them instead had to work part- or even full-time jobs to pay tuition bills.

As it turned out, the bomb failed to go off. Methodologically, *Academically Adrift* proved open to criticism, not least because it relied on a generic, content-free assessment test taken by student volunteers with nothing at stake.[17] But its findings were too powerful to ignore. The nationwide furor that ensued showed that the book had struck a nerve: a nagging fear that too many undergraduates left college having failed to learn what they needed to learn according to their own institutions' academic requirements. That question went to the heart of the University's effort to reform its core curriculum. It was an effort shaped and steered by insistent pressure from its regional accrediting agency, even though the ambition to submit the entire curriculum to learning outcomes assessment has yet to come to fruition, and probably never will.

Reforming the core curriculum is a hill that no provost, dean, undergraduate vice provost, or faculty senate president wants to die on. It is too large a task with too many rival interests at stake. Core courses offer departments a chance to showcase their specialties to students who are still exploring majors, and so they naturally contend for the most space in the cafeteria. Even if most students will never sign up for a full four-year major as a result, large lecture courses offered to the general undergraduate population generate enormous tuition revenue. At the University, the credit-hour-based New Budget Model had unleashed a competitive scramble among schools, colleges, and individual departments despite admonitions from administrators to refrain from cannibalizing each other. The law school, for example, facing a collapse in its J.D. program after the Great Recession, proposed to offer freshman-level courses on constitutional law despite the political science department having done so for a century. More positively, the music school's crowd-pleasing offerings in hip-hop received national recognition for cross-subsidizing a high-quality but deficit-prone conservatory.[18] The unsurprising result was a proliferation of new offerings. At the beginning of the decade, the University listed 735 core education courses of various stripes; ten years later there were 866.[19] In its defense, the University could point to many others that faced a similar profusion. When Harvard College reformed its own core curriculum in 2014, faculty members fought tooth and nail over whether to recertify, revamp, or remove each of the 574 core courses that august institution then offered.[20]

Although the University's regional accreditor was impressed with its vibrant and diverse core curriculum, it was far more interested in a systematic, uniform approach to learning outcomes assessment. In 2012, the University stated its aspiration to mount an assessment effort that would place it "in the upper one-half of the public universities in the AAU." As benchmarks, it held up traditional metrics of student engagement and student satisfaction, again measured by AAU standards.[21] This was a daunting goal considering how far behind it lagged on those standards on other counts (see chapter 5). Recognizing this, the accreditors called the University's bluff by insisting on a new assessment push. It was now enjoined to adopt "measurable, assessable, and verifiable" indicators of student achievement, to identify learning outcomes across all courses and degree programs, and to pledge time and resources from central leadership while also engaging faculty from the grass roots.[22] Schools and departments were required to devise discipline-specific learning outcomes and draw up "curriculum maps" to show how the structure of each academic major introduces, develops, and then assesses each learning outcome. These materials were then harvested for bragging points with which to impress the next round of site visitors and evaluators.

Accreditor demands for core curriculum assessment illustrate how and why universities turn to resources from the national student success movement under outside pressure. Realizing that its AAU ambitions smacked of hauteur, the University now dropped mention of the AAU in favor of lingo, standards, and practices popularized by dedicated assessment practitioners.[23] At accreditors' prompting, the University Senate's Core Education Council adopted a well-respected set of rubrics produced by the AAC&U, a leading player in the national assessment movement, almost word for word, to screen its many hundreds of general education courses.[24] A new team of outside evaluators profusely complimented its work. Yet it also pointed out that the University was still unable to document students' assessed mastery of core curriculum learning outcomes. Indirect measures of assessment were still being used when the real effort should instead be devoted to evaluating student learning directly.[25] Student course evaluations, for example, are suggestive, but best practice is to pluck a sample of graded assignments out of individual courses and then find another faculty member willing to regrade them using the rubrics of the overall curriculum. Assessment is not the same as grading, as its devotees never tire of pointing out. It is a new regime of evaluation imposed on top and to the side of traditional grading, and requiring large amounts of (usually uncompensated) faculty effort and a cycle of self-study and continuous improvement. Designing learning outcomes and curriculum maps is the easy part; actually deploying them to change classroom teaching and departmental curriculum planning is a wholly different task.

Somewhat comically, evaluators objected that having derived core curriculum learning outcomes from its official mission statement, the University could not yet show whether individual core courses contributed to that roster of lofty ideals. It so happened that the mission statement intoned exactly those liberal arts values that a core curriculum ought to instill: to "question critically, think logically, reason effectively, communicate clearly, act creatively, and live ethically."[26] But the idea that a document hastily cobbled together for public relations and compliance purposes under a 2014 state-level mandate should have been reverse-engineered, clause by clause, to generate a set of curricular learning outcomes, and then fleshed out into a set of detailed rubrics to guide the redesign of several hundred courses, and then simply imposed upon instructors teaching those courses, flew in the face of how curriculum development occurs in real life—which is from the ground up, by faculty members in academic departments with the expertise and authority to determine what students in their disciplines ought to learn.

Given that learning outcomes assessment fails to align with the incentives that animate institutions, departments, or individual faculty members, the University's foot-dragging and slow-walking was only to be expected. Assessment remained an activity rewarded neither by the New Budget Model nor by its successor, neither by the union contract's faculty workload provisions nor by its predecessor policies, neither by the membership criteria of the AAU nor by the qualifications that actually garner faculty appointments, promotions, tenure, raises, or peer recognition among practicing scholars.[27] Despite having been the cardinal strategy of the national student success movement in the 2010s, learning outcomes assessment cannot help but have a limited impact on real-world classrooms so long as it remains an unfunded, unwelcome mandate alien to the culture of most academic professionals. Pious accreditors cannot change that equation by fiat or by threats.

Universities comply with assessment mandates because they have to: to lose federal Title IV eligibility would be catastrophic, and to incur public humiliation is injurious to one's brand. Some admittedly have a genuine commitment to self-improvement to which accreditation evaluations can add an extra boost. They also regard the alternative, a federalized system to replace regional accreditation, as far worse. Both parties have long been engaged in a tacit bargain whereby accreditors pretend to regulate and institutions pretend to comply. Accreditors do at least provide an invaluable public service by buffering universities against external political meddling. Although often concealed, the loose coupling of authorities at all levels, from faculty to departments to institutions to accreditors to governments, has historically been a unique strength of the American system of higher education. Until oversight agencies at the state, regional, and federal levels join together in lockstep to attach high stakes to assessment, they are unlikely to progress any further than they already have. Decades of experience with other miscarried accountability reforms suggest that the effort may not be worth their time.

HOW TEACHERS SHOULD TEACH

The corollary to ensuring that students learn what they need to learn is to ensure that faculty teach how they need to teach. Strangely, on a national level, the reform of teaching evaluation has made far less headway than learning outcomes assessment despite being far more congenial to the culture of peer review that dominates practicing academics' professional lives. But the special dynamics of unionization at the University led it to become a leader among its peers in this area. Because teaching evaluations played a much more explicit part in faculty review and promotion under the new union contract, the stakes were higher than they had been under a more casual regime. The professionalization of non-tenure-track instructors made it especially important to ensure that the institution's shift toward such faculty had not compromised educational quality, and that those faculty were being fairly evaluated and duly rewarded for the work they performed. So, too, the abandonment of the always questionable presumption that research prowess and classroom ability are highly correlated among the *tenure-track* faculty necessitated that they be subjected to more rigorous oversight as well.

Recognizing these imperatives, the University Senate in 2018–19 created a task force on teaching evaluations. Its recommendations completely overhauled both the online student survey administered for each course and the criteria for peer review by fellow faculty. None other than the infamous anti-administration Blogger featured in chapter 4 coauthored the legislation.[28] Having become the Senate president after leaving his position as faculty union vice president, The Blogger was keen to show that shared governance could flourish anew and that faculty and administration could now collaborate on an issue of major consequence. The reform of teaching evaluations presented an opportunity for the Senate to become relevant again.

The initiative grew out of a real-world problem, namely, a well-documented gender bias in student evaluations of female professors. Careful sociological and statistical studies had shown that students learn just as much or more from female instructors, but women earn lower numerical teaching evaluation scores, on average, than men. Particularly women who seem strict and stern or simply confident and authoritative in the classroom are often penalized by students in course evaluations even as their male colleagues are rewarded for these same behaviors and persona. (One female professor at the University was even said to have "brass balls" in a student's written evaluation, although in context this was clearly meant as a compliment.) To the extent that their promotions, merit raises, and overall professional advancement depend on favorable student evaluations, women faculty are therefore put at a systemic disadvantage.[29]

The new student course survey tackled the problem of gender bias by adopting a key precept of the student success movement: that good teaching required meeting students where they are, not where their professors want them to be. The *old* survey had polled for quick gut reactions on course quality, teaching quality, instructor availability, and the like. Therein lay the problem: gut reactions had been shown to produce speciously objective results that were in fact biased against women. The *new* survey was more nuanced than this crude popularity contest. It took a more granular focus on issues of instructor inclusivity, support, feedback, assignment clarity, and active-learning strategies. Students judged fully thirteen course components as "beneficial to my learning," "neutral," or "needs improvement to help my learning." Such phrasing indicated that students' own judgments of whether they learned or not constituted valid reflections of their instructors' teaching abilities. This subtle but decisive shift in the burden of learning from students to their instructors revealed the direct influence of the student success philosophy. To put it in gendered terms, the new student survey feminized teaching evaluations by substituting an ethic of solicitude and support for a prior ethic of authority and charisma, one that had always favored male instructors. It was now incumbent on all faculty, irrespective of gender, to adopt more inclusive and supportive teaching practices. Ironically, students also incurred new burdens in the process. Response rates plummeted because the new survey bombarded them with so many questions about how they felt about their learning. But those students who did respond left lengthier and more thoughtful comments than they had under the prior system.[30] The new teaching evaluation instrument went on to win plaudits from the *Chronicle of Higher Education*, which featured a photo of The Blogger at the top of the story.[31]

A complementary reform of the ways faculty evaluated their own peers arose from another faculty-administration collaboration. Teams of faculty were gathered together to brainstorm about specific teaching challenges, including classroom diversity, mental health, career preparation, and student success writ large. Four new pillars of teaching excellence were developed to ensure "professional, inclusive, engaged, and research-informed" instruction, as measured by faculty-designed rubrics. The reform effort drew heavily from the new science of teaching and learning (SoTL). SoTL is a body of scholarship devoted to studying how college students learn and applying the lessons to the redesign of classroom and online teaching. If student engagement is student success 1.0, and learning assessment is student success 2.0, then SoTL—reflexively applying the lessons of university-level research to the practice of college teaching—is student success 3.0, the next frontier in a national movement. Combining the insights of psychology and the cognitive sciences with systematic attention to ethnic, racial, sexual, socioeconomic, neurological, and other dimensions of diversity, SoTL provides an invaluable tool kit from which every modern instructor can draw peer-reviewed best practices. References to the SoTL literature featured prominently in the University's teaching reform materials. With a politically canny accent on STEM disciplines, they cited such famous physicists as Eric Mazur (Harvard) and Carl Wieman (Stanford), who lent the prestige of their disciplines and institutions to what might otherwise have been derided as the pet agenda of do-gooders in para-academic administrative positions.[32]

Unlike the quest to stay in the AAU narrated in chapter 5, there is no external benchmark of teaching quality analogous to metrics of research productivity. The motivation to improve instead originates from within institutions, in response to authentic underlying needs for ongoing updates to curriculum, pedagogy, and quality control. If learning assessment shows how universities remain deeply resistant to monitoring, much less policing, what faculty do in the inner sanctum of the classroom, then teaching evaluations illustrate how traditional shared governance can thrive when focused on the university's core educational mission. This is because shared governance recognizes and reinforces ingrained practices of peer review, collegial self-scrutiny, local control, and autonomous professionalism that are the bedrock principles of faculty life.

At the end of the day, universities ensure good teaching by hiring the most talented faculty and trusting them to do what they do best. In short, they unfetter them. Creating and sustaining an authentic culture of teaching excellence is difficult to achieve. But affording faculty the chance to critique, collaborate, and compete with one other for recognition—including recognition by students—is far more effective than top-down management and surveillance by nonacademics. Still, even when earnestly and sincerely adopted, faculty commitments to student success cannot accomplish what is required to ensure timely college completion. As the following section shows, the largest share of that heavy lift was assumed by the growing ranks of para-academic administrators.

CLOSING ACHIEVEMENT GAPS

When President Five issued strict marching orders to crank up graduation rates in five years, it was not the faculty who had to hop to and make it happen. Both learning assessment and teaching evaluations had shown how little their professional lives fundamentally changed under the student success push. Instead, that task fell to twenty-three academic advisors and four career counselors who were installed in the new Student Success Building. These professionals were set to work helping individual students bob and weave their way through the many curricular, financial, social, and personal obstacles they faced on the way to a degree. A large share of the steep increase in para-academic staff traced in chapter 4 came from this team of advisors and counselors, plus similar ones scattered across the University. Academic advising was professionalized, largely ceasing to be a faculty responsibility, and explicitly refounded upon the student success imperative. With faculty retaining control over curriculum and academic standards, the duty of closing achievement gaps to improve college completion rates fell squarely on administrative leaders and staff.

It should come as no surprise that the University Commitment borrowed its blueprint for academic advising from a national nonprofit advocacy group called Complete College America (CCA). Founded in 2009 and headquartered (once again) in Indianapolis, CCA has been supported more recently by the megaphilanthropist Mackenzie Scott, who in good corporate style uses "rigorous, outcomes-based evaluation" to identify "high-impact organizations" working to improve outcomes for underrepresented minorities.[33] CCA's 2015 report, "The Four-Year Myth," was issued with the endorsement of thirty-five governors, most from states with performance funding schemes that, as shown in chapter 1, employ monetary incentives to promote desired outcomes on degree completion and workforce development.[34] Its provocative contention was that university leaders had tacitly abandoned the ideal of a four-year college degree and defaulted to bragging about six-year graduation rates as a grossly unacceptable alternative. What some students bemusedly call their "super-senior" (fifth and sixth) years cost them inordinate amounts of money. The solution was to invest resources in intrusive advising to keep students on track and prevent them from needlessly accumulating extra credits or more debt. A cleverly named GPS (Guided Pathways to Success) system would help students plot out the shortest possible distance to a degree, and not get lost dithering among majors or picking up superfluous credentials. Students would pledge to stick to a structured schedule of courses and electives, and in return institutions would provide degree maps, monitor their progress, hire more advisors, and ensure that needed courses were actually offered with enough seats. Citing behavioral psychology research, the report stressed "the paradox of choice": that having too many options in a degree cafeteria actually leads to disaffection and failure.

The CCA report was aimed at state politicians and public university presidents. It ended with a lengthy appendix showing how each of the fifty U.S. states stacked up in terms of on-time four-year graduation rates, accumulation of surplus degree credits, and foregone postgraduate earnings. Students at the University, for example, were shown to graduate in an average of 4.3 years with sixteen more student credit hours than they actually needed. Those who stayed a full extra year came out $67,865 behind when one added a year of tuition, fees, and living expenses to what they could have earned during that time in their first jobs.[35] This was rightly regarded as an eye-popping figure, and cited by President Five as a call for swift and decisive institutional action. "The best strategy to reduce the cost of college," he argued in citing the CCA report, "is to ensure that more of our students graduate on time."[36]

On cue, the twenty-three new academic advisors destined for homes in the new Student Success Building adopted large swaths of the CCA strategy with mostly cosmetic modifications.

For example, the report's call for "meta-majors" dictated a strategy of grouping the University's dozens of academic degree programs into helpful clusters that shared a common theme and assigning a pod of dedicated advisors to each cluster. Rebranded as a set of "flight paths"—the University's mascot is a bird—meta-majors were created on such subjects as healthy communities (everything from biology and human physiology to architecture and family services); industry, entrepreneurship, and innovation (business, economics, and journalism); global connections (for foreign languages, anthropology, history, and the like); and scientific discovery and sustainability.[37]

The faculty were not entirely marginalized in the process. Academic departments remained tangentially involved in the advising push. To help design flight paths, they were asked to repurpose the curriculum maps commissioned for assessment purposes to create suggested four-year plans. But not all academic majors imposed a linear sequence of requirements to begin with. Advisors did their best to accommodate the quirks and subjectivity of individual majors' academic requirements, attempting to remove roadblocks in degree programs that had originally been designed for intellectual and academic reasons rather than to optimize degree completion metrics. They spent much of their time assisting individual students to navigate a labyrinth of academic rules and consulting with departmental faculty on the many occasions where exceptions needed to be made. It rapidly became clear that a full-blown GPS strategy, mapping and mandating the shortest possible path to a degree, was simply unworkable in a world where faculty retained authority over academic degree programs.

As a result of this often thankless work, the new advisors did get hundreds of undergraduates on track. The number of "undeclared" students without a stated major, relabeled as "exploring" to remove pejorative connotations, dropped steeply over the decade. Proactive advising reduced by nearly 40 percent the number of students who, whether from indecision or genuine curiosity, had not yet decided what major to pursue.[38] As a result, the University met President Five's mandate to improve four-year graduation rates a year early. Whereas only 50 percent of students who entered in 2010 graduated on time, that number had increased to 61 percent by 2019, a bit more than the promised ten-percentage-point gain.[39] Completion rates for underrepresented minorities (a category including Blacks, Hispanics, Native Americans, and Pacific Islanders, but not Asian Americans) also showed dramatic improvement, as did the number of Pell Grant–eligible (financially needy) students. The greatly expanded Division for Student Services and Enrollment Management (SSEM) plowed a $25 million philanthropic gift into a highly effective scholarship and bespoke advising program for Pell-eligible state residents, with positive results.

Notably, achievement *gaps* persisted over the course of the five-year experiment even as all groups advanced. Both before and after, underrepresented minorities lagged whites by 10 percentage points, just as Pell-eligible students lagged financially secure ones by the same amount.[40] The University's ability to improve its diversity indicators remained particularly constrained. In a mostly white state, there were simply not that many students of color to begin with, and still relatively few from neighboring states with the ability to pay astronomical nonresident tuition. But the challenges were deep for all underprivileged groups.

William Bowen, the dean of higher education scholars, showed just how devilish the problem of degree completion is in 2009's *Crossing the Finish Line*. Beyond individual institutions or state university systems, beyond national networks of educators and policy activists, Bowen and his collaborators implicated an entire ecosystem, from high schools and state-level transfer articulation agreements to federal financial aid policies and the groaning inequities of American society itself.[41] Insofar as these disparities reflected injustices and inequalities that began far before students enrolled in college, but rather in their K–12 educations and in local communities, there was only so much any university could do to compensate for them. Even if it somehow could act in a coordinated fashion, the higher education sector cannot alone address the complex set of societal problems that retard college completion. The deeper burdens on students, brought to the surface by COVID-19, are what I turn to now.

COVID-19: THE END OF AN ERA?

Only six months after the Student Success Building opened in late September 2019, its halls fell silent. COVID-19 arrived in March 2020, forcing students, faculty, and advisors to move all of their work online in a matter of days. More than a year of Zoom-based learning ensued before in-person classes resumed in the fall of 2021.

Student success instantly became a universal imperative when the pandemic struck. Faculty knew it was their job to get students through the ordeal even before official policy gave them new guidelines on grading, late assignments, student engagement, and other academic logistics. Learning outcomes assessment and teaching evaluations were but a few of the nonessential processes put on hold while the University focused on mission-critical functions. Everyone in a position of academic authority suddenly had a new license to be compassionate. Faculty took the occasion to rethink old practices, such as penalties for missing deadlines or timed closed-book examinations, that now seemed to have lost their rationale and effectiveness. Something like an authentic commitment to the real-life meanings of student success took root among instructors who now had to strip down their pedagogy to focus on what was most important: that somehow, through awkward interactions in Zoom boxes, it was their burden to ensure that their students learned, and help them put one foot in front of the other for as long as this period of abnormal life continued. The silver lining of an otherwise terrible pandemic was that it succeeded, if only temporarily, in making faculty take student success to heart in a way that a decade or more of policy prescriptions, unfunded mandates, and well-meaning harangues had failed to do.

Different students and different faculty, of course, had different experiences. But one nearly universal takeaway was that the millenarian hopes previously invested in online learning proved to be a mirage. Whether touted as an alternative to the often denigrated "sage on a stage" pedagogy, or as a way to cut costs and realize productivity gains, or as a way to widen student access and promote student success, or as a way to transcend physical campuses and perhaps even human contact, online education disappointed anyone who had once sought a magic bullet for higher education's challenges. Thrown on Zoom, everyone simply figured out how to teach and learn as best they could, and just about everyone discovered that they would prefer to be back in person. Online teaching methods will henceforth have a place in every college instructor's tool kit. Universities offering courses or full degrees online will invest significant amounts to make them run well because that is what the best online providers already do. But traditional classrooms, lectures and seminars, and the ancient living bond between students and teachers are not going anywhere. Fanciful notions of a wholesale e-learning revolution or of a "disruptive innovation" heralded by business prophets, still surprisingly popular in the late 2010s, thankfully became a casualty of that decade because of the worldwide experiment COVID-19 forced upon us.

The pandemic was not just a crisis in physical health. Students' mental health now joined escalating debt, achievement gaps, and social injustice among the prime concerns of the student success and college completion movements. The traumas of lockdown and the fragility of a social safety net that, but for trillions of dollars in emergency federal assistance, showed many families living in precarious conditions, will no doubt scar a whole generation of high school and college students who came of age in or around 2020. As often happens with large-scale crises of any sort, the pandemic merely uncovered and intensified mental health problems that had long been festering among students.

Well before the pandemic, a large number of college-goers labored under unsustainable pressures, taking out loans, working part- or even full-time jobs that stole precious time from studying, fretting about picking a major with a decent return on investment, and completing academic degrees while juggling all manner of real-life challenges—all while navigating the road to adult maturity in a world beset by traumas from the murder of George Floyd to the authoritarian turn in American politics to the looming impact that climate change would have on their later lives. Frontline advisors realized this well before administrative leaders did. During the planning of what became the Student Success Building, their most insistent request was for private counseling rooms and Kleenex boxes. Advisors did not need, nor did they want, exciting open spaces to brainstorm future possibilities with eager students, or clever studies to prove to them the superb marketability of the liberal arts. Rather, they needed secluded rooms to talk students through the painful process of dismantling the unrealistic expectations that society has instilled in them. Tears often flowed when students faced their anxieties in these private confessionals. That was what the Kleenex boxes were for.

If nothing else, COVID-19 offered a frame-breaking respite from this carousel of worries by forcing everyone into the same miserable boat. But that was transitory, and by the time things reverted to normal, much had been forgotten. The pandemic closed the book on a lost decade of pedagogical reform: what could have been—and almost was—a time for colleges and universities to work creatively and systematically to improve the way they teach and the way students learn. A decade of external prodding and top-down mandates left behind a veritable cutting-room floor of missed opportunities to meaningfully improve student success at the local, face-to-face, institutional level. The abortive initiatives touched upon in this chapter—career counseling for arts and sciences majors, a renaissance of the core curriculum, experiments drawn from the science of teaching and learning, new digital teaching modalities inspired by educational possibilities rather than by makeshift necessity, holistic advising that spans students' academic, social, psychological, and financial challenges—and many others like them, harbored true potential to change the lives and futures of students, and still do.[42] But through it all, what remained unexamined was the underlying assumption of the college completion agenda: that a bachelor's degree is the sine qua non for success in an economically precarious world. It turns out that that assumption also bedevils our efforts to diversify higher education. This is the subject of the next chapter.

7

DIVERSITY

What do diversity, equity, and inclusion initiatives actually accomplish?

For Halloween 2016, a white law professor at the University dressed up in blackface and an Afro wig for a class party at her own home. It was an incomprehensibly misguided attempt to call attention to racial discrimination in the United States. Livid that students at the party had been subjected to such an offensive costume, twenty-three law school faculty jettisoned all concern with due process and in an open letter demanded their colleague's immediate resignation. The ensuing furor led President Five to hire an outside law firm to determine whether the offending professor had committed discriminatory harassment. Indeed, the firm found that she had.[1] She was relieved of duties and put on administrative leave, returning to work some months later without incident.

In hindsight, the campus community clearly overreacted to what no one would deny was a gross lapse of judgment about blackface. Similar instances of "cancel culture," humiliating those who violate progressive norms around race, gender, and other dimensions of diversity, were rife on American campuses during the 2010s. More than four hundred cases of scholars punished for constitutionally protected but politically controversial free speech were documented from 2015 to 2020 alone.² Such attacks gave ammunition to critics, mainly on the right, who conflated cancel culture with the effort to diversify higher education. The censoriousness of the left often set back the very causes for which the liberals were fighting.

Debacles like this caught both universities and the nation in a racial tinderbox. The years between the Black Lives Matter movement's origin in 2013 and the murder of George Floyd in 2020 were a period of racial turbulence not seen since the civil rights era. Let us not forget that eight days after that 2016 Halloween party, America elected a president who built his campaign on the birther lie that his Black predecessor, Barack Obama, was not actually born in the U.S.A. The presidency of Donald Trump, who professed to "love the poorly educated," put higher education on notice. His political base of non-college-educated whites inverted the coalition of racial minorities and college-educated professionals that Obama himself personified. During what seemed to many on the left like a four-year emergency for American democracy, colleges and universities doubled down on their efforts to redress racial, ethnic, gender, and sexual inequities. But in a society where dark skin and the possession of a bachelor's degree had become two of the most powerful predictors of partisan allegiance, those efforts could not help but enflame political polarization even further.

Well before the 2010s, diversity was a cardinal value, a civic obligation, and an institutional imperative for academic institutions, but it was not yet a central component of every college or university mission. One was more likely to encounter buoyant praise for multiculturalism, touting diversity for its educational benefits, than the soul-searching critique of structural racism that has dominated university discourse in recent years.

Previously defended as a cardinal job skill in the international economy during the heyday of globalization in the early century, facility with diversity was now recast as an essential component of domestic citizenship for an era when Americans retreated inward to focus on homegrown pathologies. As a species of civic religion, diversity might even be said to have filled the moral vacuum left by the excessively careerist, instrumentalist view of higher education ascendant in the early millennium.

That said, the reckonings of the 2010s merely accelerated trends that had long been underway in academia. With the U.S. population slated to become "majority minority" by midcentury, multigenerational demographic changes made it imperative for colleges and universities to recruit more diverse students, faculty, staff, and senior leaders. A string of Supreme Court cases dating back to the 1970s, and centering on universities' admissions policies, routinely put higher education in the crosshairs of political and moral disagreements about the efficacy and legitimacy of affirmative action. The academic study of race, ethnicity, gender, sexuality, and identity, for which detractors coined the term "political correctness" around 1990, became one of the few areas in which the humanities and humanistic social sciences enjoyed a decisive impact on our vocabulary and ways of thinking, both on and off campus. And, as ever, universities in perennial competition with one another scrambled to diversify themselves on every metric, whether by copying what peer institutions were doing or, increasingly, by borrowing best practices from the corporate world.

For all of these reasons, the values of "diversity, equity, and inclusion" (DEI) moved from the margins to the center of higher education's mission during the first two decades of the twenty-first century. Vocal commitments to DEI could now be found in college and university mission statements, in public celebrations and symbolic rituals, and in marketing and branding materials.

Tangible accomplishments in DEI work now counted as explicit job qualifications for most administrative leadership posts and increasingly for regular faculty and staff positions and promotions as well. Academic curricula, faculty hiring initiatives, undergraduate admissions policies, and student success programs now looked to DEI values as stars to navigate by. Corporate-style strategic plans injected DEI action items and accountability benchmarks into every layer of institutional decision-making. At hundreds of institutions nationwide, a chief diversity officer (CDO) joined the president's cabinet with other vice presidents, signaling to campus communities and constituencies that the promotion of DEI was a mission-critical, executive-level function. As one CDO put it, "diversity is everyone's responsibility, and a university cannot achieve excellence without diversity."[3] Those two mantras could now be heard at practically any mainstream institution.

If research and teaching remain the two core missions of public universities, diversity and social impact (the subjects of this chapter and the next) are their critical adjuncts and indispensable supports. Reaching beyond the Ivory Tower, they stake out a role for the university in wider society. But DEI initiatives, despite being universally adopted across academia, have not proven as effective in securing social justice as their champions had hoped. Nor, as its detractors allege, does DEI amount to a system of thought control, a catechism of politically correct pieties, or the instrument of a "woke" faction bent on canceling nonbelievers. DEI is too hemmed in—triply constrained by constitutional law, administrative implementation, and public policy—to count as either the redeemer or the despoiler of American higher education.

DEI's fortunes are instead tied to a broader college for all agenda that tends to equate social progress with degree completion. It is but the latest incarnation of a centuries old national belief that public education is the surest route to upward mobility and therefore the best remedy to societal inequities, and of an even more ancient view that treats college as central to the moral formation of young adults and not just to the transmission of knowledge. DEI's efficacy is sharply limited by this distinctively American equation of social justice with public (and now higher) education, and it has been positively compromised by a populist backlash against DEI's moral fervor. In a society in which college education all but defines class status, class conflict cannot help but take the form of anti-intellectualism. The culture wars that have erupted around DEI are a result of this political impasse. They have left some of America's greatest social ills outside the purview of what universities can be expected to address in the first place.

DIVERSITY, EQUITY, AND INCLUSION

For all their popularity, diversity, equity, and inclusion are three words whose meaning is hardly self-evident. Critics of DEI point out that its constituent terms have never been stably defined, that their combined meaning keeps changing, and that recent alternatives—such as the admittedly catchy "justice, equity, diversity, and inclusion" (JEDI)—are even more vague. Others defend DEI for its admirable capaciousness. Beyond the remediation of past racial oppression and sexual discrimination, it embraces, more positively, a panoply of identities centered on gender, sexual orientation, ethnicity, cultural tradition, religious belief, physical (dis)ability, cognitive style (neurodiversity), and intersectionality—the overlapping of two or more dimensions of inequality and identity, such as race and gender.

As this list grows, political affiliation (aka "viewpoint diversity") is still often overlooked, whether in practice or on principle. That is because DEI is indeed an ideological concept that has always been anchored in post-civil-rights-era liberalism. Irrespective of its multiple meanings today, the word "diversity" first entered mainstream higher education via a conscious political effort to remedy racial inequality. Dating to the 1970s, the diversity rationale in university admissions emerged as a legally palatable alternative to other, more intrusive forms of affirmative action (itself an odd circumlocution), specifically quotas, which had mandated the redistribution of scarce opportunities to designated racial and ethnic minorities. "Equity" and "inclusion" were only added later, following the model of major corporations driven by a mixture of farsighted and profit-seeking motivations. Combined, the ideology of educational diversity and the practices of corporate equity and inclusion explain the proliferation of chief diversity officers and DEI infrastructure in U.S. higher education by the early 2000s.

Legal and Constitutional Constraints

The main reason university leaders invoke "diversity" when they mean "racial justice" is that the U.S. Supreme Court has all but told them to say one thing while thinking another. In 1974, a white student named Allan Bakke sued the University of California at Davis for rejecting him from its medical school. Bakke argued that Davis's policy of reserving sixteen out of one hundred admissions slots for minority students was an unconstitutional racial quota. Four years later the Court agreed. But in a tortured decision, it did acknowledge racial diversity to be a "compelling state interest." Universities were thus permitted to recognize a whole host of qualifications and characteristics contributing to an academically robust student body as long as they afforded no overriding privilege to race or ethnicity. Being Black might "tip the balance" between two meritorious candidates, just as, for example, "life spent on a farm" might bring the unique perspective of a rural applicant.[4] Diversity could be fully justified for its "educational benefits" without recourse to notions of remedying past wrongs or redistributing future opportunities.[5]

The diversity rationale propounded by *Bakke* was immediately controversial. At issue were two rival conceptions of fairness, one centered on substantive social outcomes and the other on procedurally colorblind meritocracy, each with deep roots in American moral and civic traditions.[6] It took twenty-five years for the Supreme Court to clarify how universities could justify race-conscious admissions policies. In a pair of similar cases brought by white students against the University of Michigan, the justices in 2003 deferred to universities on academic judgments of what, precisely, the educational benefits of diversity might be. The majority opinion provided some helpful suggestions: cross-racial understanding, breaking down stereotypes, livelier classroom discussions, good citizenship, workplace skills, the training of future leaders, exposure to different ideas and viewpoints, legitimacy in the eyes of the citizenry, and national security (since a diverse military made it a better fighting force). As long as universities adhered to "individualistic, holistic" application review, eschewed quotas, reduced reliance on numerical formulas, and gave *majority* students the opportunity to showcase their own contributions to diversity, race-conscious admissions policies passed constitutional muster.[7]

It was no accident that the most elite public research universities provided the targets for litigation in such cases. In addition to California and Michigan, Texas's flagship Austin campus was sued near the turn of the millennium, as was North Carolina at Chapel Hill in the mid-2010s. Unlike the vast majority of public institutions, even most other state flagships, the admissions policies of these and other so-called public Ivies are not only selective but highly competitive. The white students who brought suit against them were supported by conservative activists, but they spoke to an anxiety about educational credentials that was shared by affluent students and their parents across the political spectrum. Then as now it was *non*selective public institutions, from community colleges to urban comprehensive universities to sub-flagship-level research institutions, that served underrepresented and disadvantaged populations in the greatest numbers. But as a matter of constitutional law and public debate, "diversity" remained a concept framed around schools frequented by the upper middle class.

It was only to be expected that elite institutions, both public and private, began to tout diversity not just for its educational benefits but as inherently indispensable to academic "excellence"—a word to conjure with, as shown in chapter 5. The University of Michigan took the lead by yoking diversity to excellence forcefully and early on, pioneering what became the national gold standard for campus-wide DEI initiatives. The so-called Michigan Mandate, adopted in the late 1980s, was subtitled "a strategic linking of academic excellence and social diversity." This large-scale administrative effort took as its premise the ideas that "diversity is a necessary condition for the achievement of excellence" and that "our ability to achieve excellence in teaching, research, and service, in a future increasingly characterized by its pluralism, will be determined by the diversity of our campus community."[8] Every student—not just minorities—would benefit as a result. The Michigan Mandate put teeth into that rhetoric. It recaptured one percent of annual budgets to create a centralized pool for all manner of diversity programs and hired a vice provost to coordinate it all. By the late 1990s, on the eve of being sued, Michigan's Ann Arbor campus had more than doubled its minority student population (even if most Black students still came from middle- rather than working-class families) and significantly diversified its faculty ranks as well.[9]

If the Michigan cases of 2003 articulated a more eclectic, civic-minded view of diversity than what *Bakke* grudgingly conceded, the 2013 and 2016 Texas cases narrowed the diversity rationale back down to utilitarian economic concerns. As one amicus brief put it, the "robust exchange of ideas" on a diverse campus was essential to "equip professionals and business leaders to interact with diverse customers, clients, co-workers, and business partners" in an "increasingly globalized and heterogeneous economic world." Other amici tilted even further toward the business case for diversity and away from its educational benefits, to say nothing of the moral imperative of eradicating racism. Harvard, Yale, and Stanford, in a joint brief, bent over backward to stress that training "leaders for a heterogenous society" was a far cry from the more radical aim of "remedying generalized discrimination."[10] The timing of the Texas decisions was telling. Landing between Black Lives Matter and Trump's election, which reminded Americans that racism was hardly an issue of the past, they signified the high-water mark of a naïvely postracial conception of diversity. Even DEI's most vocal supporters defended it in these terms, as a benign multiculturalism whose primary benefits were economic and financial. Given the premium that consumers of higher education had come to put on return for investment in an era of high tuition, global competition, and a recession-prone economy, it is difficult to fault those with a sincere commitment to social justice for making their case in opportunistic terms as well.

Corporate Models and Practices

The second major influence on DEI initiatives in American higher education came from the corporate world, which has long been vulnerable to antidiscrimination litigation resulting in expensive settlements. Surprisingly, the diversity rationale that provided the dominant justification for DEI in college admissions has never figured prominently in corporate cases. Indeed, two legal scholars note that "the compelling state interest in diversity has never been invoked or even addressed in the employment realm."[11] Lawsuits against employers typically rely on Title VII of the 1964 Civil Rights Act, which forbids employers (including colleges and universities) from using race, sex, or certain other characteristics when making hiring decisions, instead of giving them constitutionally permissible ways to *encourage* diversification. Affirmative action as it has been practiced in businesses, governments, educational institutions, and elsewhere has long had to operate within those guardrails. The common ground that they all share as employers of human resources has promoted cross-pollination across sectors, including with colleges and universities.

Corporations have instead adopted many of *Bakke*'s diversity insights voluntarily.[12] By the early 2000s—contemporaneously with the Michigan and Texas cases that stressed the business case for diversity in higher education—enterprises embraced the rhetoric of "inclusion" to cast diversity as a core competency essential for all employees, critical to teamwork, customer relations, and creative innovation.[13] Defining "DEI work" as an explicit component of job descriptions and employee evaluations, thus giving employees of all backgrounds a chance to demonstrate their DEI contributions, is an elegant way to avoid reverse discrimination and pass muster with Title VII law. Corporate DEI became a multibillion-dollar industry, dominated by the lucrative business of diversity trainings offered by a burgeoning profession of specialized consultants, and taking a host of other forms as well.[14]

Two widespread practices that register the direct influence of corporate DEI on higher education include CDOs and DEI strategic plans. CDOs were quite rare in academia at the beginning of the century, but by 2016 more than two-thirds of institutions had such a position, most being created at the tail end of the prior decade.[15] Often originating as "special assistants" with minimal staff, the recent trend has been to appoint CDOs to vice provost or vice president positions and, within the portfolios of these executive-level leaders, to gather multiple offices together in institutional organization charts.[16] These subunits might range from designated minority affairs offices and cultural centers for Black or Hispanic students to the ombudsperson and affirmative action and equal opportunity (AAEO) compliance office. Almost universally, CDOs are in charge of developing campus-wide strategic diversity plans by convening collaborators from every major university unit, harvesting their best practices, and coordinating local efforts across the institution. At universities further along on the corporatization spectrum, diversity plans are consciously aligned with both the campus-wide academic plan and the overall campus-wide strategic plan, whereas other, loosely managed universities find it convenient or beneficial to cast the CDO as more of a free agent who operates by building networks and alliances rather than through formal bureaucratic power. Having a midlevel staff of capable individuals who themselves build networks among other midlevel peers across an institution is often seen as an optimal happy medium between these extremes.[17]

DEI initiatives in American higher education rely on two assumptions. First, diversity is far more likely to withstand constitutional scrutiny when couched in expansive terms. It is better framed as an educational and career benefit for all students rather than as a moral imperative to remedy injustices done to specific oppressed groups. Second, the best way to implement DEI is through executive leadership appointments, strategic planning efforts, and other managerial practices borrowed from the corporate world. And as in that world, it is implicitly motivated by the need to compete with and conform to what peers are doing. DEI has thus become a form of industry-wide best practice that is now baked into administrative structures and standards of professionalism everywhere.[18] What that attempt at institutional reprogramming looks like is the subject of the next section, which analyzes why and how the University escalated its own efforts to improve campus diversity.

DEI AS CULTURAL REPROGRAMMING

The University conducted two comprehensive DEI strategic planning cycles between 2006 and 2020, revising its approach between the two iterations and intensifying its tactics in response to the national racial traumas of the mid-2010s. Each cycle produced mixed results that positioned it as a leader in some areas and a laggard in others. But in general, its efforts were broadly typical of other universities. Like them, it attempted to infuse more inclusive values, practices, attitudes, and policies into every corner of the institution while refraining as a matter of principle from treading on its core freedoms of teaching and research. DEI, almost universally, is a strategy that seeks to reprogram the culture of university life at an almost cellular level without compromising or dismantling any of the deep structures that make it run.

Strategic Plans and Moral Exhortations

The University was relatively early to adopt an institution-wide DEI strategy, but this was partly because it had been forced to do so. To settle a series of antidiscrimination lawsuits brought by a Black employee beginning in the mid-1990s, the University agreed to create a new vice provostship for diversity and fund a new Office of Institutional Equity and Diversity for a period of at least five years.[19] In 2006, the office issued the University's first Diversity Strategic Action Plan after extensive collaborations with more than one thousand faculty, staff, and students. The plan led with the standard arguments that diversity was essential to academic quality and knowledge creation; that diversity was a key skill to possess in a rapidly globalizing world; and that the evolving demographics of the state and the nation made it imperative to more actively recruit diverse students, faculty, and staff.[20] Diversity of demographic origin was touted alongside diversity of (political) opinion as part of a bipartisan commitment to "pluralism," and international understanding was prominently highlighted along with awareness of domestic problems. Viewpoint diversity and global diversity would later become far less salient under a new, sharpened focus on social injustice within the United States. Administratively, the plan was quite modest. It required the creation of diversity committees and action plans in every college and top-level administrative unit but otherwise pledged to work within established personnel and governance policies and practices. The hope was to avoid any intrusion, or perceived intrusion, into local academic judgments and prerogatives.[21]

Notwithstanding its cautious incrementalism, the plan's rollout was marred by controversy because its initial draft had proposed mandatory "cultural competence" training and standards for all employees. Influential faculty on the University Senate objected to this ill-defined concept, and especially to the recommendation that it be used in tenure and promotion reviews, where strictly academic peer judgments of research, teaching, and service had long been held sacrosanct. An article in the national higher education trade press called the plan a "train wreck" due to the cultural competence debacle.[22] Bowing to criticism, its final draft stressed that "cultural competence should not be viewed as advocating political correctness or as any sort of infringement on academic freedom."[23]

That glitch aside, the 2006 plan captured the national state of debate by offering a snapshot of the critiques made against DEI before the reckonings of the 2010s. Some critics wondered whether a diversity plan was needed to begin with, a question that would have been seen as heretical a decade later. Many argued that at a time of chronic public disinvestment, the added expense and bureaucratic apparatus required for DEI initiatives could not be financially justified. Diversity, they said, should not be the priority when boosting faculty salaries and promoting academic excellence were more pressing needs. Others pointed out the inconsistency between the plan's broad and expansive definition of diversity and the need for targeted interventions and strategies to help specific racial and ethnic minorities and women. Filling the pipeline of future college-goers and faculty members was more likely to succeed than ex post facto diversity initiatives on the other end of that pipeline, just as focusing on socioeconomic deprivation, and not just race and ethnicity, was critical to any comprehensive approach to the problem of inequality. Still others frankly denied that diversity should be so blithely equated with excellence, warning that standards of academic quality could easily be compromised when faculty or students are rewarded based on "criteria other than academic qualification."[24]

Following a postmortem on the 2006 plan after five years in operation, the University greatly increased its investment in DEI infrastructure. Here, too, it followed trends at peer institutions. The vice provost for diversity was elevated to a vice presidency in 2012, and a national search yielded its first incumbent to lead a newly established Division of Equity and Inclusion. Also reflecting evolving best practice, the new vice president was given a portfolio of subunits rather than functioning as a free-floating networker and coordinator, as her predecessor had been constrained to do. These reporting units included a faculty development center, a multicultural student center, an academic advising staff catering to underrepresented students, and a longhouse for the Native American community.[25] That said, the DEI office's total $2.6 million budget remained fairly small both before and after the administrative reorganizations of the 2010s, growing at a slightly lower rate than the other vice presidential portfolios charted in chapter 4.[26]

After another extensive round of cross-campus consultations, a new strategic plan and a new set of tactics were issued in 2015–16. Two mnemonics helped campus constituencies recall its key precepts. The plan itself was titled "IDEAL," which stood for inclusion, diversity, evaluation, achievement, and leadership. As is standard for corporate-style strategic plans, a list of substrategies was itemized under each heading, with individual tactics broken out under those.[27] The DEI office reported with dubious precision that of the 657 identified tactics in the IDEAL plan, 58 percent of them had been met or were in progress by 2020.[28] Separately, a framework of moral values called "LACE" was promulgated to encourage love, authenticity, courage, and empathy in interpersonal interactions among members of the University community. An exhaustive list of surprisingly practical, down-to-earth resources, tips, and tactics was posted on two LACE websites, one for faculty and one for students.[29]

Implementation and Results

Like most DEI initiatives at other institutions, the University made no real incursions into established faculty and staff hiring and promotion policies or student admissions policies. Many of the steps taken in response to Black Lives Matter (BLM) were symbolic and performative, if undeniably important. President Five launched an elaborate and thoughtful process to remove the names of racist forebears from University buildings in cases where this was warranted by careful historical research and thoughtful consideration of past and present contexts.[30] Funds were raised for a brand new Black cultural center and an academic residential community for first-year Black students. Five distinct "strategies groups" were set up to provide networking opportunities and peer support for Blacks, Asians, Hispanics, Native Americans, and white allies from among the University's employees, mixing faculty and staff. The University Senate passed several resolutions against racism and instituted a major overhaul of the undergraduate core curriculum's 1990s-era multicultural requirement.[31] And when, under cover of darkness, a group of students unceremoniously toppled an iconic statue of a stereotypically white frontiersman opposite the central administration building, the campus police elected not to pursue the culprits.

The impact of BLM on the daily lives of faculty and other employees, together with that of the contemporaneous movement against sexual harassment called #MeToo, otherwise remained sharply limited. Roughly seventy new diversity committees were established that, in contrast to the prior (2006) plan, were now required in every department and administrative unit, not just in the schools and colleges and at the top levels of the administration. A campus-wide climate survey by the well-respected Gallup Organization was launched in response to staff concerns that too many workplaces had become toxic environments marred by harassment and bullying.[32] Units were required to draft workplace norms documents listing the fundamental civilities and courtesies—such as not interrupting colleagues or pressuring office staff to work after hours—shown to have a disproportionate impact on women. Inventories of DEI-related resources were drawn up to make the University's radically dispersed efforts more accessible and transparent, even if these same lists revealed how siloed those efforts remained.[33]

Tweaks, but no structural changes, were made to the University's core academic function of recruiting, retaining, and promoting faculty. The union contract required faculty to describe their contributions to diversity, equity, and inclusion as part of their cases for tenure and promotion. Yet in contrast to written standards for research, teaching, and committee service, no explicit guidelines were drawn up for deans or personnel committees to refer to in determining whether faculty had met, exceeded, or not met expectations in DEI. Those who sat on search committees for new faculty members were required to watch a short video on implicit bias, and trained search advocates (often junior administrators with little clout) were installed as observers to flag instances of biased behavior that sometimes crept into freewheeling discussions of candidate applications. Finally, the University-wide Institutional Hiring Plan required departments, schools, and colleges competing for new tenure-track appointments to be explicit in analyzing how such hires would enhance the racial, ethnic, and gender diversity of their departments relative to the demographic composition of their likely applicant pools.³⁴ A bevy of (mostly nonfinancial) resources was made available to assist departments in devising active recruitment plans to seek out and recruit underrepresented minorities who might not otherwise have applied for faculty positions, to ensure that their visits to campus as candidates were as welcoming and culturally sensitive as possible, and to make special accommodations for dual-career couples so that those with family obligations, whatever their gender or ethnicity, could more easily consider relocating. But at the end of the day, standards of promotion remained focused on academic merit, just as they always had been.

Progress in undergraduate recruitment and retention was far more significant, for two reasons detailed in earlier chapters. The phenomenal growth and consolidation of Student Services and Enrollment Management (SSEM) put real resources, both financial and human, behind outreach efforts and scholarships that benefited low-income, first-generation, minority, and other underrepresented students. And the parallel consolidation and reorganization of Undergraduate Education and Student Success (UESS) professionalized undergraduate advising and significantly improved four-year graduation rates for both underrepresented students and the general undergraduate population, even if the achievement *gap* between them stayed essentially the same as the two populations improved in tandem with one another.³⁵ The glaring exception was Black students, who were alone among underrepresented groups in not registering real gains in graduation rates during the 2010s. So, too, Black faculty, whom the University courted assiduously in part to serve as role models and mentors for Black students, were three times more likely to leave the University than any other underrepresented faculty group.³⁶

Table 7.1 Demographic diversity

	2010	2020
Students		
Nonwhite	16%	32%
Women	51%	55%
Tenure-related faculty		
Nonwhite	14%	20%
Women	35%	41%

Source: Office of Institutional Research. For 2010 figures, see "Student Demographics 06/07 to 16/17," https://perma.cc/KFK9-JE5T, and "Faculty Demographics 05/06 to 16/17," https://perma.cc/RZP6-W98L. For 2020 figures, see Office of Institutional Research, "Detailed Enrollment (Ethnicity)," https://perma.cc/9RNQ-VGDB, and "Faculty and Employees," https://perma.cc/PB5E-A7JJ.

The results, reflecting the combined impact of all these efforts plus exogenous factors beyond the institution's control, are shown in table 7.1. The proportion of minority students doubled from one-sixth to one-third during the 2010s, led mainly by Hispanic and Asian American students. Meanwhile, on the faculty side, lesser but still significant gains were made in the hiring of minorities and women. Among students, women increased their majority as part of a national trend whose flip side—the declining numbers of men seeking college educations—has only recently begun to receive due attention. And among tenure-related faculty, women very much remained in the minority despite making small gains. This chronic deficit was a combined result of pipeline factors, the historic exclusion of women from the science fields that were favored under Institutional Hiring Plan priorities, traditionally heavy family responsibilities including child care and "two-body problems" (the need to find work for trailing spouses or partners), and in rare cases overt gender discrimination.

Tellingly, international students never figured prominently in any of the University's DEI strategies despite a massive increase in their numbers and campus presence during the 2010s. As was the case across the United States, Chinese students were far and away the largest cohort among them, and they were actively recruited and welcomed for the hefty out-of-state tuition they paid. At the height of this nationwide enrollment boom, the University hosted some three thousand matriculated students from other countries, roughly two thousand of them from China, plus a contingent of several hundred nonmatriculated students who enrolled in its ESL (English as a second language) program. As a result of the severe growing pains the ESL program experienced, an abortive attempt was made to overhaul its structure and financing, but its promise was cut short when the international student bubble deflated again after 2016—the result not just of Trumpian xenophobia but of various other factors, including the regular boom-and-bust cycles that beset this sector of academia. An enormous opportunity had been lost to better integrate this population of international students—speakers of different languages, hailing from radically different cultures, bringing authentic diversity and unparalleled educational benefits—into the cultural, social, and intellectual life of the University.[37]

The fact that so few U.S. universities treated international students as a cultural resource and not just as a revenue stream reflects a large gap between DEI's stated ideals and its realization in practice. Typically, international students, whatever their race or ethnicity, do not count toward institutional diversity metrics except as a separate, stand-alone category of "nonresident aliens." So, too, the substantive moral impulse behind DEI initiatives remains focused on domestic minorities (including actual immigrants from other countries, notably the large population of undocumented "Dreamer" students) and the obstacles they face that are specific to American society. International students only transiently resident in the United States count for little in that equation. However critical to America's centuries old civic project, DEI strictly speaking remains bounded by the provincial concerns of one admittedly very large and influential nation-state, not to promoting authentic interculturalism at a transnational scale.

All told, the University's DEI efforts in the 2010s showed what was possible and not possible when it came to promoting social justice goals while acting within a framework that remained institutionally conservative. Tools and best practices of corporate managerialism could not help but have a limited effect on such institutions because tenure and departmental self-governance were enshrined in faculty union contracts and woven into the fabric of American academia at large. The set of strategies it actually implemented left the institution's two most important third rails untouched. First, its practices and policies on faculty tenure and promotion remained aligned with AAU peers and standards of AAU excellence. And second, the University continued to exploit its considerable latitude in adjusting the mix of resident and nonresident students, and the tuition they paid, to meet revenue needs. In the next section I delve deeper into this second factor—whether the University served or neglected in-state minorities—by exploring the wider field of public policy, statewide DEI goals, and postsecondary higher education across the University's home State.

DEI AND THE FIFTY STATES

The nation's fifty states are where inequities of race, ethnicity, gender, and class will ultimately either be rectified or not, both in the sphere of education and in the broader worlds of work and citizenship that education leads into. The reason for this is that in the United States, the states, not the federal government, are the fifty laboratories where systems of public education from K–12 through research universities are designed, managed, and funded. The details of state-level policy making are therefore of overwhelming importance to DEI goals that focus on college completion and other postsecondary credentials, and how such goals relate to the critical prior stages in students' educational journeys as children and young adults. But there is a catch. When state disinvestment collided with the college for all agenda in the years around 2010, higher education became a private consumer good at the very moment that its importance to public policy became greater than ever before. This ensured that the semiprivatization of public universities and the shortcomings of performance funding have rendered states progressively less able to achieve coherent reforms that bridge K–12 to college and remedy key educational gaps.

As mentioned in chapter 1, the University's home State sought in the early 2010s to become a national leader in creating frictionless pathways all the way from preschool through graduate school. The Higher Education Coordinating Commission (HECC) was established to implement the Legislature's 40-40-20 goal: the plan that by the year 2025, 40 percent of working adults would hold a bachelor's degree, another 40 percent some other postsecondary credential, and the final 20 percent a simple high school diploma. DEI goals stood at the very center of HECC's mission, whose official "equity lens" cites changing demographics and workforce skill development as commanding priorities.[38] Among its specific tactics were efforts to streamline the pathway and transfer of credits among the state's community colleges and universities, educator equity plans for the various teacher training programs typically housed in universities' colleges of education, and—most important—a new funding model for all public universities that uses financial performance incentives to improve the recruitment and retention of underrepresented minority students.[39]

The centerpiece of HECC's commitment to DEI was a performance funding scheme established in 2015 and titled the Student Success and Completion Model (SSCM). As the name suggests, its motivation was the selfsame student success and college completion policy agenda that, as shown in chapter 6, inspired the University's efforts to improve its four-year graduation rates.[40] A significant DEI component was baked into the SSCM funding formula by adding bonus dollars for each bachelor's degree awarded to any in-state student from an underrepresented minority. That amount was intended as an incentive for universities to recruit more racial and ethnic minorities but also as compensation for the substantial extra costs, from recruitment and scholarships to academic advising and social support services, needed to see them through to degree completion. Numerically, roughly 8 percent of the total state appropriation to universities was pegged to this DEI goal. Put another way, for each in-state undergraduate minority student a given public university graduated, it could expect to receive about $6,450 in extra money from the State.[41]

Performance funding is limited in its efficacy, as was shown in chapter 1, and the SSCM scheme was no exception to that rule. Under the SSCM formula, the University already received less funding per student than any other public university in the State.[42] Its DEI-specific incentives contributed only about $6.5 million to a total general fund budget of $461 million. That number may or may not have correlated with the actual added costs of student success services for underrepresented minorities. A few drops in the bucket, however welcome, could not be expected to materially affect the University's enrollment calculations and student success investments. This was especially true when its top financial priority lay in recruiting enough high-paying out-of-state students, of whatever race or ethnicity, to balance the books. At nearly $9,000 per year, the differential tuition paid by an out-of-state student easily exceeded the equity incentive attached to each in-state minority student.[43]

This fact raises the broader question of what impact the semiprivatization of public universities has on the DEI goals that they share with the states that fund (or underfund) them. Scholars have asked whether wooing out-of-state students enables universities to subsidize in-state minorities or crowds them out of precious slots in freshman classes. Recent work suggests that most public universities below the elite level do not suffer a *general* trade-off between resident and nonresident students.[44] But when one trains the focus specifically on low-income and underrepresented minority students, there is a strong correlation between enrolling students from out of state and diminished access for disadvantaged in-state residents. This is in part because admissions offices devote their limited resources to recruiting from affluent out-of-state high schools, which tend to be more white, and because financial aid offices often rely on costly tuition discounting to lure affluent students away from other expensive public and private universities. Some institutions have shifted the overall financial aid mix from need- to merit-based scholarships to boost metrics of academic quality, which again disadvantages minorities who tend to have lower average test scores. The result is that "public research universities become less racially diverse as they increase nonresident enrollment."[45] Enrollment management in a semiprivatized high-tuition environment suffers from an "iron triangle" of constraints. Forced to choose among access, revenue, and academic quality, they sometimes sacrifice the first of these goals to satisfy some combination of the other two.[46]

Finally, there is the policy problem of putting so many eggs in the bachelor's degree basket. When the State reviewed its 40-40-20 goals in 2019, the most conspicuous gap was not at the four-year but the two-year level. Whereas 37 percent of the desired 40 percent of adults now held at least a bachelor's degree, only 19 percent of the aspirational goal of 40 percent held an associate's degree, and another 19 percent had some college but no credential.[47] Clearly, the priority should have been on closing the two-year degree gap.[48] Yet the political will, policy tools, and financial resources all continued to align overwhelmingly behind the four-year degree as the most prized credential. HECC did launch a smorgasbord of initiatives to open up alternative pathways to the State's 40-40-20 goal: college credit for rigorous high school classes and for prior learning in the workplace, pilot partnerships with industry groups to promote workforce development in high-demand skilled occupations, and various programs to subsidize apprenticeships, technical training, and nondegree credentials.[49] But the State's few concerted policy initiatives devolved into small-bore interventions such as a new law on college textbook prices. The associate's degree has in any case come to function less as a terminal degree than as a springboard to a four-year university. Community colleges, given their very low tuition and articulation agreements ensuring that public universities will accept their courses for required credits, now often serve as inexpensive two-year transfer platforms for students heading on for their third and fourth years elsewhere, rather than as destinations in their own right.

The stark choice between a bachelor's degree and underemployment is one that America as a whole now faces after decades of policy choices that make it an outlier by international standards. As a nation, the United States is recognized as having the developed world's finest set of public universities and one of its most mediocre K–12 schooling systems. Not only that but among the world's leading economies, the United States is nearly alone in lacking a formal vocational track at the secondary level.[50] Leaving aside a smattering of vocational classes, American high schools are geared around getting students into college, and four-year colleges at that. Above all, our system of primary and secondary public education is scandalously inadequate. Between the failure of No Child Left Behind in the early 2000s and the gross defects in schooling revealed by the COVID-19 pandemic, K–12 education was all but abandoned as a national policy priority. Aside from limited right-wing and center-right efforts to promote school choice, vouchers, and charter schools, the financing and quality of K–12 education simply dropped off the policy agenda. Policy makers instead rallied around the wishful notion that higher education can compensate for K–12's failings. Some even indulged in the motivated reasoning that the BA is essential in the new knowledge economy rather than what it in fact often is: a surrogate for an increasingly meaningless high school diploma.

As long as the educational ladder is missing so many middle rungs, our education system will continue to reproduce a system of class inequality founded on the attainment of a four-year college degree. In the final section I turn to the larger system of class stratification that the college for all agenda licenses, and to the populist backlash against DEI that it has unleashed.

RACE, CLASS, AND HIGHER EDUCATION

DEI as implemented in the 2010s amounted to a noble but unfulfilled and perhaps unfulfillable quest. Because constitutional and civil rights law sharply circumscribes the use of race, ethnicity, gender, and other characteristics in university admissions and employment decisions, DEI efforts in American universities are in little danger of somehow engineering widespread reverse discrimination against white men and other privileged groups. So, too, because universities are rightly determined to preserve academic structures that govern critical functions such as faculty tenure and curriculum design, DEI practices borrowed from corporate HR departments at best exert an incremental, symbolic impact on their core research and teaching missions. DEI is, in short, neither a battering ram for political correctness nor a systematic program for social justice within the academy, much less outside of it. Where DEI does enjoy overwhelming influence, albeit far from unanimous support, is in the nation's longstanding commitment to public higher education as a privileged route to upward social mobility. Financed by federal loan subsidies and realized by the fifty states, the ambition to provide college for all centers on creating new opportunities for disadvantaged and underrepresented groups—precisely those segments of the population whom leaders really have in mind when they invoke "diversity" as an all-purpose catchword.

For all of its undeniable benefits, the close alignment of the DEI and college for all agendas has created a bevy of unintended consequences. In recent decades, college education has also become aligned with both socioeconomic class and partisan affiliation. By extension, DEI efforts in colleges and universities are implicated in inequalities of income, wealth, and social opportunity that have become weaponized by political polarization and cultural conflict. In a deeply worrisome trend, Democrats and Republicans, who at the beginning of the 2010s were both highly supportive of higher education, have dramatically parted ways in their opinions of it: by the end of the decade, two-thirds of Democrats harbored a positive view of college whereas nearly 60 percent of Republicans felt the opposite.[51] Right-wing populist legislation, such as the 2022 Stop WOKE Act targeting Florida's public universities, plus numerous campaigns to ban "critical race theory" in schools and colleges, are but the latest round in a generations-long debate over multiculturalism whose terms of discourse have changed very little since political correctness first became a hot-button issue around 1990.[52] The endless culture war against DEI is a result of the policy straightjackets that this stalemate has produced.

In the 2010s, possession of a bachelor's degree became highly predictive not just of socioeconomic class and party affiliation but even of life and death itself. During that decade, "deaths of despair" skyrocketed among those who lack a four-year degree, whether the cause was alcohol, drugs, or suicide.[53] This crisis has no analogue in Western Europe, where the challenges associated with the postindustrial knowledge economy are comparable, as indeed are those associated with multiculturalism. It is rather a product of America's overwhelming focus on higher education as a one-stop policy solution to social ills. Britain has universal health care, France has free child care, Germany has robust labor unions and vocational tracking, and Scandinavia has a wall-to-wall welfare state. The United States has the bachelor's degree.

Among those who desperately want higher education and are well-qualified for it, racial and ethnic minorities are overrepresented among those who embark on a college degree without finishing one. These students too often end up saddled with debt in a country where the average white person is six times wealthier than the average Black person.[54] They get lost in the system, exploited by bad actors, and diminished in dignity and adult independence. The many for-profit colleges that grew in the 2000s and 2010s frequently capitalized on the easy availability of student loans to soak their students for tuition. The recent deflation and, in some cases, outright collapse of such degree mills is a welcome sign that the system may now be righting itself. But the underlying dynamics have not gone away. Students still too often suffer from leaky pipelines that allow too many dropouts to disappear against their wishes, from a Kafkaesque financial aid system that is inefficient and frequently exploitative, and from underinvestment in vocational paths and training opportunities that can serve as alternatives to the four-year degree.[55]

As progressive scholars themselves point out, DEI can act as a convenient distraction from these nettlesome systemic issues. Performative or symbolic celebrations of diversity and multiculturalism allow educational leaders to congratulate themselves for endorsing progressive ideals without, however, diverting resources or changing structures that perpetuate inequality. The specific indignities and prejudices attached to being Black, Hispanic, Asian, gay, transgender, or a member of any other minoritized group, not to mention multiple intersecting identities, are flattened out and effaced when such differences are condensed into an omnibus definition of diversity.[56] Identity politics are inherently divisive, not only pitting the weak against the strong but disadvantaged groups against one another, thus limiting coalition building along either universal or class-based principles. The very categories universities use to measure difference, like the federal government's crude typologies of race and ethnicity, help produce and reify invidious distinctions without capturing authentic underlying identities.[57] As for affluent whites, many are only too happy to strike a "diversity bargain" that gives them the educational and career advantages of associating with diverse peers and colleagues in college, but only insofar as the inclusion of those others does not deprive them of their own places in the socioeconomic and educational hierarchy.[58]

Contrast the ongoing disadvantages experienced in distinct and disparate ways by racial and ethnic minorities with the improving situation of women, taken as a group, in higher education. Although still underrepresented in faculty ranks and still subject to harassment, discrimination, and structural disadvantages as both employees and students, women in 2020 outnumbered men in the college-going population by an even greater margin—roughly 55 percent to 45 percent and growing—than they did a decade earlier.[59]

Women gained in power as well as in numbers. In the 2010s, Title IX civil rights protections aimed at combating gender discrimination were dramatically expanded beyond their traditional role of requiring that colleges offer women's sports. In 2011, the federal Office of Civil Rights obligated higher education institutions, under Title IX, to investigate and punish acts of sexual harassment and violence on their own campuses, separately from the police. That mandate was later rescinded for having prompted numerous university administrators to mount inquisitions and tribunals whose methods grossly violated the due process rights of accused sex offenders.[60] The career of Title IX in the 2010s is thus an ambiguous story of feminist empowerment and bureaucratic overreach. Yet, coinciding as it did with the #MeToo movement, it is at the same time a telling illustration of how women, as a group, enjoyed greater access to power than underrepresented minorities. Meanwhile, the striking dearth of *men* among today's college-goers, and the attendant, social, economic, and psychological problems that accompany this trend, is a problem that has proven difficult to even conceptualize as a DEI issue.[61]

All of these inequities, and many more, pertain to America at large and by no means to higher education alone. It is unfair to hold colleges and universities responsible for failing to rectify society's ills, or to chastise them for putting themselves forward as solutions to a knotty set of problems that few other broad-based American institutions are even capable of recognizing, much less committed to solving. The political riptides to which higher education has been subjected are far more to blame for this failing than whatever missteps or hypocrisies have sometimes marred its sincere efforts to promote diversity, equity, and inclusion. Colleges and universities *do* enjoy unique advantages to attack DEI problems that K–12 schools, businesses, governments, churches, and voluntary organizations do not. They are configured to study and teach about diversity, equity, and inclusion, domestically and globally, scientifically and humanistically, in as many different ways as the dozens of disciplines under their roofs allow. As institutions, they are uniquely able to tackle the subtleties and the complexities, the nuances and the paradoxes—in short, the rigorous academic and intellectual work—that other institutions are not designed to engage.

After the Supreme Court all but struck down race-based admissions—effectively gutting *Bakke* and its successors in two 2023 opinions—universities faced the difficult task, already faced in Michigan and California, of finding other ways to enhance diversity. The silver lining is that they are well-positioned to do so. Universities can begin by submitting their own shibboleths about DEI to rigorous and ongoing scrutiny. Among these are the idea that diversity as an omnibus concept is superior to a more targeted and transparent focus on concrete racial, ethnic, gender, and other disparities; that diversity, so conceived, is justified primarily as an educational benefit or career skill rather than, more forthrightly, as a way to right past and present wrongs; that diversity is an ineluctable component of academic excellence instead of a distinct and often rival good that can be weighed alongside properly academic standards; that college for all can compensate for prior inequities in K–12 education; that the "knowledge economy" demands college for all despite the value of vocational and alternative postsecondary credentials; and that strategic planning, diversity training, and other corporate best practices can change hearts and minds and make campus communities havens of inclusion and tolerance in a bitterly divided and politically toxic society.

Values of diversity, equity, and inclusion not only speak to national societal imperatives but also tap into higher education's historic identity, self-conception, and mission. Moral education and character development had been the central goals of colleges and universities from colonial times up through the early 1900s.[62] Submerged but never entirely abandoned, the moral mission of higher education has been periodically revived in various guises throughout the twentieth century, and now through DEI into the twenty-first. The rearguard moral panic that DEI has provoked is paradoxically the surest sign that efforts to diversify higher education remain on the right track.

8

IMPACT

How are universities reforming themselves to tackle twenty-first century problems?
A new instrumentalism took hold on university campuses in the first quarter of the twenty-first century. An ethic that stresses the practical, economic, social, and even moral impact of knowledge displaced an older commitment, already waning, to the pursuit of knowledge for its own sake. Universities have never been Ivory Towers. They have always been expected to produce benefits for the public good and for private interests. But their academic cores, centered on the arts and sciences, have long been driven by open-ended curiosity and exploration, not real-world application. Since about 2000, however, the dynamic of growth and expansion at research universities has shifted from problems and questions that are intrinsic to the academy to pressures and opportunities that originate outside of it.[1]

That reorientation toward tangible impact springs from deep changes in the pursuit of knowledge itself. But it has been propelled by the decline in state financial support that makes public universities, like their private counterparts, dependent on continually having to prove their worth to other external patrons. Governments, businesses, foundations, philanthropists, and individual consumers of education and knowledge all seek a more tangible return on their investment than they have in the past. This remains true whether that return is counted in dollars or in broader metrics of societal impact. Universities have become too costly and too valuable to be left to their own devices. Just as they have become far more expensive to the students they teach, they have also become far more lucrative for the research they produce. Instrumental concerns have begun to prevail over pure curiosity in a way that was far less the case when their primary functions were education and exploration. Once subsidized at arm's length by generous state and federal governments, those functions are now much more tied to practical payoffs, and again, not just crude economic and financial returns but moral and social benefits as well.

The last decade registered a long-term sea change in our views on the uses of knowledge. No one, aside from throwbacks and curmudgeons, bothers to defend the Ivory Tower anymore. Concerns that the new instrumentalism might somehow corrupt higher education's public and academic missions largely evaporated while hardly anyone noticed. As late as the early 2010s, university leaders, policy makers, and scholars fretted deeply about "academic capitalism," the dense web of contacts between universities and corporations that grew up around biotechnology, microelectronics, materials science, and other high-tech fields starting around 1980.[2] The search for profit and the search for knowledge had once been seen as rival goals, their interaction fraught with moral hazard and conflicts of interest. Steep firewalls had to be erected to ensure that the values of the marketplace did not erode the values of disinterested science. Today, in contrast, academic capitalism is universally regarded as a matter to be managed, not overcome. Philosophical questions about its propriety are rarely even raised. Universities are instead scrambling to promote "innovation and entrepreneurship," spawning research parks, separate campuses, and entire urban innovation zones to expand industry partnerships further.

Chapter 7 focused on a very different illustration of the new instrumentalism: diversity, equity, and inclusion. DEI initiatives are founded on the now universal belief that colleges and universities have an intrinsic obligation to combat discrimination and real-world inequities based on race, ethnicity, gender, sexuality, and other characteristics. That commitment, too, has been in place since the 1970s if not longer. And yet, only a generation ago, the injunction to factor demographic considerations and histories of oppression into admissions policies, faculty hiring and promotion decisions, and the academic curriculum was seen as controversial and potentially corrupting, or at least worthy of debate, and not just by right-wing critics of political correctness. Certainly the comprehensive scrutiny of mores and policies that accompanies DEI was not on the agenda. Today, in contrast, the idea that DEI might be philosophically inconsistent with meritocracy, excellence, and academic freedom appears wrongheaded on its face. The question is not whether to pursue DEI goals but how to do so.

Alongside teaching, research, and DEI, "impact" now ranks as the fourth cardinal mission of the public university. Impact is the manifestation of a new instrumentalism, applied to the university not in its capacity as an educating and moralizing institution, as is the case for DEI, but in its capacity as a producer of research and applied knowledge for economic and social benefit. In this chapter, I explore how the University made a dramatic bid to enhance its impact mission in the late 2010s. This followed closely on the heels of its efforts to improve its research profile, teaching practices, and DEI commitments as a natural next step. Its foray into this domain is still quite young. The fascinating unresolved question is whether the University's new impact mission will simply grow as an adjunct to its long-standing commitments to teaching and research, or whether innovation on the periphery will have a reciprocal effect on the core. Whatever the answer turns out to be, it will depend on what peers and competitors are doing in this space. As the world confronts large-scale problems from climate change and social injustice to the challenges of artificial intelligence and global security and beyond, universities everywhere will be expected to articulate what role they intend to play in providing solutions to them.

IMPACT-DRIVEN PHILANTHROPY

Why should a semi-independent university that thrives on undergraduate tuition and a respectable portfolio of federally funded research have felt a need to plant a flag for economic and social impact? The simplest answer, perhaps also a simplistic one, is that this is what a new class of major donors wants. Between 2016 and 2022, the University received the largest and the fifth largest philanthropic gifts ever bestowed on an American public university at the time. The first came in two half-billion-dollar installments from the Big Donor and his wife. Those went toward the creation and funding of a New Campus for Accelerating Scientific Impact, sited across the street from the University's main campus. The second, at $425 million, went toward the acquisition of a defunct college a hundred miles away in the State's main metropolis, and now slated to be repurposed as the home for a new Children's Behavioral Health Institute.[3] That donation, too, was funded by a billionaire entrepreneur and his wife, but in this case it was the wife, not the husband, who was an alumna (and later a trustee) of the institution.

Philanthropy being gendered, especially among the generations old enough to give, women are more likely to donate to social causes, whereas men are more likely to favor scientific and economic innovation.[4] Either way, today's donors are often more interested in making gifts that have a tangible impact than merely naming buildings, funding regular academic programs, or shoring up the endowment, as donors often did in the past. Among recent donors in the $100+ million category, one major focus is on scholarships for underprivileged and less affluent students: clearly a major DEI imperative. But the other is on high-impact science, whether the theme is sustainability, nanotechnology, cures for cancer, or other cutting-edge applications. At the megadonation level, there is an especially high correlation between (largely male) entrepreneurs and support for STEM fields. And among STEM fields, interdisciplinary science receives the largest and most numerous gifts, in part because the biggest and most complex problems require tools from many different fields.[5] As a class, the new donors have an entrepreneurial mindset and a large appetite for high-risk/high-reward propositions. They are particularly keen to leverage their generosity to help universities take on major societal and global challenges, and they prod them to reconfigure old ways of doing business to meet those challenges.[6] All these statements hold true for the University's four megaphilanthropists.

Together the two new applied science campuses showed what it meant for a newly emancipated public university to dream big for the first time. Granted formal autonomy, it now had the cash in hand to devise two entirely new satellite ventures from scratch. The first new campus is a novel play in a by now well-established innovation ecosystem dominated by the likes of Stanford and MIT. The second suggests ways that the same impact-minded ethos extends beyond academic capitalism to embrace solutions to pressing social problems. To use the cliché, the University aspired not just to do well but also to do good: emulating far richer universities while also attending to inequities in its own backyard.

Accelerating Scientific Impact

The three-word mission of new campus number one is "science advancing society." This is defined as shortening the timeline between the discovery of a scientific innovation and the impact that discovery has on society. Underlying this mission are two ambitious goals: to "redefine the modern research university by fostering world-changing research unfettered by traditional academic boundaries" and to "improve the health and well-being of the citizens of [the State], the nation, and the world."[7] These could be taken word for word as a slogan for the new instrumentalism.

Precursor concepts for some kind of applied sciences school or college had long been burbling among the University's faculty. Administrators once remained wary of treading on the State's other major research university, which historically had a monopoly on engineering programs as a close cousin of applied science. But key groups of innovative faculty researchers continued to agitate from within the arts and sciences in such subfields as materials science (housed in chemistry, but also coming together in a distinct Materials Science Institute) and neuroscience (spanning psychology and biology, who collaborated in a well-regarded Institute of Neuroscience).

The New Campus for Accelerating Scientific Impact gathered these dispersed clusters of activity into one institutional home and added still others. It also gave them a new mandate to translate their work with all due urgency into real-world applications. Although the planning stages were dominated by faculty from biology and chemistry, a year of strategic planning and campus conversations identified more than fifty subfields across the university whose research was prominent and promising enough to contribute to the new endeavor.[8] Laid out in specific applications, the campus produced for the Board of Trustees a list of practical innovations on which researchers were busy at work, including:

- implantable and wearable medical sensors and devices.
- implantable interfaces to the brain and peripheral nervous system.
- building biological parts (proteins, peptides, and nucleic acids) by repurposing biological cells as factories allowing large-scale low-cost manufacturing of complex macromolecules.
- what is missing from the engineer's toolbox: 3D structures, tools, and devices at the interface of materials chemistry and biomedical engineering.

Faculty were also given assistance launching startup companies, for example, to harness 3D printers to design customized patient-specific implants and a novel therapy for visual problems caused by diabetes.[9]

The guiding philosophy behind these efforts is known in contemporary academia as "innovation and entrepreneurship." That philosophy entails a series of structural and policy changes—things like clearer policies on intellectual property and licensing rights, which are discussed later. But equally important, it signals a culture shift that departs from the conservative norms of academic research while borrowing inspiration from the entrepreneurial spirit of the business world. The embrace of failure is perhaps foremost among those business values, which is anathema to conventional career-minded professors who are used to painstakingly marching from one carefully designed experiment to another. So, too, is a willingness to stray beyond the confines of one's academic training, formal credentials, and professional comfort zone. As the new campus's strategic plan put it, researchers and students should feel free to wander beyond traditional academic boundaries to embrace a new culture of innovation founded on "resilience through failure, collaboration, diversity, responsiveness, and creativity."[10]

The innovation mindset expected of the new campus's faculty goes deeper than mission-statement exhortations, trustee-friendly strategic plans, or catchy marketing materials. It is baked into its formal promotion, tenure, and governance policies. Unlike conventional arts and sciences faculty, who are evaluated by peer-reviewed publications aimed at the academic community, faculty who are based at the new campus are explicitly evaluated and rewarded based on activities to develop new products and launch new ventures.[11] DEI values figure prominently in a new campus culture that prides itself on breaking down old hierarchies that impede the free exchange of ideas. Combining different modes of expertise from different quarters of academia and different walks of life in the wider world applies a DEI lens to the challenge of growing a new campus culture assembled from innovators from a plethora of diverse fields and backgrounds.[12]

Innovation in the Social Sector

The University's new impact orientation is not just about the nexus of scientific innovation and commercially lucrative application. It also embraces a socially conscious component and a genuine desire to improve the lives of the disadvantaged. If the first new applied sciences campus touted sexy new technologies from customized brain implants to 3D printing, the second campus was designed to attend to a more troubling and less glamorous aspect of its home state: an epidemic of behavioral and mental health challenges among young people. Taking inspiration from what the U.S. surgeon general identified as a national crisis, but one that was particularly acute in the University's backyard, the New Institute for Children's Behavioral Health bid to transform the entire region into a national model for successful interventions whose successes could be replicated elsewhere.[13]

The University had long boasted one of the nation's top colleges of education among public research universities. That college's reputation was founded—tellingly—not on training K–12 teachers, which is a critical albeit unglamorous function of education schools at prestigious research institutions, but on federally funded social and behavioral science, with a specific accent on special education for children with behavioral and other difficulties. A long-standing Child and Family Center had served both clinical and research functions by offering services to troubled children and adolescents and their families in the local area. A new institute dedicated to a new interdisciplinary field called "prevention science" grew from that seed, just as materials science and neurosciences institutes had served as proofs of concept for the other applied science campus.[14]

Access to a major metropolis made the new behavioral-sciences campus different in kind from these prior efforts. One hallmark of the University's new impact mission is a thicker set of networks and collaborations with nonuniversity partners that only big cities can offer at scale. Joint ventures with the State's largest K–12 school district are one concrete form this will take.

Another is a suite of academic offerings for a large pool of mid-career professionals, whether teachers, school counselors, or day care providers, who need (re)training in how to deal with an increasingly complex set of juvenile mental health challenges. In another hallmark of the new instrumentalism, the gulf that traditionally separates researchers from practitioners is expected to be broken down by physical proximity and intellectual collaboration in an urban setting. Students from the undergraduate through adult professional levels will participate alongside an interdisciplinary research faculty drawn from the fields of psychology, neuroscience, early childhood development, and education. In this way, the institute aspires to close the gap that leaves the State's schoolchildren chronically underserved by psychological professionals relative to the national norm.[15] Tacitly, its mission acknowledged the profound insufficiency of public K–12 school systems to do all that is asked of them—which is a major DEI deficit examined in chapter 7.

It is too early to tell whether either of these new campuses will become national leaders in their respective domains. Yet one thing remains clear. This new species of megaphilanthropy did not merely spring from the idiosyncratic passions of wealthy patrons. Instead, donors accelerated powerful developments that were already underway at the institution and in academia at large. Both new campuses grew out of existing initiatives within the academic core that were previously pursued in more conventional ways. Both conjoined donors' ideals with long-standing faculty research interests in collaborations catalyzed by a novel impact orientation shared by both groups. Eagerly facilitated by the University's top leadership, these marquee projects signaled to the outside world and to on-campus constituents that the University was placing big bets on creating knowledge with real-world instrumental value. That was something novel. But to understand what made it novel requires a look back at older conceptions and concerns about the purposes of knowledge and how they were being displaced during the early millennium.

ACADEMIC CAPITALISM

What one might call the *old* instrumentalism, to contrast with the new, has a storied past in American higher education. Ever since the Morrill Act of 1862, when the federal government used grants of land to fund public universities, those universities have been expected to provide tangible benefits to society. Most notably, they opened agriculture and engineering schools to serve practical needs. Many also provided extension services to bring useful ideas and inventions, such as new farming techniques, directly to the populace. Later, in the 1900s, universities pioneered other ways to provide social and economic benefits through research and public service. Easily the best examples are the hospitals, clinics, and laboratories that sprang up around university medical schools. University health centers have since become massive complexes that often dwarf their host campuses both physically and financially. On a smaller but still important scale, midcentury universities began to host a wide variety of specialized research centers and institutes. These might be devoted to specific scientific applications, policy issues, social services, studies of world regions, or various interdisciplinary problems that cannot be tackled within a conventional academic discipline alone.[16] Yet another example are the world-famous high-tech innovation zones in biotechnology and computing that grew up in greater Boston, Silicon Valley, North Carolina's Research Triangle, and Austin, Texas, in the 1970s and 1980s. The "triple helix" of university, corporate, and governmental collaboration that sustains these regional clusters has precedents going back to the 1920s.[17] Academic entanglements with industry and with public policy are nothing novel and nothing unusual.

The old instrumentalism cohabited well with the pursuit of pure knowledge right down to the end of the twentieth century because the boundaries between them remained clear and reasonably stable. As shown in chapter 5, the grand political bargain that guaranteed this division of labor was the one struck after World War II, when the federal government committed to supporting basic science through what became the NSF and the NIH, rather than insisting, as the U.S. Congress nearly did, on funding only practical and applied research. Science after that time was typically treated as a resource for economic growth rather than as an actual driver of it. University-based basic research was expected to produce foundational and freely available knowledge for public use, whereas it was industry's job to apply it to patentable inventions and useful products, taking the risks and reaping the rewards. The bargain was never perfect—classified university research for the Department of Defense came under heavy attack during the Vietnam War, for example—but the values of disinterested inquiry that demarcated academia from outside entities at least provided a clear set of principles to argue over.

It was only during the last two decades of the 1900s, when the push provided by entrepreneurial faculty met the pull of declining federal research dollars, that a new constellation of interests called academic capitalism began to coalesce. That change would lay the groundwork for the innovation and entrepreneurship initiatives that most every major research university has now adopted as part of its impact mission.

Origins

The pivotal year for what is now called academic capitalism was 1980, when the congressional Bayh-Dole Act permitted and in some instances required universities to patent and market inventions developed under federal research grants and programs. The prior decade had seen revolutionary innovations in recombinant DNA and other biotechnologies with massive potentials to generate both profit and life-enhancing benefits through pharmaceuticals and other medical therapies. Following the examples of Genentech and Biogen, founded in the 1970s, roughly two hundred new biotechnology firms were founded between 1980 and 1984 alone. Universities spawned research centers and institutes, and in some cases whole research parks, to cultivate relationships with drug companies, microelectronics firms, and a host of other knowledge-intensive industries. State governments got into the act with various programs, policies, and incentives to stimulate university-anchored regional economic development. Industry funding of university research tripled over the decade too.[18]

If the 1980s saw a headlong rush into various experiments from patents and licenses to corporate partnerships and venture-funded startups, the 1990s presented a paradox. As research stagnated in universities' academic cores, it thrived on its margins, especially in university-based research centers and institutes that maintained an amphibious capacity to partner with outside entities. Whether offshoots of an individual faculty entrepreneur's research agenda, or captives of the corporations that cosponsored them, or anything on the spectrum in between, organized research units played a decisive role in linking academic science to economic needs by forging new networks of people and new channels for ideas to cross back and forth between both sectors.[19] Technology transfer offices (TTOs) were another institutional innovation of the 1980s and 1990s. Designed to proactively catalyze the application of scientific knowledge to real-world use, they focused on licensing, patenting, and contracting with corporate firms. Originally, these offices developed a reputation for blocking rather than facilitating technology transfer. In part this was because universities' interests in intellectual property revenues were at odds with the individual faculty entrepreneurs who created lucrative innovations. But it was also because the whole idea that universities should be involved in business ventures in the first place was greeted with political and philosophical skepticism.

The main arguments made against commercializing academic research were that the search for profit distorts research agendas, creates conflicts of interest, and encourages secrecy that prevents the open sharing of ideas. Two of the most controversial and widely publicized illustrations of these dangers came in 1994, when a firm called Myriad Genetics tried to patent the BRCA1 gene, discovered by NIH-funded scientists at the University of Utah, in order to profit from the breast cancer screening services it provided;[20] and in 1999, when the Novartis pharmaceutical corporation offered the University of California at Berkeley $25 million for the right to profit from discoveries made in its plant and microbial biology department, a controversy magnified by pervasive concerns about GMOs (genetically modified organisms). The breaches—or perceived breaches—of academic ideals suspected in cases like these provided fodder for a series of exposés and critiques cresting in the early 2000s. Books titled *Buying In or Selling Out* (2004), *University, Inc.* (2005), and *Science for Sale* (2007) drew attention to some of the many scandals that attended, or were feared to attend, the deals that universities made with corporate patrons. Even academia's elder statesman, the former Harvard president Derek Bok, weighed in with

Universities in the Marketplace (2003), albeit optimistically and with more measured concerns.[21]

A New Millennium

By the dawn of the 2000s, it seemed as if a whole cluster of threatening trends was being fused together that favored the new instrumentalism at the expense of the old. The free, public, disinterested pursuit of knowledge was yielding to a different ethic that instead stressed marketability, profit, and performance, potentially reducing every university activity to a measurably impactful pursuit. This was not because universities had somehow been captured or colonized by corporate interests. Rather, entrepreneurial actors within universities themselves were forming networks with external business entities. As these networks coalesced around powerful financial and political incentives, they began to exert a distorting effect on universities at large. At the ground level, "interstitial" organizations, such as research institutes and spin-off companies, placed department-based faculty in close contact with external partners, acting as porous membranes where experts and expertise could migrate between academia and industry. Meanwhile, presidents and trustees formed interlocking networks at the topmost level of institutional strategy and fund-raising, for example, by sitting on the same corporate boards. Universities were becoming "restratified" both internally and among themselves. Individual faculty members, academic departments, and entire institutions saw their value, prestige, and resources increasingly measured by market proximity and economic impact.

To theorists of academic capitalism, the commercialization of science is but one key element of this much larger puzzle. Other components included public disinvestment, escalating undergraduate tuition, marketing and branding universities to student "customers," the incursion of corporate-style managerialism into traditional academic governance, the conversion of tenured faculty into untenurable adjuncts, bean-counting student credit hours and other metrics of academic productivity, producing and copyrighting of "courseware" for online educational delivery, and even licensing university logos and mascots. All these controversial developments on the student/teaching side of the university were purportedly of a piece with all that was happening on the research/discovery side.[22]

In previous chapters I have investigated most of these trends in great detail: public disinvestment in chapter 1, quasi-capitalist budget models in chapter 2, restructuring faculty roles in chapter 3, and the spread of corporate-style management and marketing in chapter 4. Although each of these phenomena is traceable to the semiprivatization of public higher education, academic capitalism in the strict sense—market-driven partnerships between scientific researchers and industry—is by no means implicated in them. Universities' traditional research and teaching missions may have been buffeted by these changes but have survived essentially intact. This definitely held true for the University, whose struggles for independence, financial health, and academic excellence were almost wholly unaffected by commercialized research ventures, which remained small and confined to the periphery—at least until its four megadonors made the new campuses possible.

What instead happened in American academia is that our values changed, and with that our prior concerns dissipated. After a burst of journalistic exposés and academic theories in the first decade of the new millennium, the entire critique of academic capitalism simply went dark around 2010. In part, this was because universities and policy makers had taken those critiques to heart and instituted policies and safeguards to prohibit the worst abuses. In part it was because they came to accept a new normal that traded high tuition and aggressive marketing in return for continued support of the traditional academic missions of teaching and research. But it was also because the economic and social benefits of applied knowledge and industry partnerships had proven too compelling to ignore, much less disparage.

A Rechristening

Defenders of what has since been rechristened "innovation and entrepreneurship" acknowledged the potential pitfalls of academic capitalism. But they argued that universities have done an admirable job of managing and containing their more deleterious side effects. Not only have technology transfer offices been streamlined and improved, but the underlying conflict of interest and intellectual property issues have been worked out. A standard set of legal and administrative policies and practices has been developed to promote fairness, clarify incentives, mitigate conflicts of interest, and render the relationships between universities and private outside entities more transparent. To be sure, some of the freewheeling spontaneity that marked early startup culture has now been sacrificed to bureaucratic routine, but the benefit is a stable and replicable set of arrangements that universities can apply as new opportunities arise, confident that they will not create unintended consequences that compromise their core academic missions.[23] Disinterested inquiry has, to the extent feasible, been reasserted as a guiding principle of university-affiliated research.

Far from subjugating academic research laboratories to private corporations, the power dynamic has if anything put universities in the driver's seat when it comes to choosing how they engage with business interests. It is too early to render a definitive conclusion on the effect of corporate-sponsored research, but preliminary assessments are surprisingly positive. One recent study suggests that its benefits are at least as great as those attached to federal grant-funded research.[24] Corporate-sponsored inventions are licensed and cited more than federally sponsored ones. They also produce more "spillovers" in the form of unanticipated side discoveries that emerge from a given line of inquiry. Top scientists may even by coaxed by industry patronage to wander into cutting-edge problems beyond the safer and more conservative research topics favored by their academic peers and by federal funding agencies. For their part, firms are less interested in capturing and hoarding profit-making inventions than they are in having regular access to scientific exploration at the frontiers of knowledge, plus steady streams of graduates produced by university research laboratories. Many companies are only too happy to invest in speculative science, leaving the traditional right to publication and open dissemination intact, if that results only indirectly in lucrative profit-making opportunities down the road. One should not romanticize corporate farsightedness, such studies suggest, but neither should one assume that the profit motive inherently corrupts university science. Commercial interests do privilege applied science, but that does not necessarily mean that they harm basic science.[25]

Academic capitalism having been domesticated in the last twenty years, there is every reason to believe that universities can enhance their impact missions without compromising their teaching and research in other, more traditional spheres. Innovation and entrepreneurship efforts will likely continue to prove additive and complementary, not a threat to core academic values or missions.[26] They remain fully consonant with universities' centuries-long tendency to seek out and disseminate knowledge wherever and however that path may lead. But it is worth returning to the University's impact mission to put these hypotheses and predictions to the test. Placing its new campuses in the broader context of its overall institutional trajectory helps us to assess to what extent a new instrumentalism was displacing the old, not just on the periphery but also closer to the core.

INNOVATION AND ENTREPRENEURSHIP

During the 2010s, innovation and entrepreneurship came into vogue nearly everywhere, not just at research powerhouses but up and down the educational hierarchy. The University responded with the same strategy it had conceived when it first began clamoring for its independence. As an arts-and-sciences-based flagship in a midsized college town, it had long been confined to a narrow lane of activity in demonstrating its wider impact, even relative to other research universities in the State. The latter included a traditional land-grant university with prominent engineering, agricultural, veterinary, and extension programs, but also a big-city commuter school, plus a metropolitan medical school-cum-health sciences complex that expanded dramatically after its own unfettering from the state system. That was a classic division of labor by twentieth-century standards. It made public policy sense by avoiding duplication of effort and parceling out precious state dollars wisely and strategically. But it hampered the University in its competition with national peers. By taking fellow AAU institutions as its pacesetters rather than the needs of the State and its citizens, the University adopted a ready-made tool kit of best practices to promote innovation and entrepreneurship as the spearhead of an enhanced impact mission. Because it was a newcomer to that field of activity, its rhetoric and approach were even more overtly tinged by the new instrumentalism than was the case among more established players. Parts of the academic core prospered as never before, even as other parts seemed to fall behind.

After formal independence came a long preparatory phase during which the University put in place the infrastructure and professional networks needed to mount a bid for impact and innovation. First, the central Research Office was overhauled from top to bottom to improve the University's grant-winning and federal policy compliance support and internal financial plumbing.[27] Later, template forms and contracts for intellectual property, patenting, licensing, copyright, data management, and conflicts of interest were made available to would-be faculty entrepreneurs. Customized project management and networking services were offered to those seeking industry contacts or desiring to create stand-alone spinoff businesses based on research they had done for the University.[28] New policies governing innovation were designed to secure the traditional values and freedoms that attach to all university research. Thus, given the "open-ended inquiry nature [sic] of research with inherently unpredictable results," University contracts could not commit to specific deliverables the way an industrial company would. Corporate partners were also barred from restricting the open publication and free dissemination of research findings in academic venues, aside from a brief review period to determine whether any proprietary data were being inappropriately shared.[29] These principles reflected the state-of-the-art research standards worked out during the taming of academic capitalism.

On top of new policies, the University Research Office forged new partnerships with local, regional, statewide, and national "incubators" to facilitate technology transfer in areas such as nanoscience. A regional "accelerator" explicitly adopted a DEI mission in order to "reduce barriers to entrepreneurship and innovation for underrepresented populations and communities." Startup support helped faculty and students to commercialize their research and "get out of the building" to meet real-world potential customers.[30] Some of the ventures University faculty and nonfaculty researchers could boast a hand in having created are listed here.[31] They reflected a burgeoning innovation ecosystem in the local vicinity, touted with a healthy dose of marketing lingo:

- revolutionary laundry products for activewear
- genomic services for plant and animal researchers
- new targeted chemotherapy
- custom fitted padding for the sport of lacrosse
- flour, brownie mix, and more made from crickets
- noninvasive geodesic technologies to monitor and interpret brain activity
- language assessments focused on real-world proficiency

None of these were world-beating technologies, none of them the "next big thing." Laundry products, lacrosse pads, and cricket-based brownie mix are small fry. But their humble practicality illustrates what an ambitious university situated well outside major East Coast and West Coast high-tech hubs could aim for and achieve. Beneath and beyond revolutionary gene therapies or pharmaceuticals that attract the most money and the most attention, it is this type of innovation and entrepreneurship that in future years will become even more routinized and regularized within the impact portfolios of second- and third-tier research universities.

In the early 2020s, the University issued a splashy report that cannily recast its new role as an "agent of change and innovation" as a simple extension of its 150-year-history of working for a better world rather than the experimental departure that it in fact was.[32] Hype aside, its accent on impact *was* something new. In truth, there is an inverse correlation between how much universities boast about innovation in their strategic plans and PR materials and how much they actually do in this space. The MITs and Stanfords of the world have no need to brag in front of the up-and-comers.[33] That said, the University's impact and innovation strategy was more than skin deep. Its signature initiatives were all distilled from Institutional Hiring Plans (see chapter 5) that had been thoughtfully designed to grow the faculty in areas formally identified as competitive priorities.[34] Those plans were then subsumed under a written strategic framework whose production had been the preoccupation of top leadership since the late 2010s.[35] A selection principle was applied that singled out for more resources and attention those initiatives whose value could be articulated in the real-world terms of the new instrumentalism. All were multiyear efforts, deeply grounded in the academic core of the University's various schools and colleges. All were systematically coordinated across the domains of budgeting, planning, hiring, communications, and consultations that spanned institutional silos. Successful or not, the University will have staked its reputation and resources on the decisive embrace of a new impact mission that reflects neither donor wishes nor public relations opportunism but rather its own institutional trajectory in a field of research university rivals all turning in this same direction.

The University's new impact focus will inevitably produce winners and losers. Fields with ready connections to real-world economic and social applications will likely prosper, whereas those grounded in more traditional conceptions of knowledge will likely suffer, at least in relative terms. As evidence of this trend, a widening gulf between the traditional liberal arts and the market-oriented STEM fields had already weakened the college at the academic core that housed them both. In the late 2010s, the College of Arts and Sciences consistently lost power to the central administration over such critical matters as budgeting, tenure-track faculty hiring, fund-raising and friend-raising, student success, and research support—all subjects treated in earlier chapters. The neglect of the arts and sciences was not necessarily caused by the University leadership's focus on impact and on courting big donors, but the College's declining clout and coherence were certainly correlated with a major shift in strategic vision and priorities at the top.

With the task of matching intellectual priorities to resource commitments now thoroughly centralized at the top level, the College was sidelined as an academic entity and relegated to a largely administrative role. In 2018, the president and provost even questioned whether it should continue to exist. They convened a faculty task force to investigate whether the College of Arts and Sciences ought to be broken up, perhaps into separate divisions for humanities, social sciences, and natural sciences. The idea was dropped after its study revealed zero appetite among the rank and file for yet another administrative revolution. (Tellingly, the principal exception came from faculty working with industry partners, who preferred "highly specific collaborations" in their areas of business focus to "more diffuse" engagements with the arts and sciences as a whole.[36]) Arts and sciences departments were later regrouped willy-nilly under eight "academic support units" dedicated purely to providing shared administrative services. With the College consumed by managerial rather than intellectual questions, latent divisions between STEM and non-STEM fields, between those close to and remote from the market, and between those with an impact orientation and those without, all went unaddressed. Optimistic departments that were tapped into resources and external opportunities faced different futures from despairing ones that felt deprived of favor. Lacking a formal strategic plan of its own, and suffering disruptive instability in its leadership, the future of the University's largest academic unit remained uncharted and uncertain in the early 2020s. The historic mission of curiosity-driven teaching and research that defines the arts and sciences was left up for grabs.[37]

THE ARTS AND SCIENCES

One litmus test for the new instrumentalism in years to come will be the fate of the arts and sciences. Although their composition varies from place to place, the arts and sciences encompass the set of disciplines, whether physics or history, literature or economics, whose questions, methods, and agendas are driven by open-ended curiosity and intellectual exploration, not by practical application. Whether at flagship public universities, at elite private institutions, or at any level of American higher education, these fields have long served as the academic core of teaching and research. Even the 1862 Morrill Act stressed both "liberal and practical education" for this reason, which is why designated land-grant institutions share this key feature with other public and private universities. One can be confident that the arts and sciences will prosper in the long term, but the question of what organizational and intellectual form that will take remains anyone's guess.

A great many academic leaders and observers have begun to ask why distinct arts and sciences disciplines should continue to exist when so many of the world's greatest challenges require interdisciplinary solutions that cross multiple subfields. Perennial complaints about Ivory Tower thinking find ready targets in traditional academic departments that are organized around these disciplines. These institutional structures protect and defend the pursuit of arcane, subspecialized academic concerns that seem not only remote from real-world problems but even sometimes from the ideas and methods of fellow academics in neighboring fields. Turf battles—over curriculum offerings, faculty positions, space, and symbolic recognition—are the natural result.

Persuasive arguments have been made in favor of reforming the academic core inasmuch as department-based disciplines are no longer convincingly aligned with either the public's need for knowledge or the flourishing of intellectual creativity for its own sake.[38] And yet disciplinary departments, numerous times over the century or more since they were first created, have proven resistant to dissolution because they remain such an efficient means for gathering scholars in groups to simultaneously deliver teaching and conduct research.[39] Their tenacious persistence amid widespread calls for interdisciplinary and problem-based teaching and research seems to call into question the whole idea that the new instrumentalism will ever achieve priority over the traditional pursuit of open-ended inquiry.

And yet if universities aspire for real-world impact, disciplines will remain not only indispensable but all-powerful in their capacity to organize knowledge and stimulate creativity. The opposite of disciplinarity, after all, is not interdisciplinarity but *undisciplined*. Academic departments are merely the local campus franchises of the worldwide, spontaneously self-organizing networks of scholarly creativity and quality control that we call "disciplines." Their proliferation over centuries has been driven by the natural division of labor as knowledge has expanded and scholars developed different tools to annex more and more of it to human understanding. An invisible hand guides the competition among disciplinary practitioners for the favor of their peers, who alone can recognize and validate innovations in scholarship and research that depend on highly specialized expertise. It also guides the competition among disciplines themselves for the favor of the universities that house them, and that provide the venues whereby disciplinary scholars propagate their methods through a fusion of teaching and research. This freewheeling system has spawned dozens of academic disciplines and subdisciplines over the centuries and the list is still growing. The university's dynamic core has always been the arts and sciences precisely because these fields are unfettered by real-world constraints and concerns, responding to intellectual curiosity and creativity alone.

Even professional schools, which are defined by their service to the outside world, have long since been captured by the arts and sciences. This is overwhelmingly the case for medicine, which is founded on biology, chemistry, and physics. And what these same fields are to engineering, agriculture, and computing, so too political science, economics, and psychology are to law and business, and sociology and English are to journalism and communications—and so on. To the extent that the academic core's protective shell has been breached, this is because the core's influence has been projected outward, not because its autonomy has been undermined by external forces. For as long as American higher education has expanded and grown, the sovereignty of the arts and sciences has remained uncontested as the ultimate generator of innovation.

A paradox of higher education in the United States is that the arts and sciences have historically had such a secure footing here in the most practically and economically minded of nations. Europe, where the arts and sciences do not occupy such a central role in universities, has taken another path. There, the new instrumentalism is referred to as the university's "third mission" after teaching and research. (DEI in higher education, although it has analogues in Europe, remains a distinctively American phenomenon.) Partaking in the same drive for global competitiveness as American universities, and driven by the ambition to catch up with the United States, European universities have embarked on many of the same impact ventures as their counterparts across the Atlantic. Sponsored by local, regional, and national governments, and now coordinated at the level of the European Union, European universities have made strategic investments in technology transfer and economic development, drafted new rules of engagement to regulate intellectual property and conflicts of interest, and begun to inventory, measure, incentivize, and reward entrepreneurship among their faculty members.[40] They have also begun to widen their conception of the third mission from economic development to the solution of grand societal challenges that include efforts in the social sector, again paralleling developments in the United States.[41]

Across knowledge economies, whether in America, Europe, or beyond, the demands placed on higher education by the new instrumentalism can only be expected to intensify as universities are called upon ever more insistently to solve the world's problems. What began as academic capitalism and later matured into innovation and entrepreneurship will likely expand into various social and moral challenges for which market-adjacent STEM and preprofessional fields cannot be expected to provide all the answers, but where insights from arts and humanities fields potentially can. Whether new policy infrastructure to stimulate economic and scientific impact can be applied in any straightforward way to new ventures in civic and social impact is as yet untested. The changes required to unleash experimentation in what is now called social entrepreneurship, and to do so ethically, will no doubt be very different from the changes required to commercialize scientific inventions or devise profit-sharing formulas with corporate partners. The two lodestars of the new instrumentalism, DEI and academic capitalism, as yet correspond to different mores, cultures, networks, and methods. DEI is anchored in the humanities and social sciences whereas academic capitalism took root in the physical and biological sciences. Meanwhile, large swaths of the arts and sciences, from ancient literature to particle physics, cannot easily be yoked to *any* impact goal, imperative, strategy, or metric.

Much of the academic core should and most likely will remain driven by pure curiosity, exploration, and interpretation as it has been in the past. We may simply see the continued disaggregation of fields and functions once presumed as unitary—STEM from the liberal arts, research from teaching, departments from disciplines—as the steady pressure for relevance, impact, and return on investment exerts its tidal effect. The dismantling and reconfiguring of academic departments and other organizational forms may yet prove necessary. The disciplines that used to correspond with them so neatly no longer do. Spontaneous global organization in social networks is after all the hallmark of our time. Universities in general, and their arts and sciences cores in particular, must do far more to adapt than they have to date. Whatever the case, they must ask more of themselves to ensure that creativity continues to thrive, not just in peripheral side ventures but at their very centers.

CONCLUSION

Every time a public university closes a foreign language department or a classical music radio station, every time it invests in a new stadium rather than in a new chemistry lab, every time it raises tuition while also raising the president's salary, members of the public object that the university has lost its way and abandoned its public character. And they may be right to do so. But we no longer live in a world where such arguments cut any ice, if they ever did. Invoking the public good ought to be a way to inspire or at least shame universities into changing their behavior, but it isn't any longer. That has simply not been the reality that surrounds public higher education in this century. Indeed, a special danger comes from holding these treasured national institutions to too high a standard during our present age of disruption.

Writers who feel passionately about public universities are variously inclined to praise them for their virtues or condemn them for their failings based on the mistaken belief that, after all, at institutions that exist to search out the best ideas, clarion calls for reform will somehow automatically be put into practice. But that is manifestly not what universities do. Universities are not configured to apply their ideals reflexively to themselves, and they never have been. They only ever improve in response to external forces, each one acting or reacting according to its own internal capacities and culture, all in a field of competitive striving.

With an alarming uptick in the number of Americans who have lost faith in college education, the public deserves honesty and transparency, not motivated reasoning, about the universities it sponsors. By offering a bracing dose of realism, I have sought to intervene in debates often marred by simplistic arguments and wishful thinking about what public universities could be, should be, once were, or must be again. I fear that it does actual harm to invoke high ideals and earnest wishes while overlooking the messy questions, the empirical questions, the questions of fact as well as of value—the questions at the heart of this book—that reveal what the university is actually capable and not capable of doing, and willing and unwilling to do. Conversely, to probe deeply in search of answers to those questions, as I have done in this book, is a first step toward restoring the public's confidence that public universities, for all of their failings and flaws, still remain public goods.

By contrast with the elite private schools that preoccupy the nation's attention, public universities educate millions of students and conduct more than half of the nation's research. Treating them forthrightly as semiautonomous actors is our best hope for navigating a political landscape that will remain fractured and polarized for the foreseeable future. The career of public universities during the last decade offers ample reassurance that they can be trusted to chart their own paths. Their recent track record robustly disproves the left's claim that higher education has been captured by private patrons and corporate interests as well as the right's claim that it has been captured by political correctness and ivory-tower elitism. Against all expectation, public universities have continued to serve their stakeholders faithfully. With a modicum of grace from the public, they could fulfill their missions more effectively as well.

What are the broader lessons that come from studying one university, unfettered? The last thing I would urge is that every state should copy the plot of this story and emancipate its flagship research institution, much less abolish its entire public university system. The nation's fifty states continue to sponsor a remarkable variety of higher education schemes and systems. That diversity is precisely the strength of a nationwide network of public universities that has become world-beating through interstate competition. Illinois, Indiana, Minnesota, New Jersey, Ohio, Virginia, and Washington have dominant flagships orbited by smaller affiliated campuses and a variety of regional schools. Other states, including the large states of New York and Pennsylvania, have sprawling multicampus systems that integrate everything from comprehensive research powerhouses to small regional and urban commuter schools under one governance umbrella. The same holds true for the midsized states of Wisconsin and North Carolina. Each of these two university systems punches far above the weight of its home state thanks to generations of (mostly) enlightened legislators who have long recognized higher education as a source of competitive advantage.

Competition is so ubiquitous in athletics that we tend to overlook its centrality to academics. One of the most common patterns in public higher education is an in-state rivalry between the historic "flagship" and the historic "land-grant," whether Michigan and Michigan State, Florida and Florida State, Oregon and Oregon State, Arizona and Arizona State, or Texas and Texas A&M. Such pairs of universities compete with one another not just on the gridiron but also for students, resources, and renown—despite having originally been founded for the precise purpose of pursuing distinct missions and serving distinct stakeholders. That phenomenon is powerful evidence of the rivalry and competition that act as the mainspring of university behavior. It applies not just among states but also within them.

Then there is California, the biggest state, which boasts the greatest publicly funded experiment in higher education ever realized. It has been over sixty years since the world-famous California Master Plan was established to integrate the University of California, California State, and community college systems, pledging generous state funding to shuttle every deserving student as far upward as their talents and ambitions could carry them. For all the compromises and failings that have beset California in the decades since, that plan has still been able to accomplish what no other state has or perhaps ever will have the capacity to accomplish. The University of California sets the standard for the public research university, not just nationally but worldwide. The UC still boasts extravagant taxpayer support, still serves mainly Californians, and has recently added a remarkable eighth campus to the list of those that belong to the prestigious Association of American Universities. But California's shining example of comprehensive social-democratic equity is itself the product of competitive striving as much as it is of beneficent governance. Its system stands or falls, not on the elegance of its design or the attractiveness of its ideals, nor even on the generosity of California's wealthy taxpayer base, but because it has been able to prosper in a field of rivals both public and private. It is precisely California's ability to compete that is now in question, both for its universities and for its economy, infrastructure, cities, and, above all, its vaunted quality of life. Whether it succeeds or fails, the State of California is and always has been a polity that thrives on rivalry with others.

There are at least four things that politicians and policy makers should do, or rather refrain from doing, to sustain the new partnership that has taken shape with public universities. One thing that all states should abjure is any and every attempt to crimp or curtail academic freedom. To fetter free speech is a sacrilege in any self-respecting democracy. But manipulating the marketplace of ideas also simply backfires in a world of interinstitutional competition. Across our modern history, public universities have been sporadically subjected to ideological meddling by the politicians who oversee them. Our current epoch has been one such time, gripped, as has so often been the case, by exaggerated fears of left-wing indoctrination. Populist attacks on tenure in Wisconsin, and on DEI and "wokeness" in Florida, North Carolina, and Texas, all drew energy from the partisan polarization that afflicted the 2010s and accelerated in the 2020s. What makes such cases so concerning is that these states rank among those that still provide the *most* taxpayer funding to their public universities, such that their generosity only magnifies the leverage that politicians can exert over them. State capture, whereby national networks of right-wing activists produce model legislation for adoption by sympathetic red states, could easily do to higher education what it has already done to environmental regulation, voting access, labor unions, gun control, abortion rights, and other liberal causes. In the case of DEI, it already has.[1]

Yet every time a governor or a legislature turns against their own state's public universities, that state delivers up an unsolicited free gift to the other forty-nine. Innovative faculty and skilled administrators quietly decamp for more hospitable campuses in other states, sometimes sacrificing salary for intellectual freedom and professional opportunity. Students, too, take notice, even if their main role is as protestors, attracting short-lived media attention while faculty and staff go about business as usual. Universities are further protected by alumni, donors, trustees, and other patrons who buffer their alma maters against attack. Presidents and chancellors, condemned to serve as human shock absorbers even at the best of times, fall on their swords when that does not suffice. Only in rare instances do incursions into the academic core of teaching and research knock universities permanently off course. At worst, politically motivated micromanagement—for example, of faculty workloads, the academic curriculum, or DEI—spawns compliance bureaucracies that, like scar tissue, impair universities' agility without going so far as to constrain their scope of action. Most bouts of politicization are like a bad stomachache. As all-consuming as they are in the moment, they subside when politicians move on to other battles.

One cardinal point remains. Local restrictions on academic freedom cannot fundamentally alter the ground rules of a national—and global—marketplace of ideas. The worldwide network of knowledge-seekers encompasses people and institutions who are as collectively invincible as they are individually vulnerable. The marketplace of ideas may have its own biases and blind spots, but if it does lean left, then handicapping the competition to favor the right is doomed to fail in the fullness of time. In the long run, ideas triumph over politics: paper covers rock.

A second takeaway is that there is absolutely no reason to let states off the hook for funding their universities just because students and parents are willing and able to pay ever-higher tuition. Quite the opposite. States should give until it hurts, if for no other reason than sheer self-interest. Plowing money into higher education is like buying a blue-chip stock that only ever goes up in value. The simple reason is that universities are one of the very best ways for any state's citizens, via their elected state representatives, to invest in themselves, in their own children, and in attracting newcomers who, in acquiring college and university educations, will go on to become productive taxpaying citizens themselves. States are in rivalry with one another to support and subsidize the quality of life for their own citizens, and it is on this basis that they should invest as much as they can afford into public higher education. State universities should never be treated as government agencies, public utilities, or social service providers. In a crucial sense, they should not even be treated merely as educational and research institutions. Universities are magnets for talent and drivers of local, regional, and statewide economic prosperity and cultural development. They are as close as we come to one-stop shopping for ambitious policy makers.

If state leaders do have good grounds for withholding financial support for higher education, this is because primary and secondary education need even more financial support. Redressing chronic underinvestment in K–12 schooling can unburden state universities from using their own resources to compensate for deficiencies in the educational pipeline, freeing them to do what they do best. Once that pipeline is repaired, DEI initiatives in higher education stand a much greater chance of success. Then they can truly serve their stated purpose, as sources of educational benefits, rather than as remediation for past and present inequities.

Third, states should forswear any backsliding toward too-clever management doctrines, however tempting. Legislators and policy makers are rightly concerned to maintain accountability for public universities, but the existing political process and existing forms of governance and oversight can assure this. Vigilant trustee boards, arm's-length coordinating commissions, regular accreditation, statewide articulation agreements, authentic strategic plans, labor union protections, systemwide administrative services, and reasonable auditing mechanisms have proven far preferable to bureaucratic micromanagement, line-item legislation, quantified performance metrics, incentive-based budgeting schemes, or unfunded mandates of the sort that have been shown time and again to fail in practice. It is also critical that states not learn the wrong lessons from capitalist competition and its mechanisms of motivation. Wise public policy does not seek to artificially manipulate universities' inherent competitiveness with financial carrots or sticks. It focuses on missions and goals rather than the strategies and tactics to reach them, which should be left to local initiative. One of the best things states could do is help their universities choose appropriate comparators and publicly benchmark their performance against such peers, holding their feet to the fire over long periods of time. That might give everyone a viable alternative to simplistic rankings quests founded on tabulations of research dollars, student selectivity, or other reductive criteria.

In a liberal spirit, public support ought to provide a secure platform for universities to compete, safe in knowing that their basic needs and viability are a collective responsibility of each state's citizenry. State systems and coordinating bodies should focus less on internal regulation than on external competition, trusting that competition will keep universities on their toes far more effectively than bureaucratic oversight. Wealthy states have nothing to fear from such competition, and poorer ones have everything to gain. They can all experiment with novel public-private partnerships, innovation and entrepreneurship zones, workforce development schemes, joint ventures with municipal and metropolitan governments, and new ways to link up with community colleges, vocational education providers, and other four-year university systems.

A good rule of thumb is as follows. Excellence and equity are the twin missions of public universities. These two missions often coincide, but sometimes they stand in tension. When that happens, state policy should focus on promoting equity and leave individual institutions to pursue excellence, each in its own way. Put differently, the *only* reason to fetter public universities is to ensure that the benefits they spontaneously produce are equitably distributed among the publics they serve.

The depressing state of national politics is a fourth cause for worry, but one that is self-contained by the limits of federal influence. Federal agencies and federally recognized accreditation agencies should continue to stand back, set the rules of the game, establish guardrails to protect against malfeasance, and refrain from subjecting well-respected and well-established institutions to excessive scrutiny. Here, too, policy makers should avoid learning the wrong lessons from capitalism. One of the biggest mistakes in federal policy making of the early 2000s was to empower predatory lenders and for-profit degree mills in the misguided belief that market competition alone would suffice to weed out bad actors and ensure quality. The end effect was instead to burden and harass respectable public and private universities with one-size-fits-all accreditation regimes while thousands of students succumbed to exploitation, corruption, and indebtedness. If changes do need to be made, there is something to be said for shifting from regional to sectoral accreditation, grouping institutions by shared mission rather than the accidents of geography. That could make interinstitutional competition more explicitly a function of oversight bodies that already serve de facto to circulate best practices among colleges and universities, but now on a national rather than regional scale. Beyond this, accreditors should limit their focus to certifying reputable institutions for federal financial support. Properly administered, federal student loans and grants are an absolute cornerstone of American higher education policy. The billions of dollars dedicated to these purposes are worth just as much as what the nation pays for Medicare, social security, or defense. In the case of higher education, the investment has proven time and again to be worth it.

Also at the national level, we have America's private universities to thank for setting the standard for the highest level of quality found in any higher education system in the world. No public university, not even the so-called public Ivies, approaches what our private universities are able to offer in terms of resources per student or per faculty member. That fact establishes an aspirational lodestar for all of our public universities, and one that offers independent assurance of accountability and quality better than any strictly governmental system of oversight or coordination could possibly provide. One only needs to look to other countries' public university systems, none of which rivals America's set of private universities *alone* in sheer excellence, to appreciate the inestimable value of our unique hybrid system of public and private higher education.

Since January 6, 2021, we have rightly been preoccupied with national politics and with the future of the democratic constitutional order itself. All bets are off if a slide into authoritarianism fits universities, public or private, with an ideological straitjacket. A coherent far-right legislative agenda for higher education now exists where it did not at the time of Trump's shambolic climb to power in 2016, and its enactment could do long-term damage.[2] Certainly, it would jeopardize the country's global preeminence in higher learning if the federal government were to slash its financial support for scientific research and student loans, or to condition that support on conformity to particular political mandates. The intersection of class conflict, culture wars, and partisan polarization will remain combustible and unpredictable for as long as America's civic disease goes untreated. But there is a silver lining in the deadlock and dysfunction of partisan politics, assuming the status quo continues and feckless governance remains the rule. The very absence of a national higher education strategy is precisely what unfettered universities in the 2010s. That has been the default condition for decades and centuries since the nation's founding, and it has served us well.

I am in no way advocating for neoliberalism as a privatized, market-based panacea for the problems that public universities still face. Politically, financially, and academically, the best way forward is instead a kind of neofederalism: for the fifty states to embrace, with gusto, the chance to compete with all the others. Let red states compete with blue states, small states with big states, rust belt states with sun belt states, both specifically with respect to higher education and generally with respect to the quality of life. During an era of protracted political crisis in the United States, it may reduce partisan strife to concede that there is no national consensus on what public higher education ought to do, and to embrace the opportunities for state-level experimentation that an agreement to disagree implies.

It has been a long time since we looked to states as laboratories of democracy, each one competing on a level playing field established by our federal government and its institutions. State patriotism, as such, is seen at its best as a quaintly outmoded concept and at worst as a perniciously backward-looking one. In American history, the defense of states and of states' rights has rightly been associated with reactionary provincialism. But when it comes to higher education, there is no reason it cannot also take the form of a progressive cosmopolitanism. This is especially true in a country where virtually every university campus and college town skews more liberal than its host state, and that boasts deep wellsprings of serious, good-natured, bipartisan competitiveness rooted in its public universities. When someone dons a sweatshirt with the name of a state on it, it is not out of love for that state but out of some real or imagined connection to a university. It is precisely each state's public universities that provide a rallying point for intense emotional and deep practical attachments to the benefits that states provide.

States own public universities. They can do whatever they want with them. No other civic or governmental entity has that privilege or that power—not the federal government, not city government, and certainly not "the public" in abstract. The true spirit of public and civic commitment to our universities reposes in this unglamorous middle tier of government, one that has been neglected as the American citizenry consumes itself in political and cultural battles at the national level. Let states use their universities to vie with one another to improve our collective quality of life. It might just help save the Republic.

ACKNOWLEDGMENTS

I taught at the University from 2000 to 2024, serving for about half that time in various administrative and faculty leadership positions before moving to a very different public flagship institution. Few universities, nationally, could have offered a better perch, not only for observing but also for participating in the changes buffeting American public higher education in the first quarter of the twenty-first century.

My debts are first to my colleagues, mentors, and friends at the University, and even to those who may have seen matters differently, but all of whom I know to be deeply committed to the mission and values of public higher education. I would especially like to thank Bruce Blonigen, Scott Coltrane, Cheryl Ernst, Karen Ford, Bill Harbaugh, Kevin Hatfield, Dave Hubin, Laura Illig, Rob Illig, Peter Keyes, Richard Lariviere, Andrew Marcus, Randy McGowen, Gabe Paquette, Michael Redding, Lisa Ross, Hal Sadofsky, Perri Schodorf, Brad Shelton, Doneka Scott, Karen Sprague, Carol Stabile, Gordon Taylor, and Matthias Vogel. I want to give as much credit as possible to these and many other colleagues for contributing to debates about higher education that, aside from books like this one, take place largely in institutional conference rooms. But I also want to protect them from unwanted notoriety, which is one reason I have chosen to anonymize the University in these pages.

I have an American Council on Education (ACE) Fellowship to thank for the priceless experience of shadowing administrators at other institutions in 2016–17. That fellowship gave me firsthand knowledge of the way universities are managed elsewhere, through both formal training and behind-closed-doors access to upper- and middle-level administrators. Above all, I am indebted to Holden Thorp, my mentor at Washington University in St. Louis, together with many colleagues there who made me feel welcome, among them Marion Crain, Adrienne Davis, Joy Kiefer, Norah Rast, Lisa Siddens, Jennifer Smith, Bill Tate, Hank Webber, Lori White, and Mark Wrighton. Logging sixty thousand air miles crisscrossing four time zones, I also visited eleven other campuses from UCLA to Utah to Illinois to Johns Hopkins, interviewing presidents, provosts, deans, faculty, students, and frontline staff along the way. Among those who were kind enough to host me in personalized site visits were José Antonio Bowen, Ed Feser, Sunil Kumar, Nancy Brickhouse, David Mengel, Larry Singell, Ruth Watkins, Scott Waugh, and their colleagues and staffs. Mark Roche and Kathryn Bond Stockton shared invaluable documents and insights on the inner workings of their universities. My entire ACE cohort of twenty-nine midcareer administrators, drawn from a remarkable diversity of higher education institutions, was an inspiring troupe of colleagues and friends who taught me what it means to "serve the mission."

Mitchell Stevens and Emily Levine inducted me into the tribe of higher education scholars at numerous conferences, and also hosted me at Stanford to workshop the book. Five cohorts of undergraduates who took my "How Universities Work" seminar helped me understand what puzzles and what inspires those who come to higher education with fresh eyes. Gabe Paquette, Carol Stabile, and Mitchell Stevens read the whole manuscript and provided superb feedback and encouragement, as did the two anonymous reviewers whom I would also like to thank here. My editor at Columbia, Eric Schwartz, saw the book's potential and helped it come to fruition.

More than the usual caveat applies when I say that I alone remain responsible for any errors that may remain in these pages. There's an obvious challenge in penning a history of one's own time, to say nothing of one's own employer, in a way that transcends self-absorption and commands wider interest. It might seem awkward, unprofessional, or unwise to write honestly and openly about university finances, personnel, operations, and politics at a moment when higher education is beset by so many enemies and detractors. My modest and perhaps naïve hope is that I can help restore public confidence in our universities by opening the proverbial books on how they function and speaking without fear or favor about the decisions they make. Whatever the case, it is my job as a historian, and a historian of knowledge at that, to analyze institutions of higher learning with as much commitment as I can muster to evidence, reason, fairness, objectivity, and truth. I have done my best to hew to all of the canons of the historian's craft, starting with a groundedness in publicly and permanently available archival sources and acknowledging my debts to the work of others. And I can state with complete honesty that my account of the University is unclouded by sentiment or emotion, whether positive or negative. Like most professors, I work *at* an institution but *for* my profession, and that precept remains my lodestar as a scholar.

With love, affection, and profound gratitude to my family, Lisa Wolverton and Margot, Jing, and Karen McNeely, I dedicate this book to Karen, our youngest.

SOURCES

The vast majority of primary sources used for this book were originally posted on official institutional websites open to the public and created by entities within the University (or in some cases its home State). Below is a list of these entities. Their webpages post or once posted all manner of policy analyses, white papers, annual reports, budget spreadsheets, labor contracts, strategic plans, official memos, charts, graphs, and other sources. A permanent archive of these materials is housed at http://perma.cc, for which URLs are given in the notes. Many of these URLs point further to the Internet Archive's Wayback Machine, an open, free, permanent archive of the entire public internet at https://web.archive.org. Readers can use the latter to follow hyperlinks to subpages and external websites and to track changes in webpages over days, months, and years.

I. STATE ENTITIES

Governor
Higher Education Coordinating Commission (HECC)
Department of Administrative Services

[State] Education Investment Board
[State] University System

II. UNIVERSITY ENTITIES

Board of Trustees
Budget and Resource Planning
Business Affairs Office
College of Arts and Sciences
Communications Office
Department of Athletics
Diversity Advisory Committee
Division of Equity and Inclusion
Division of Student Life
Division of Undergraduate Education and Student Success
Human Resources
[New] Campus for Accelerating Scientific Impact
Office of Academic Advising
Office of Government and Community Relations
Office of Institutional Equity and Diversity
Office of Institutional Research
Office of Student Financial Aid and Scholarships
Office of the President
Office of the Provost
Office of the Registrar
Office of the Vice President for Research and Innovation
Prevention Science Institute
Statutory Faculty Assembly
Student Services and Enrollment Management
Task Force on the Structure of CAS
Tuition and Fees Advisory Board

University Housing
University Senate
University Senate Academic Council
University Senate Budget Committee
University Senate Committee on Courses
University Senate Continuous Improvement and Evaluation of Teaching Committee
University Senate Multicultural Requirement Task Force
University Senate Task Force to Address Sexual Violence and Survivor Support
University Senate Teaching Evaluation Task Force
University Tuition Website
University-Wide Diversity Committee
Vice Provost for Budget and Planning

NOTES

INTRODUCTION

1. For a guide from the middle of the decade, see Goldie Blumenstyk, *American Higher Education in Crisis? What Everyone Needs to Know* (New York: Oxford University Press, 2014).
2. Mark C. Taylor, *Crisis on Campus: A Bold Plan for Reforming Our Colleges and Universities* (New York: Knopf Doubleday, 2010); Clayton M. Christensen and Henry J. Eyring, *The Innovative University: Changing the DNA of Higher Education from the Inside Out* (New York: Wiley, 2011); Jeffrey J. Selingo, *College (Un)Bound: The Future of Higher Education and What It Means for Students* (New York: Houghton Mifflin Harcourt, 2013); Richard DeMillo, *Revolution in Higher Education* (Cambridge, MA: MIT Press, 2015); Michael Crow and William Dabars, *Designing the New American University* (Baltimore, MD: Johns Hopkins University Press, 2015); and Kevin Carey, *The End of College: Creating the Future of Learning and the University of Everywhere* (New York: Riverhead, 2016).
3. Derek Bok is ageless, but for this decade see Derek Bok, *Our Underachieving Colleges: A Candid Look at How Much Students Learn and Why They Should Be Learning More* (Princeton, NJ: Princeton University Press, 2009); Derek Bok, *Higher Education in America* (Princeton, NJ: Princeton University Press, 2015); and Derek Bok, *The Struggle to Reform Our Colleges* (Princeton, NJ: Princeton University Press, 2017). Also see Robert Zemsky, *Making Reform Work: The Case for Transforming American Higher Education* (New Brunswick, NJ: Rutgers University Press,

2009); Robert Zemsky, *Checklist for Change: Making American Higher Education a Sustainable Enterprise* (New Brunswick, NJ: Rutgers University Press, 2013); William G. Bowen, *Higher Education in the Digital Age* (Princeton, NJ: Princeton University Press, 2015); and William G. Bowen and Michael McPherson, *Lesson Plan: An Agenda for Change in American Higher Education* (Princeton, NJ: Princeton University Press, 2016).

4. Andrew Hacker and Claudia Dreifus, *Higher Education? How Colleges Are Wasting Our Money and Failing Our Kids—and What We Can Do About It* (New York: Times Books, 2010); Ellen Schrecker, *The Lost Soul of Higher Education: Corporatization, the Assault on Academic Freedom, and the End of the American University* (New York: New Press, 2010); Richard Arum and Josipa Roksa, *Academically Adrift: Limited Learning on College Campuses* (Chicago: University of Chicago Press, 2011); and Sara Goldrick-Rab, *Paying the Price: College Costs, Financial Aid, and the Betrayal of the American Dream* (Chicago: University of Chicago Press, 2016).

5. Jonathan Cole, *The Great American University: Its Rise to Preeminence, Its Indispensable National Role, Why It Must Be Protected* (New York: PublicAffairs, 2009); Jonathan Cole, *Toward a More Perfect University* (New York: PublicAffairs, 2016); and Andrew Delbanco, *College: What It Was, Is, and Should Be* (Princeton, NJ: Princeton University Press, 2012).

6. Holden Thorp and Buck Goldstein, *Engines of Innovation: The Entrepreneurial University in the Twenty-First Century* (Chapel Hill, NC: UNC Press, 2013); and Holden Thorp and Buck Goldstein, *Our Higher Calling: Rebuilding the Partnership Between America and Its Colleges and Universities* (Chapel Hill, NC: UNC Press, 2018).

7. Steven Brint, *Two Cheers for Higher Education: Why American Universities Are Stronger Than Ever—and How to Meet the Challenges They Face* (Princeton, NJ: Princeton University Press, 2018); and William Tierney, *Get Real: 49 Challenges Confronting Higher Education* (Albany, NY: SUNY Press, 2020).

8. Jason Brennan and Phillip Magness, *Cracks in the Ivory Tower: The Moral Mess of Higher Education* (New York: Oxford University Press, 2019); Arthur Levine and Scott Van Pelt, *The Great Upheaval: Higher Education's Past, Present, and Uncertain Future* (Baltimore, MD: Johns Hopkins University Press, 2021); and Will Bunch, *After the Ivory Tower*

Falls: How College Broke the American Dream and Blew Up Our Politics—and How to Fix It (New York: HarperCollins, 2022).

9. See "What You Need to Know About MOOCs," *Chronicle of Higher Education*, August 8, 2012; Kris Olds, "The MOOCs Fad and Bubble: Please Tell Us Another Story!," *Inside Higher Ed*, December 18, 2012; and Laura Pappano, "The Year of the MOOC," *New York Times*, November 2, 2012.

10. Of those over twenty-five, 23.5 percent had a bachelor's degree and another 14.4 percent had an advanced degree. See U.S. Census Bureau, "Census Bureau Releases New Educational Attainment Data," February 24, 2022, https://perma.cc/G6WG-4DKX; U.S. Department of Commerce, "Middle Class in America," January 2010, 1, https://perma.cc/Z2CZ-SDP7. Also see Anne Case and Angus Deaton, "Without a College Degree, Life in America Is Staggeringly Shorter," *New York Times*, October 3, 2023; Jon Shelton, *The Education Myth: How Human Capital Trumped Social Democracy* (Ithaca, NY: Cornell University Press, 2023).

11. Thomas Edsall, "'There Are Two Americas Now: One With a B.A. and One Without'," *New York Times*, October 5, 2022; and Yascha Mounk, "Nothing Defines America's Social Divide Like a College Education," *The Atlantic*, October 4, 2023.

12. Paul Tough, "Americans Are Losing Faith in the Value of College. Whose Fault Is That?," *New York Times*, September 5, 2023; compare to David Deming, "The College Backlash Is Going Too Far," *The Atlantic*, October 3, 2023.

13. See the acknowledgments for more on my relation to the University, and on my other credentials as a scholar-administrator. On those occasions when I rely on inside knowledge or an unpublished source, or played a bit part in the narrative, I disclose as much in the notes.

14. Many scholarly ethnographers anonymize the institutions they study because they rely on private communications and nonpublic source materials. See, e.g., Rebecca Nathan [pseudonym], *My Freshman Year: What a Professor Learned by Becoming a Student* (Ithaca, NY: Cornell University Press, 2005); Mitchell Stevens, *Creating a Class: College Admissions and the Education of Elites* (Cambridge, MA: Harvard University Press, 2007); and Laura Hamilton and Elizabeth Armstrong,

Paying for the Party: How College Maintains Inequality (Cambridge, MA: Harvard University Press, 2013. For a thinly veiled exposé of the author's home institution, see Gaye Tuchman, *Wannabe U.: Inside the Corporate University* (Chicago: University of Chicago Press, 2009). Other scholars choose to identify and critique their home institutions, including Christopher Newfield, *Unmaking the Public University: The Forty-Year Assault on the Middle Class* (Cambridge, MA: Harvard University Press, 2008); Christopher Newfield, *The Great Mistake: How We Wrecked Public Universities and How We Can Fix Them* (Baltimore, MD: Johns Hopkins University Press, 2016); Benjamin Ginsberg, *The Fall of the Faculty: The Rise of the All-Administrative University and Why It Matters* (New York: Oxford University Press, 2011); and Kelly Nielsen and Laura Hamilton, *Broke: The Racial Consequences of Underfunding Public Universities* (Chicago: University of Chicago Press, 2021).

15. But see John Lombardi, *How Universities Work* (Baltimore, MD: Johns Hopkins University Press, 2013); Larry Nielsen, *Provost: Experiences, Reflections, and Advice from a Former "Number Two" on Campus* (Sterling, VA: Stylus, 2013); and Mark Roche, *Realizing the Distinctive University: Vision and Values, Strategy and Culture* (Notre Dame, IN: University of Notre Dame Press, 2017), written, respectively, by a former president, a former provost, and a former dean.

16. Emily Levine, *Allies and Rivals: German-American Exchange and the Rise of the Modern Research University* (Chicago: University of Chicago Press, 2021); William Kirby, *Empires of Ideas: Creating the Modern University from Germany to America to China* (Cambridge, MA: Harvard University Press, 2022); Ian F. McNeely with Lisa Wolverton, *Reinventing Knowledge: From Alexandria to the Internet* (New York: Norton, 2008); and especially David John Frank and John W. Meyer, *The University and the Global Knowledge Society* (Princeton, NJ: Princeton University Press, 2020).

I. THE PUBLIC

1. A seventh, the State's medical school, already had an independent governing board and had prospered under that arrangement, a fact The Hat cited to make his own case.

1. THE PUBLIC • 279

2. Office of the President, "Preserving Our Public Mission Through a New Partnership with the State," August 2010, https://perma.cc/VUU3-P6XW. An archive on the New Partnership is posted on the Internet Archive Wayback Machine as the live page linked to https://perma.cc/2YP8-USC8.

3. Statutory Faculty Assembly, "Motion on the Replacement of [University President]," November 30, 2011, https://perma.cc/V8E7-HRBQ.

4. Disclosure: I wrote the 2011 motion after consulting with a senior colleague who had signed the 1987 resolution and sent me the original text. See Statutory Faculty Assembly, "Meeting Featuring System Chancellor," December 1, 2011, https://perma.cc/P9UQ-AWW9, at 1:33:30; "human being" question at 1:14:40.

5. See, e.g., Doug Lederman, "Flexibility—But for (and From) Whom?," *Inside Higher Ed*, February 27, 2011; Dan Berrett, "What's Next for Wisconsin?," *Inside Higher Ed*, June 5, 2011; Kris Olds, "On the Failure of Legacy Governance at the University of Virginia," *Inside Higher Ed*, June 14, 2014; and Jack Stripling, "An Academic Reputation at Risk: The U. of Oregon's Big Brand Masks Its Fragile Standing," *Chronicle of Higher Education*, September 14, 2015.

6. Christopher Newfield, *The Great Mistake: How We Wrecked Public Universities and How We Can Fix Them* (Baltimore, MD: Johns Hopkins University Press, 2016).

7. Office of the President, "Preserving Our Public Mission," 2.

8. University Senate Budget Committee, "Preliminary Report on the Proposed 'New Partnership'," November 9, 2010, https://perma.cc/NRH9-VCTQ.

9. University Senate Academic Council, "Academic Implications of New Partnership Proposal," January 24, 2011, https://perma.cc/PLX9-W3YL. Disclosure: I wrote this report, which was then endorsed by the full council.

10. Juan Pablo Pardo-Guerra, *The Quantified Scholar: How Research Evaluations Transformed the British Social Sciences* (New York: Columbia University Press, 2022).

11. University Senate Meeting, May 12, 2010, https://perma.cc/MR7J-9959, at 00:03:47.

12. [State] University System, "Q&A: Higher Education Reform Proposal," December 9, 2010, https://perma.cc/HW7P-FCGZ; [State]

University System, "Governance Proposal," July 2, 2010, 1, 5–6, https://perma.cc/NPJ5-5CDG.
13. President Emeritus, "The Coming Crisis in College Completion: [The State's] Challenge and a Proposal for First Steps," November 2009, 29, 31, 34–44, https://perma.cc/AS9M-SKHW, including mention of the 6,300 line items.
14. [State] Education Investment Board, "[The State] Learns: Report to the Legislature from the [State] Education Investment Board," December 15, 2011, https://perma.cc/8L56-N8K3.
15. Letter from University President to Governor, March 29, 2011, https://perma.cc/FW29-HRAV; and Letter from Governor to University President, March 29, 2011, https://perma.cc/W64D-68JN. See also Letter from Governor to [State] Education Investment Board, December 1, 2011, https://perma.cc/BSF9-5KWD, sent in the immediate aftermath of The Hat's firing, reiterating the governor's support for independent institutional boards by 2013–14.
16. Betsy Hammond, "[Governor's] Once-Powerful Education Board Will Die," [State Metropolis Main Newspaper], May 21, 2015.
17. Newfield, *The Great Mistake*, 28–32.
18. The term "risk shift" is from Jacob S. Hacker, *The Great Risk Shift: The New Economic Insecurity and the Decline of the American Dream* (New Haven, CT: Yale University Press, 2006).
19. On the 2010s, see Goldie Blumenstyk, *American Higher Education in Crisis? What Everyone Needs to Know* (New York: Oxford University Press, 2014), 49–51; on tax revolts, see Michael McLendon and Christine Mokher, "The Origins and Growth of State Policies That Privatize Higher Education," in *Privatizing the Public University: Perspectives from Across the Academy*, ed. Christopher Morphew and Peter Eckel (Baltimore, MD: Johns Hopkins University Press, 2009), 22–23; and Robert B. Archibald and David H. Feldman, "State Higher Education Spending and the Tax Revolt," *Journal of Higher Education* 77 no. 4 (2006): 618–44.
20. The Pew Charitable Trusts, "Federal and State Funding of Higher Education: A Changing Landscape," June 2015, 1, 4–5, 7–8, https://perma.cc/D2LM-KEVZ.
21. McLendon and Mokher, "Origins and Growth," 14, 17, 25.

22. For this and the next two paragraphs, see Kevin Dougherty and Rebecca Natow, *The Politics of Performance Funding for Higher Education: Origins, Discontinuations, and Transformations* (Baltimore, MD: Johns Hopkins University Press, 2016); and Amy Li, "Performance Funding in the States: An Increasingly Ubiquitous Public Policy in Higher Education," *Higher Education in Review* 11 (January 2014): 1–29.
23. Joseph Burke, "Reinventing Accountability: From Bureaucratic Rules to Performance Results," in *Achieving Accountability in Higher Education*, ed. Joseph Burke (San Francisco: Jossey-Bass, 2004), 216–45.
24. Gabriel Kaplan, "Governing the Privatized Public Research University," in *Privatizing the Public University: Perspectives from Across the Academy*, ed. Christopher Morphew and Peter Eckel (Baltimore, MD: Johns Hopkins University Press, 2009), 109–33.
25. Peter Eckel and Christopher Morphew, "The Organizational Dynamics of Privatization in Public Research Universities," in *Privatizing the Public University: Perspectives from Across the Academy*, ed. Christopher Morphew and Peter Eckel (Baltimore, MD: Johns Hopkins University Press, 2009), 90–92, 96–97, 103 (for quotation).
26. Sondra Barringer, "The Changing Finances of Public Higher Education Organizations," in *The University Under Pressure*, ed. Elizabeth Popp Berman and Catherine Paradeise (Bingley, UK: Emerald Group, 2016), 253–56.
27. Donna Desrochers and Steven Hurlburt, "Trends in College Spending 2003–2013" (Washington, DC: American Institutes for Research, 2016), 6, 10, 14, 17, 20, part of the Delta Cost Project.
28. John Thelin and Richard Trollinger, *Philanthropy and American Higher Education* (New York: Palgrave MacMillan, 2014).
29. On the priorities of patrons, see Steven Brint, *Two Cheers for Higher Education: Why American Universities Are Stronger Than Ever—and How to Meet the Challenges They Face* (Princeton, NJ: Princeton University Press, 2018), 7, 203–48.
30. Compare Rob Reich, *Just Giving: Why Philanthropy Is Failing Democracy and How It Can Do Better* (Princeton, NJ: Princeton University Press, 2018); and Francie Ostrower, *Why the Wealthy Give: The Culture of Elite Philanthropy* (Princeton, NJ: Princeton University Press, 1995).

31. Susan Svrluga, "With the Largest Gift Ever to a Public University, the [University] Has Big Plans," *Washington Post*, October 18, 2016. The University held the record until 2021, when Western Michigan University received $550 million from a private donor, but when the Big Donor's two separate $500 million gifts for the new campus are combined, it remained in first place as late as 2023.
32. Around the [University] (Communications Office bulletin), "Gifts Last Year Were the Third Highest in [University] History at $689M," September 14, 2022, https://perma.cc/LV96-LCYL.
33. Higher Education Coordinating Commission, "State Educational Attainment Goals and Equity Lens," December 15, 2021, https://perma.cc/ENW6-BDQL, plus various subsidiary webpages and posted reports.
34. Office of Institutional Research, "Historical Enrollment (Enrollment by Level and Residency)," https://perma.cc/VB68-HUUV, undergraduates between 2009–10 and 2019–20.
35. University Tuition Website, "State Appropriations," https://perma.cc/E3VQ-SZDL.
36. Office of the President, "Five Years of Institutional Governance at the [University]," December 5, 2019, 4–5 (for the statistics cited), https://perma.cc/6H5L-ZG5X.
37. Office of the President, "The [University] Commitment to Student Access and Success," November 10, 2015, https://perma.cc/46RT-LVB7.
38. Gabriel Kaplan, "Do Governance Structures Matter?," in *Restructuring Shared Governance in Higher Education*, ed. William Tierney and Vincente Lechuga (San Francisco: Jossey-Bass, 2004), 23–34, finds "few significant relationships between how governance [including shared governance] organizes and shares authority, on the one hand, and outcomes, on the other." Peter Mandler, *The Crisis of the Meritocracy: Britain's Transition to Mass Education Since the Second World War* (Oxford: Oxford University Press, 2020), likewise focuses on irrepressible student demand in the UK, with a commensurate deemphasis on the efficacy of public policy.
39. Karin Fischer, "The Shrinking of Higher Ed," *Chronicle of Higher Education*, August 12, 2022.

2. STUDENTS

1. See David Labaree, *A Perfect Mess: The Unlikely Ascendancy of American Higher Education* (Chicago: University of Chicago Press, 2017).

The world's other great "system" of research universities, in nineteenth-century Germany, was likewise a market free-for-all in which that disunited country's many state-level governments competed vigorously with one another for the best faculty and student talent. Similar precedents reach back through medieval Europe to the rival city-states of ancient Greece.

2. Intercollegiate athletics and medical centers are two other auxiliaries; they range in size from massive to nonexistent on any given campus, but again, are budgetarily separate entities.

3. At the University, internal student aid of this sort increased by 126 percent in real terms over the 2010s, winding up at an average of about $2,000 per student. See Office of Institutional Research, "Revenue and Expenditures," https://perma.cc/9LBC-UZXP, for expenditures for student aid, FY09–11 vs. FY19–21 averages, adjusted for 19 percent cumulative inflation, ending at about $44 million (averaged) for roughly 22,000 students.

4. For this discussion, see Vice Provost for Budget and Planning (VPBP), "[New] Budget Model Primer," https://perma.cc/P3VS-Q3E9; and VPBP, "Introduction to Responsibility Centered Management," https://perma.cc/XE7N-KKUG, both ca. December 2010.

5. Henceforth, I will use "Schools" to refer to the seven schools and colleges, including for arts and sciences, and "College" to refer to the College of Arts and Sciences in particular.

6. Credit hours are accounting units for college courses. A typical course at the University carries four credit hours.

7. In contrast, some universities either charge a fixed tuition amount irrespective of the number of credit hours or adopt a jagged series of escalating plateaus.

8. VPBP, "[New] Budget Model: Frequently Asked Questions," ca. December 2010, https://perma.cc/9E5E-3NAA.

9. VPBP, "[New] Budget Model Primer."

10. See Scott Carlson, "Colleges 'Unleash the Deans' with Decentralized Budgets," *Chronicle of Higher Education*, February 9, 2015.

11. Robert Birnbaum, *Management Fads in Higher Education: Where They Come From, What They Do, Why They Fail* (San Francisco: Jossey-Bass, 2000), 229; Edward L. Whalen, *Responsibility Center Budgeting: An Approach to Decentralized Management for Institutions of Higher Education* (Bloomington: Indiana University Press, 1991); Douglas M. Priest,

William E. Becker, Don Hossler, and Edward P. St. John, eds., *Incentive-Based Budgeting Systems in Public Universities* (Cheltenham, UK: Edward Elgar, 2002); Darren Deering and Creso Sá, "Do Corporate Management Tools Inevitably Corrupt the Soul of the University? Evidence from the Implementation of Responsibility Center Budgeting," *Tertiary Education and Management* 24 no. 2 (2018): 115–27; James C. Hearn, Darrell R. Lewis, Lincoln Kallsen, Janet Holdsworth, and Lisa M. Jones, "'Incentives for Managed Growth': A Case Study of Incentives-Based Planning and Budgeting in a Large Public Research University," *Journal of Higher Education* 77 no. 2 (2006): 286–316; and John Bethell, Richard Hunt, and Robert Shenton, "Harvard A to Z," *Harvard Magazine*, May–June 2004.

12. Jon Strauss and John Curry, "Responsibility Center Management: Lessons from 25 Years of Decentralized Management" (Washington, DC: NACUBO, 2002), https://eric.ed.gov/?id=ED469330; Robert Heath, "Responsibility Center Budgeting: A Review and Commentary on the Concept and the Process," *Journal of the Association for Communication Administration* 1 (1993): 1–10, at 8–9; and Stephanie Simon and Stephanie Banchero, "Putting a Price on Professors," *Wall Street Journal*, October 22, 2010, on Texas.

13. Deering and Sá, "Do Corporate Management Tools Inevitably Corrupt the Soul of the University?," 121–24.

14. David Kirp, *Shakespeare, Einstein, and the Bottom Line: The Marketing of Higher Education* (Cambridge, MA: Harvard University Press, 2004), 110–28; and Whalen, *Responsibility Center Budgeting*, 163–76, on the "monster."

15. For publicly posted financial information used in this and subsequent chapters, see Budget and Resource Planning, "Budget Reports," https://perma.cc/MHL4-PCTQ; and Business Affairs Office, "Financial Reports," https://perma.cc/2WDH-57EW, with links to live pages.

16. Composite tuition rate = (resident tuition rate × % of resident students) + (nonresident tuition rate × % of nonresident students), per undergraduate credit, averaged over the 2016–17 through 2020–21 academic years. The University's resident (in state) population averaged 54.9 percent during this time. Residency percentages are from the Office of Institutional Research, "Detailed Enrollment (Residency)," https://perma.cc/E5X4-74FS.

2. STUDENTS • 285

17. Office of Institutional Research, "Operational Metrics," accessed Fall 2022 and in the author's possession. See https://perma.cc/PWZ8-96DB for a sample. Metrics used here include primary operational metric #7 (total unit-level expenditures per SCH) and type I, IIA, IIB, and type III expenditures. Sources of moderate inaccuracy include the following: schools are assumed to have spent all the budget model revenue they collected; summer session tuition and certain graduate programs are charged at different rates; and the New Budget Model was being phased out during the last two fiscal years of the decade.

18. Office of the Registrar, "Historical Tuition and Fees," https://perma.cc/7K4N-LLFD, averaging figures for in-state and out-of-state tuition for the academic years 2016–17 through 2020–21.

19. Office of Institutional Research, "Revenue and Expenditures (Revenue)," https://perma.cc/ZD74-BWSM, showing an average state appropriation of $74 million for FY17–FY21; and Office of Institutional Research, "Operational Metrics," showing University-wide average of 923,000 total student credit hours for FY17–FY21. Simple division results in an overall state subsidy of about $80 per credit, which is about one-third of the $236 difference between the $455 (composite) and $219 (in-state) rates per credit hour. A source of moderate inaccuracy is that those credits include those for graduate programs, charged at differing rates, but the discrepancy is not large enough to undermine the overall point.

20. See note 19. FY21 is anomalous because of the pandemic-related federal stimulus.

21. Taken together, the schools spent an average of $279 per credit hour, or 61 percent of the $455 composite undergraduate tuition rate. Office of Institutional Research, "Operational Metrics."

22. These categories mimic federal Integrated Postsecondary Education Data System (IPEDS) categories (which are given close attention in chapter 4) with some exceptions noted in the text. Also, IPEDS figures are based on overall institutional expenditures whereas I am focusing only on expenditures from the general fund (state appropriations plus student tuition).

23. In this book, the term "liberal arts" refers to the humanities and social sciences in contrast to the natural sciences (STEM) and preprofessional fields. Historically, however, the liberal arts have included the natural sciences, as does the more or less synonymous term "arts and sciences."

24. See Elizabeth Capaldi and Craig Abbey, "Performance and Costs in Higher Education: A Proposal for Better Data," *Change: The Magazine of Higher Learning* 43 no. 2 (2011), 8–15, at 11. This study by the provost at Arizona State University showed that the social sciences and to a lesser extent the humanities generated more revenue than science and engineering fields, which were far and away the biggest money losers. When scientific grant support was added to the equation, it became even more clear that the liberal arts heavily subsidize STEM fields. See also the Delta Cost Project's data brief, "How Much Does It Cost Institutions to Produce STEM Degrees?" (Washington, DC: American Institutes for Research, 2013), https://files.eric.ed.gov/fulltext/ED558229.pdf, table 1; Christopher Newfield, *The Great Mistake: How We Wrecked Public Universities and How We Can Fix Them* (Baltimore, MD: Johns Hopkins University Press, 2016), 93–104; Steven W. Hemelt, Kevin M. Stange, Fernando Furquim, Andrew Simon, and John E. Sawyer, "Why Is Math Cheaper Than English? Understanding Cost Differences in Higher Education," National Bureau of Economic Research Working Paper 25314 (November 2018), https://doi.org/10.3386/w25314.
25. On salaries, see Martin J. Finkelstein, Valerie Martin Conley, and Jack H. Schuster, *The Faculty Factor: Reassessing the American Academy in a Turbulent Era* (Baltimore, MD: Johns Hopkins University Press, 2016), 339–41, table 9.4; and Paula Stephan, *How Economics Shapes Science* (Cambridge, MA: Harvard University Press, 2012), 36–42. On workloads and demand for non-tenure-track faculty, see John Cross and Edie Goldenberg, *Off-Track Profs: Nontenured Teachers in Higher Education* (Cambridge, MA: MIT Press, 2011), 47–48, 67–75, and 149.
26. This does not even include the costs of *non*instructional research laboratories for STEM faculty, which themselves often run at a net loss even when supported by prestigious federal grants. Again, at Arizona State "the $18 million differential [between what engineering programs brought in grant revenue and what they actually cost] was subsidized by the tuition paid by undergraduate students in the fields where costs are less than tuition." See Capaldi and Abbey, "Performance and Costs," 14.
27. Office of Institutional Research, "Detailed Enrollment (Majors)," https://perma.cc/EG47-DGY3, comparing figures for 2009–10 with 2019–20. The social sciences grew by 8 percent.

28. William Bowen, *The Economics of Major Private Universities* (Berkeley, CA: Carnegie Commission on the Future of Higher Education, 1968), 16; see also W. J. Baumol and W. G. Bowen, *Performing Arts: The Economic Dilemma* (New York: Twentieth Century Fund, 1966).
29. This was dramatically the case at the University; see Tuition and Fees Advisory Board, "Recommendations of the FY17 Tuition and Fee Advisory Board," February 9, 2017, https://perma.cc/7RLQ-NFM6, attributing $18 million of a total $25 million in known cost increases to a combination of faculty and staff compensation and retirement benefits. Also see University Tuition Website, "Tuition and Fee Cost Drivers," accessed December 29, 2022, https://perma.cc/QS6E-2BPS.
30. Earl Cheit, *The New Depression in Higher Education: A Study of Financial Conditions at 41 Colleges and Universities* (Berkeley, CA: Carnegie Commission on Higher Education, 1971); and Earl Cheit, *The New Depression in Higher Education: Two Years Later* (Berkeley, CA: Carnegie Commission on Higher Education, 1973).
31. For this paragraph and the next, see David Feldman and Robert Archibald, *Why Does College Cost So Much?* (New York: Oxford University Press, 2010), 87–91, 97, 109, 113, 196.
32. Robert Zemsky, *Checklist for Change: Making American Higher Education a Sustainable Enterprise* (New Brunswick, NJ: Rutgers University Press, 2013), 21–30, calls this the "academic ratchet," reaching a similar diagnosis but with a harsher conclusion.
33. Robert Archibald and David Feldman, "College Cost: Overhyped and Misunderstood," in *The Rising Costs of Higher Education A Reference Handbook*, ed. John R. Thelin (Santa Barbara, CA: ABC-CLIO, 2013), 125–30; Feldman and Archibald, *Why Does College Cost So Much?*, 196.
34. Jennifer Ma and Matea Pender, *Trends in College Pricing and Student Aid 2022* (New York: College Board, 2022), 3–4.
35. Office of Student Financial Aid and Scholarships, "The [University] Guarantee," https://perma.cc/2FBL-VUL5.
36. Charles Clotfelter, *Buying the Best: Cost Escalation in Elite Higher Education* (Princeton, NJ: Princeton University Press, 1998), 139–58, 253–59.
37. On the origins of federal student loan subsidization in the 1980s-era financial deregulation, see Elizabeth Popp Berman and Abby Stivers, "Student Loans as a Pressure on U.S. Higher Education," in *The*

University Under Pressure, ed. Elizabeth Popp Berman and Catherine Paradeise (Bingley, UK: Emerald Group, 2016), 129–60.
38. Natasha Quadlin and Brian Powell, *Who Should Pay? Higher Education, Responsibility, and the Public* (New York: Russell Sage Foundation, 2022).

3. FACULTY

1. See, e.g., The Blogger, "Card Check Party Jan 24," January 19, 2012, https://perma.cc/N5WD-HVKF, and other posts under "Tagged AAUP-AFT Union?"
2. Charlie Sykes, *ProfScam: Professors and the Demise of Higher Education* (Washington, DC: Regnery, 1988); and Roger Kimball, *Tenured Radicals: How Politics Has Corrupted Our Higher Education* (Chicago: Ivan R. Dee, 2008). See also the far more scholarly analysis edited by Richard Chait, *The Questions of Tenure* (Cambridge, MA: Harvard University Press, 2002).
3. For two contrasting but complementary histories of shared governance, see Larry G. Gerber, *The Rise and Decline of Faculty Governance: Professionalization and the Modern American University* (Baltimore, MD: Johns Hopkins University Press, 2014); and William G. Bowen and Eugene M. Tobin, *Locus of Authority: The Evolution of Faculty Roles in the Governance of Higher Education* (Princeton, NJ: Princeton University Press, 2015).
4. In this book, "tenure-track" faculty refers both to pre-tenured faculty (assistant professors) and post-tenured faculty (most associate and full professors), not just the former. I also use "professors" for tenure-track faculty and "instructors" for non-tenure-track faculty, i.e., those who are ineligible to be considered for tenure.
5. This analysis comes from a November 2012 document I authored titled "% of SCH [student credit hours] by TRF [tenure-related (i.e., tenure-track) faculty] vs. comparators," based on faculty workloads in the College of Arts and Sciences averaging 2007–8 and 2009–10 academic years, and also contrasting 2000–1 with 2010–11. These figures were compared against similar figures from a sampling of twelve other AAU public flagship institutions included in the Delaware Study, a nationally

recognized comparative study of faculty workloads. At these comparators, the percentage of credit hours generated by tenure-track faculty ranged from 35 percent to 58 percent, with most falling below 50 percent. See University of Delaware Office of Institutional Research, "The National Study of Instructional Costs & Productivity," October 2012, https://perma.cc/83A5-ES5E.

6. The Blogger, "A Union Is Not Going to Happen," May 3, 2010, https://perma.cc/9DQN-GRPE.
7. University Senate, "Results from University Senate Survey on Unionization," April 28, 2010, https://perma.cc/8XJW-JDWG, with further links to data for tenure-related faculty and non-tenure-track instructional faculty. Administrative staff were also polled and opposed the union three to one.
8. Martin J. Finkelstein, Valerie Martin Conley, and Jack H. Schuster, *The Faculty Factor: Reassessing the American Academy in a Turbulent Era* (Baltimore, MD: Johns Hopkins University Press, 2016), 59, figure 3.2. From 1979 to 2013, the percentage of tenured and tenure-track faculty went from 45.1 percent to 24.2 percent and part-time faculty went from 24.0 percent to 43.0 percent; whereas the sum of full-time non-tenure-track faculty and graduate students went from 30.9 percent to 32.7 percent. See also Jack H. Schuster and Martin J. Finkelstein, *The American Faculty: The Restructuring of Academic Work and Careers* (Baltimore, MD: Johns Hopkins University Press, 2006), 231–32, who observe that stabilization in the percentage of full-time non-tenure-track faculty is a novel and noteworthy phenomenon.
9. A. J. Angulo, "From Golden Era to Gig Economy: Changing Contexts for Academic Labor in America," in *Professors in the Gig Economy: Unionizing Adjunct Faculty in America*, ed. Kim Tolley (Baltimore, MD: Johns Hopkins University Press, 2018), 3–26, at 9, figure 1.3.
10. Charles Petersen, "Serfs of Academe," *New York Review of Books*, March 12, 2020.
11. Gary Rhoades, "Bread and Roses, and Quality Too? A New Faculty Majority Negotiating the New Academy," *Journal of Higher Education* 88, no. 5 (2017): 645–71, at 645, 649.
12. Kim Tolley, ed., *Professors in the Gig Economy: Unionizing Adjunct Faculty in America* (Baltimore, MD: Johns Hopkins University Press, 2018);

Herb Childress, *The Adjunct Underclass: How America's Colleges Betrayed Their Faculty, Their Students, and Their Mission* (Chicago: University of Chicago Press, 2019); and Joe Berry, *Reclaiming the Ivory Tower: Organizing Adjuncts to Change Higher Education* (New York: Monthly Review, 2005).

13. *National Labor Relations Board v. Yeshiva University*, 444 U.S. 672 (1980).
14. William G. Bowen and Julie Ann Sosa, *Prospects for Faculty in the Arts and Sciences: A Study of Factors Affecting Demand and Supply, 1987 to 2012* (Princeton, NJ: Princeton University Press, 1989).
15. Christopher Jencks and David Riesman, *The Academic Revolution* (New York: Doubleday, 1968). For the best contemporary diagnosis of graduate student overproduction, with proposed solutions, see Leonard Cassuto, *The Graduate Student Mess: What Caused It and How We Can Fix It* (Cambridge, MA: Harvard University Press, 2015).
16. For this paragraph and the next, see John G. Cross and Edie N. Goldenberg, *Off-Track Profs: Nontenured Teachers in Higher Education* (Cambridge, MA: MIT Press, 2011), esp. 35–51 on hiring; see also 67–84 on non-tenure-track faculty, and 85–102 on business (budget) models, which criticizes RCM from a slightly different perspective, seeing it more as a deliberate corporatization strategy.
17. On unbundling, see Finkelstein, Conley, and Schuster, *Faculty Factor*, 454–56.
18. Finkelstein, Conley, and Schuster, *Faculty Factor*, 327, figure 9.1, 363–64.
19. Finkelstein, Conley, and Schuster, *Faculty Factor*, 243, table 7.1.
20. On union premiums, see Finkelstein, Conley, and Schuster, *Faculty Factor*, 331, 346–48.
21. On disciplinary differentiation, see Finkelstein, Conley, and Schuster, *Faculty Factor*, 335–38, 458. For an earlier snapshot of this trend, see Schuster and Finkelstein, *American Faculty*, 258, 283–84.
22. Finkelstein, Conley, and Schuster, *Faculty Factor*, 365 (for quotation), and 10–19, 467.
23. Collective Bargaining Agreement with United Academics, 2013–15 (henceforth: CBA 2013–15), https://perma.cc/A639-SZP2.
24. Set to last for an initial period of two years, from 2013 to 2015, the CBA was renegotiated and revised for the 2015–2018 period, extended again with minor changes after 2018 and 2021, and continually amended in the

interim via ad hoc agreements. See Collective Bargaining Agreement with United Academics, 2015–18 (henceforth: CBA 2015–18), https://perma.cc/NRA6-B6UW; and Collective Bargaining Agreement with United Academics, 2024 (henceforth: CBA 2024), https://perma.cc/CWS7-WUW3.
25. Article 4 lays out this process for departmental internal governance policies, and articles 17–20 and 26 mimic it for various other policies.
26. Office of the Provost, "Department and Unit Policies," multiple dates (e.g., September 15, 2018), https://perma.cc/7QF8-A6AP.
27. CBA 2013–15, Article 15, 15–16.
28. CBA 2013–15, Article 19, 24–30.
29. CBA 2013–15, Article 16, 18–19; see CBA 2015–18, Article 16, 26–30, for a much more elaborate set of protocols on contract renewal.
30. CBA 2024, Article 16, section 10, 31–32.
31. Office of Institutional Research, "Faculty Salary Comparisons," accessed May 23, 2022, https://perma.cc/77Y8-5HNC, including exhaustive unit-by-unit comparisons with peer institutions, with statistics on newly hired faculty and salary compression among established faculty.
32. University Tuition Website, "Tuition and Fee Cost Drivers," accessed December 29, 2022, https://perma.cc/FF58-KT7T.
33. Disclosure: In 2016, I led this study of faculty workloads. Historically, departments taught only 75 percent to 80 percent of their nominally assigned course load because faculty were released from teaching for various service and administrative roles. One goal was to approximate the de facto teaching load at competitor institutions to which the University might otherwise lose faculty.
34. See, e.g., United Academics, "Statement on Faculty Workloads," February 25, 2015, https://perma.cc/KJV6-MGW4.

4. ADMINISTRATORS

1. The Blogger, "Administrators Gone Wild," November 2, 2011, https://perma.cc/37VZ-W4VH; and The Blogger, "[University] Administrative Bloat," February 7, 2014, https://perma.cc/UV82-Y9QK.
2. The Blogger, "[The Blogger] Joins Union Organizing Committee," June 27, 2012, https://perma.cc/P4YW-AB2P.

3. Benjamin Ginsberg, *The Fall of the Faculty: The Rise of the All-Administrative University and Why It Matters* (New York: Oxford University Press, 2011), 25, 28–33, 35, 87–96, 97, 120, 125–26, 161. For a more balanced and informed treatment, compare with Steven Brint, *Two Cheers for Higher Education: Why American Universities Are Stronger Than Ever—and How to Meet the Challenges They Face* (Princeton, NJ: Princeton University Press, 2018), 249–86.
4. See, e.g., Philip Mousavizadeh, "A 'Proliferation of Administrators': Faculty Reflect on Two Decades of Rapid Expansion," *Yale Daily News*, November 10, 2021; and John Londregan, Sergiu Klainerman, Michael A. Reynolds, and Bernard Haykel, "Academic Administrators Are Strangling Our Universities," *Tablet*, September 18, 2022.
5. The secondary literature on university administration and management is much more developed for Great Britain and Western Europe than it is for the United States. See Ian F. McNeely, "Research Excellence and the Origins of the Managerial University in Thatcher's Britain," *Contemporary British History* 37, no. 1 (2023): 1–26, https://doi.org/10.1080/13619462.2022.2098720, and the literature cited therein; and Cláudia S. Sarrico, Maria J. Rosa, and Teresa Carvalho, eds., *Research Handbook on Academic Careers and Managing Academics* (Cheltenham, UK: Edward Elgar, 2022). For the United States, the best and most entertaining guide overall is Robert Birnbaum, *Management Fads in Higher Education: Where They Come From, What They Do, Why They Fail* (San Francisco: Jossey-Bass, 2000).
6. National Center for Educational Statistics IPEDS Glossary, https://perma.cc/B6AQ-CLZ4, includes entries for core expenses.
7. Actually, the University is categorized as having "*very* high research activity," even though it lacks the medical and engineering schools that account for the lion's share of research in that category. Federal statistics are unavailable for public institutions in this uppermost tier, however. Private universities in this elite stratum, which include the world's wealthiest institutions, spend vast sums per student in every category, making benchmark comparisons somewhat pointless.
8. National Center for Education Statistics, IPEDS Data Feedback reports for the University, three-year averages for 2013–15 and 2018–20, https://nces.ed.gov/ipeds/use-the-data; reports give data on the prior

fiscal year. Earlier and later years were untabulated or unavailable. Faculty includes postsecondary teachers and staff.

9. Donna M. Desrochers and Rita Kirshstein, "Labor Intensive or Labor Expensive? Changing Staffing and Compensation Patterns in Higher Education" (Washington, DC: American Institutes for Research, 2014), 3, 7, 9, 16, 24–26, appendix tables 2 and 3. The study, part of the Delta Cost Project, covers the period 2000 to 2012.

10. Desrochers and Kirshstein, "Labor Intensive or Labor Expensive?," 9, 14, figure 5b.

11. Desrochers and Kirshstein, "Labor Intensive or Labor Expensive?"; see also Jürgen Enders and Rajani Naidoo, "The Rise and Work of New Professionals in Higher Education," in Cláudia S. Sarrico, Maria J. Rosa, and Teresa Carvalho, eds., *Research Handbook on Academic Careers and Managing Academics* (Cheltenham, UK: Edward Elgar, 2022), 89–98.

12. On enrollment management, see Craig Tutterow and James A. Evans, "Reconciling the Small Effect of Rankings on University Performance with the Transformational Cost of Conformity," in *The University Under Pressure*, ed. Elizabeth Popp Berman and Catherine Paradeise (Bingley, UK: Emerald Group, 2016), 265–301, at 281–25; and Matthew S. Kraatz, Marc J. Ventresca, and Lina Deng, "Precarious Values and Mundane Innovations: Enrollment Management in American Liberal Arts Colleges," *Academy of Management Journal* 53, no. 6 (2010): 1521–45.

13. Budget and Resource Planning (BRP), "Level 5 Expenditure Report for FY21," https://perma.cc/3ZWR-DTDU. On customer relations management and related activities, see Student Services and Enrollment Management, "What We Do," https://perma.cc/D3SR-FT78.

14. For budget figures in this section, see BRP, "Level 4 Expenditure Report FY08–11," https://perma.cc/K6QP-MZKY; and BRP, "Level 4 Expenditure Report FY18–21," https://perma.cc/VYU4-2UFT, three-year averages (2009–11 and 2019–21). Dollar figures for 2010 are adjusted to 2020 constant dollars based on 19 percent overall inflation.

15. Student Services and Enrollment Management, "Strategic Plan 2022," April 14, 2022, https://perma.cc/V2NU-HH3D; and Division of Student Life, "Student Life Strategy," October 19, 2018, https://perma.cc/CQ77-2FDY.

16. Communications Office, "Letter From [University] President About Reorganization of [University] Central Administration," April 2, 2013, https://perma.cc/H34Q-4RNB.
17. See the concluding section of chapter 1.
18. See William McMillen, *From Campus to Capitol: The Role of Government Relations in Higher Education* (Baltimore, MD: Johns Hopkins University Press, 2010).
19. State appropriations grew from $44.8 million in FY12 (or $52.9 million in FY21 dollars, assuming 18 percent cumulative inflation) to $82.5 million in FY21. Office of Institutional Research, "Revenue and Expenditures (Revenue)," https://perma.cc/ZD74-BWSM.
20. David Kirp, *Shakespeare, Einstein, and the Bottom Line: The Marketing of Higher Education* (Cambridge, MA: Harvard University Press, 2004).
21. "Scaling Back on Branding," *Inside Higher Ed*, January 19, 2016.
22. BRP, "Level 5 Expenditure Report for FY21."
23. Like strategic communications, the University's information services administration was treated to its own thorough reorganization and centralization during the 2010s. See Office of the Provost, "IT [Information Technology] Strategic Plan," February 2017, https://perma.cc/B4SW-GG7A.
24. The best guide to intercollegiate athletics is Charles Clotfelter, *Big-Time Sports in American Universities*, 2nd ed. (Cambridge: Cambridge University Press, 2019). For two serious exposés from the mid-2010s, see Joshua Hunt, *University of Nike: How Corporate Cash Bought American Higher Education* (Brooklyn, NY: Melville House, 2018), esp. 169–229; and Jay Smith and Mary Willingham, *Cheated: The UNC Scandal, the Education of Athletes, and the Future of Big-Time College Sports* (Lincoln, NE: Potomac, 2015),
25. University Senate Task Force to Address Sexual Violence and Survivor Support, "Twenty Students Per Week," November 5, 2014, 2, https://perma.cc/LV3F-KHGG. The case attracted national attention. See, for example, "Student Sues [University], Coach Over Alleged Gang-Rape," *CNN* January 9, 2015. The survivor sued the University only to be countersued by it in return, which was a public relations disaster.
26. BRP, "Level 5 Expenditure Report for FY21," account 267830. The sole exception is the $2.3 million the University spent on academic advising

4. ADMINISTRATORS • 295

for student-athletes to keep this function under the oversight of the Provost's Office. See Department of Athletics, "Financial Information," https://perma.cc/85XU-QD5B, for a full suite of obligatory financial documents and disclosures, including "Public Football Bowl Subdivision Institutions—University Support," https://perma.cc/F4U3-AABZ, listing the University as one of only twelve out of sixty-nine institutions *not* receiving institutional revenue for athletics in 2009–10.

27. The Upshot, "N.C.A.A. Fan Map: How the Country Roots for College Football," *New York Times*, October 3, 2014.
28. Disclosure: As an administrator, I once pursued claims by a student (not involved in sports) that athletes were receiving A grades for courses they were not in fact taking. This turned out to be a piece of copycat mischief inspired by a scandal at another prominent institution. But it did give me direct (and ultimately reassuring) entrée into academic advising practices and protocols for student athletes.
29. NCES, IPEDS Data Feedback report for 2021, 11, figure 24.
30. Human Resources, "Executive Broadband Structure Effective 7/1/2021," https://perma.cc/BBR7-GKMG.
31. Data come from publicly posted salary reports available at the Office of Institutional Research, "Salary Reports," https://perma.cc/9PQ4-44AX, specifically "Unclassified employees with a record of employment during the 7/1/2020 to 6/30/2021 period," https://perma.cc/CXF4-Z5JS. According to Human Resources, "OA Compensation Structure Effective 7/1/2021," https://perma.cc/4GTH-UPR5, salaries in OA (Officer of Administration) categories eleven through fifteen are permitted to exceed my benchmark of $145,026 (even though not all of them do).
32. Keyword search for "chief of staff" or "COS" in salary reports cited in note 31 (for 2021) and "Unclassified employees with a record of employment during the 12/1/2009 to 2/28/2010 period" (for 2010), https://perma.cc/5FE3-SMZG.
33. Fringe benefit rates for twelve-month faculty and administrators are in the range of 77 to 80 percent, a large figure reflecting the high costs of health care and the legacy of generous state pension programs in prior decades.
34. See Human Resources, "Officers of Administration Compensation Information," https://perma.cc/KEC9-S8KF, with further links to OA Salary Band Project and OA Job Family Framework Project.

35. Robert Birnbaum, *How Colleges Work: The Cybernetics of Academic Organization and Leadership* (Hoboken, NJ: Wiley, 1991), 3–4, 154–75; and Michael Cohen, James March, and Johan Olsen, "A Garbage Can Model of Organizational Choice," *Administrative Science Quarterly* 17, no. 1 (March 1972): 1–25, with specific attention to universities on 11–16.
36. The shell metaphor is from John Lombardi, *How Universities Work* (Baltimore, MD: Johns Hopkins University Press, 2013), 2–8.

5. RESEARCH

1. *U.S. News and World Report*, "Best National University Rankings," accessed May 24, 2024, https://www.usnews.com. The one previous exception, Notre Dame, joined the AAU in 2023.
2. The R2 and R1 categories have recently been renamed "high research activity" and "very high research activity," but the earlier abbreviations persist in common parlance because they are easier to rattle off in speech.
3. "Extended List: Research Financing of AAU Members and Nonmembers," *Chronicle of Higher Education*, April 22, 2010.
4. Guy Maynard, "Stunned [University] Says Goodbye to [The Hat], Welcomes [President Two] Back," April 1, 2012, https://perma.cc/FPQ4-DFDX. Disclosure: I helped recruit President Two.
5. Office of the Provost, "Academic Plan" (originally 2009, revised draft on October 12, 2011), 8, https://perma.cc/GVK7-NVA2. Emphasis added.
6. Office of the Provost, "Ad Hoc Report to Accreditor," May 21, 2012, https://perma.cc/3LXR-WSDC; and Office of the President, "Self-Evaluation Report to Accreditor," February 28, 2011, https://perma.cc/5D44-ZTR4.
7. Tenure policies and standards of professionalism were explicitly tied to AAU norms in the inaugural Collective Bargaining Agreement with United Academics, 2013–15, https://perma.cc/A639-SZP2, article 17, preamble, page 20; article 20, section 3, page 30, and its successor agreements. The 2021–24 iteration further recommended that external reviewers for promotion cases should generally come from comparable AAU institutions; see https://perma.cc/CWS7-WUW3, article 20, section 21, page 54.

8. On the challenges of the 1990s, see Jonathan R. Cole, Elinor G. Barber, and Stephen R. Graubard, *The Research University in a Time of Discontent* (Baltimore, MD: Johns Hopkins University Press, 1994); and Hugh D. Graham and Nancy Diamond, *The Rise of American Research Universities: Elites and Challengers in the Postwar Era* (Baltimore, MD: Johns Hopkins University Press, 1997), 215–20.

9. Brent D. Maher, "Technically Allowed: Federal Scrutiny of Stanford University's Indirect Cost Expenditures and the Changing Context for Research Universities in the Post-Cold War Era," *History of Education Quarterly* 59, no. 1 (February 2019): 97–127; Robert Rosenzweig, "The Politics of Indirect Cost," *50th Anniversary 1948–1998* (Washington, D.C.: Council on Governmental Relations, 1998), 1–12; and Paula Stephan, *How Economics Shapes Science* (Cambridge, MA: Harvard University Press, 2012), 116, 141–42. For an overview of university science funding, see Paula Stephan and Ronald G. Ehrenberg, eds., *Science and the University* (Madison: University of Wisconsin Press, 2007).

10. The Wikipedia article on STEM is a good resource.

11. National Academy of Sciences, National Academy of Engineering, and Institute of Medicine, Committee on Prospering in the Global Economy of the 21st Century, *Rising Above the Gathering Storm: Energizing and Employing America for a Brighter Economic Future* (Washington, D.C.: National Academies Press, 2007).

12. National Research Council, *Research Universities and the Future of America: Ten Breakthrough Actions Vital to Our Nation's Prosperity and Security* (Washington, D.C.: National Academies Press, 2012).

13. Association of American Universities, "Guiding Principles for the America COMPETES Act Reauthorization," 2013, https://perma.cc/DS66-TZY5.

14. Association of American Universities, "Undergraduate STEM Education Initiative," ca. 2018, https://perma.cc/87TW-84XQ.

15. See, e.g., Heather Gonzalez and Jeffrey Kuenzi, "Science, Technology, Engineering, and Mathematics (STEM) Education: A Primer," Congressional Research Service Report for Congress, August 1, 2012, https://sgp.fas.org/crs/misc/R42642.pdf.

16. Bill Readings, *The University in Ruins* (Cambridge, MA: Harvard University Press, 1996) was among the first to call attention to this trend.

17. Office of the Vice President for Research and Innovation (OVPRI), "Sponsored Project Services Annual Reports," fiscal years 2009–2020, https://perma.cc/34U7-6ZCS.
18. For this paragraph and the next, see Association of American Universities, "Membership Policy," accessed November 22, 2022, https://perma.cc/XEM4-6M5N.
19. Office of the Provost, "Academic Planning Benchmarks and Metrics," December 10, 2013, and January 14, 2014, linked to https://perma.cc/3AJ8-MD8Z.
20. Office of the Provost, "Benchmarking [the University]," November, 4, 2013, 1, https://perma.cc/H5G6-ESGN. Emphasis added. Further materials are available at the Academic Planning website, ca. 2015, https://perma.cc/3AJ8-MD8Z.
21. Office of the Provost, "Benchmarking [the University]," 2–13.
22. In contrast, the *second*-lowest ranked public AAU spent more than four times as much of its own funds on research support than did the University. Figures come from OVPRI, "Sponsored Project Services Annual Reports" for fiscal years 2009–2021.
23. National Center for Science and Engineering Statistics, "Higher Education R&D Expenditures at Public Institutions, Ranked by All R&D Expenditures, by Source of Funds: FY 2022," https://perma.cc/89F8-VFYM.
24. Karen Holbrook and Paul Sanberg, "Understanding the High Cost of Success in University Research," *Technology and Innovation* 15, no. 3 (2013): 269–80; and Henry R. Bourne and Eric B. Vermillion, *Follow the Money: Funding Research in a Large Academic Health Center* (San Francisco: University of California Medical Humanities Press, 2016).
25. Stephan, *How Economics Shapes Science*, 121–22; Association of American Universities, "Frequently Asked Questions About Facilities and Administrative (F&A) Costs of Federally Sponsored University Research," https://perma.cc/P4FK-G4ZW; and Rosenzweig, "The Politics of Indirect Cost."
26. Office of the Provost, "Benchmarking [the University]," 26.
27. For an introduction to global metrics and rankings, see Catherine Paradeise and Ghislaine Filliatreau, "The Emergent Action Field of Metrics: From Rankings to Altmetrics," in *The University Under Pressure*,

ed. Elizabeth Popp Berman and Catherine Paradeise (Bingley, UK: Emerald Group, 2016), 87–128.
28. Yves Gingras, *Bibliometrics and Research Evaluation: Uses and Abuses* (Cambridge, MA: MIT Press, 2016).
29. Diana Hicks, Paul Wouters, Ludo Waltman, Sarah de Rijcke, and Ismael Rafols, "Bibliometrics: The Leiden Manifesto for Research Metrics," *Nature* 520 (April 23, 2015): 429–31.
30. Office of the Provost, "Institutional Metrics," Winter 2018, https://perma.cc/HG6U-WSTB, and the materials archived there, including "Executive Vice Provost . . . CAS Metrics Blog Post" and "Notes from the Provost's March 16 Town Hall." Also "Research Metrics Overview and Data Definition Standards 11-29-18" (document in author's possession).
31. "MOU Between [Provost] and United Academics Regarding Local Level Metrics," March 16. 2018, https://perma.cc/HG6U-WSTB.
32. Office of the President, "Aligning Our Resources for Academic Excellence," January 6, 2016, https://perma.cc/RDU7-D9XN.
33. For this whole section, see Office of the Provost, "Academic Allocation Model," July 1, 2018, https://perma.cc/T2S7-C48E, with links to the "Academic Allocation Model Handbook"; Provost presentation on "Academic Allocation Model Implementation," in Board of Trustees, "Finance and Facilities Committee," June 7, 2018, 36–41, https://perma.cc/8NXL-X7G5; and "Operational Metrics Glossary," November 7, 2021, in author's possession.
34. Office of the Provost, "Big Ideas," https://perma.cc/6R94-7FCN; Office of the Provost, "Big Ideas Archives," https://perma.cc/Y6N5-CCLV; and Office of the Provost, "Big Ideas Forum," https://perma.cc/8WV7-ZHHU (all Summer 2009).
35. Office of the Provost, "AY2023–24 Institutional Hiring Plan," ca. December 2022, https://perma.cc/QY3R-PGMB, with archive of previous hiring plans going back to 2017–18, including the "IHP Proposal Template" and "IHP Proposal Template Guidance," and finalized "Institutional Hiring Plan" documents for each year. Also see Provost presentation to Board of Trustees on "Academic Excellence: How Do We Measure and Define It," in Board of Trustees, "Meeting of the Board," December 8, 2017, 88–106, https://perma.cc/EM5C-9CKM.

36. Annual Institutional Hiring Plan documents for AY2017–18 through AY2022–23, archived on Office of the Provost, "AY2023–24 Institutional Hiring Plan" website sidebar.
37. Of twelve identified institutional initiatives, six were squarely in the physical and biological sciences, two in the health and behavioral sciences, two in the social sciences, and two in the humanities or humanistic social sciences. These were later grouped into five top-level hiring initiatives. See Provost's "Academic Initiatives," ca. December 2021, https://perma.cc/3UG3-37HL, with subpages on the five initiatives named.
38. Kevin Carey, "Building a New AAU: The Case for Redefining Higher Education Excellence," June 2014, https://perma.cc/Z6NJ-KFML. Relatedly, the Carnegie Foundation, whose Commission on Higher Education pioneered R1 and other classifications in the 1970s, announced major changes to the 2025 classification founded on "multidimensional categories that better reflect the breadth and diversity of colleges and universities today," including recognition of social and economic mobility as well as community engagement. See https://carnegieclassifications.acenet.edu.
39. Juan Pablo Pardo-Guerra, *The Quantified Scholar: How Research Evaluations Transformed the British Social Sciences* (New York: Columbia University Press, 2022).
40. Nicholas Bloom et al., "Are Ideas Getting Harder to Find?," Centre for Economic Performance Discussion Paper No. 1496 (London: London School of Economics and Political Science, 2017), https://doi.org/10.1257/aer.20180338; Max Kozlov, "'Disruptive' Science Has Declined—and No One Knows Why," *Nature* 613 (January 4, 2023): 225; and Michael Park, Erin Leahey, and Russell J. Funk, "Papers and Patents Are Becoming Less Disruptive Over Time," *Nature* 613 (January 4, 2023): 138–44.
41. Pat O'Connor, "A Typology of STEM Academics and Researchers' Responses to Managerialist Performativity in Higher Education," in *Research Handbook on Academic Careers and Managing Academics*, ed. Cláudia S. Sarrico, Maria J. Rosa, and Teresa Carvalho (Cheltenham, UK: Edward Elgar, 2022), 189–201.
42. Jay Bhattacharya and Mikko Packalen, "Stagnation and Scientific Incentives," National Bureau of Economic Research Working Paper 26752 (February 2020), https://doi.org/10.3386/w26752.

43. Johan S. G. Chu and James A. Evans, "Slowed Canonical Progress in Large Fields of Science," *PNAS* 118, no. 41 (October 4, 2021).
44. Roberta Ness, *The Creativity Crisis: Reinventing Science to Unleash Possibility* (New York: Oxford University Press, 2014).

6. TEACHING

1. Office of the Provost, "About [Student Success Building]," ca. 2019, https://perma.cc/GP2Z-RWHT. Disclosure: I served on the vision and academic program design team for this building.
2. Debra Humphreys and Patrick Kelly, "How Liberal Arts and Sciences Majors Fare in Employment: A Report on Earnings and Long-Term Career Paths" (Washington, D.C.: Association of American Colleges and Universities, 2014), https://perma.cc/5PSB-GLEH; and Hart Research Associates, "It Takes More Than a Major: Employer Priorities for College Learning and Student Success. An Online Survey Among Employers Conducted on Behalf of: The Association of American Colleges and Universities," April 10, 2013, https://perma.cc/CJ7K-BXTQ. During the 2010s, both of these studies, and many others echoing their conclusions, were widely quoted in trade publications, by national advocacy organizations, and at professional conferences for administrators.
3. Office of the President, "The [University] Commitment to Student Access and Success," November 10, 2015, https://perma.cc/UH4J-5QDL.
4. On "college for all," see Steven Brint, *Two Cheers for Higher Education: Why American Universities Are Stronger Than Ever—and How to Meet the Challenges They Face* (Princeton, NJ: Princeton University Press, 2018), 116–57.
5. Barack Obama, "Address to Joint Session of Congress," February 24, 2009.
6. Commission on the Future of Higher Education [Spellings Commission], "A Test of Leadership: Charting the Future of U.S. Higher Education" (Washington, DC: U.S. Department of Education, 2006), x, 14–15, 20–21, 25, for other quotations in this section, https://files.eric.ed.gov/fulltext/ED493504.pdf.
7. For context, see Joseph Burke, ed., *Achieving Accountability in Higher Education* (San Francisco: Jossey-Bass, 2004), 89–95, 104–17, 216–45.

8. Shirley Tilghman, "The Uses and Misuses of Accreditation," Reinvention Center Conference, Arlington, VA, November 9, 2012, https://perma.cc/2AN6-BVVQ.
9. Boyer Commission on Educating Undergraduates in the Research University, *Reinventing Undergraduate Education: A Blueprint for America's Research Universities* (Princeton, NJ: Carnegie Foundation for the Advancement of Teaching, 1998).
10. Peter T. Ewell, "Assessment and Accountability in America Today: Background and Context," *New Directions for Institutional Research* S1 (Autumn 2008), 7–17.
11. Jillian Kinzie, Stanley O. Ikenberry, and Peter T. Ewell, "The Bigger Picture: Student Learning Outcomes Assessment and External Entities," in *Using Evidence of Student Learning to Improve Higher Education*, ed. George D. Kuh (New York: Wiley, 2015), 160–82; and Katherine Hughes, *The College Completion Agenda: 2012 Progress Report* (New York: College Board, 2013).
12. Arthur M. Hauptman, "Increasing Higher Education Attainment in the United States: Challenges and Opportunities," in *Getting to Graduation: The Completion Agenda in Higher Education*, ed. Andrew P. Kelly and Mark Schneider (Baltimore, MD: Johns Hopkins University Press, 2012), 17–47, at 27–31, esp. table 1.4.
13. Nabih Haddad, "Philanthropic Foundations and Higher Education: The Politics of Intermediary Organizations," *Journal of Higher Education* (2021): 1–30.
14. See George D. Kuh, Jillian Kinzie, John H. Schuh, Elizabeth J. Whitt, and Associates, *Student Success in College: Creating Conditions That Matter* (New York: Wiley, 2005); George D. Kuh et al., *Piecing Together the Student Success Puzzle: Research, Propositions, and Recommendations* (New York: Wiley, 2007); and George D. Kuh et al., *Using Evidence of Student Learning to Improve Higher Education* (New York: Wiley, 2015).
15. Compare with Brint, *Two Cheers for Higher Education*, 296–315, who treats these as separate strands.
16. Richard Arum and Josipa Roksa, *Academically Adrift: Limited Learning on College Campuses* (Chicago: University of Chicago Press, 2011), 30–37, 54, 94–99.

6. TEACHING • 303

17. For a fuller critique by a distinguished expert, see Alexander W. Astin, "In 'Academically Adrift,' Data Don't Back Up Sweeping Claim," *Chronicle of Higher Education*, February 14, 2011.
18. Scott Carlson, "Colleges 'Unleash the Deans' with Decentralized Budgets," *Chronicle of Higher Education*, February 9, 2015.
19. Office of the Registrar, "Group Satisfying & Multicultural Courses," June 9, 2010, https://perma.cc/PW5J-R3VE; and Office of the Registrar, "Areas of Inquiry and Cultural Literacy Courses," November 23, 2020, https://perma.cc/8PBF-52CC.
20. John S. Rosenberg, "General Education Under the Microscope," *Harvard Magazine*, May 6, 2015.
21. Office of the Provost, "Ad Hoc Report to [Accreditor]," May 1, 2012, 6, https://perma.cc/2M7M-V6SA. On the absence of a plan, compare with the Office of the Provost, "Self-Evaluation Report to [Accreditor]," February 28, 2011, 9, https://perma.cc/ABC7-PKXB. A full set of accreditation materials, including these, is posted at Office of the Provost, "Regional Accreditation—Historical Documents," https://perma.cc/XG7U-447M.
22. Office of the Provost, "Accreditation Reaffirmation," July 27, 2017, 3, https://perma.cc/XG7U-447M, citing Spring 2013 recommendations.
23. Office of the Provost, "Demonstration Project," March 15, 2017, https://perma.cc/3YPY-K992.
24. Compare AAC&U, "VALUE Rubrics," https://perma.cc/WX9Y-GMHS, with rubrics posted at Office of the Provost, "Changes to Core Education Group and Multicultural Requirements," Fall 2018, https://perma.cc/X6ET-NXUK, plus sample templates at https://perma.cc/ZA2U-V3HL. See also University Senate, "Creation of Core Education Council," February 14, 2018, https://perma.cc/85HQ-9KP9; and University Senate, "Learning Goals for Methods of Inquiry," May 9, 2018, https://perma.cc/T9MG-FNRA.
25. Office of the Provost, "Mid-Cycle Peer Evaluation Report," April 20–21, 2020, 6, https://perma.cc/9B9U-T5U6.
26. Board of Trustees, "University Mission Statement (Trustees motion)," November 5, 2014, https://perma.cc/25NA-N7A6, following Office of the Provost, "Mission Statement Revision Draft Language," Fall 2014, https://perma.cc/3RHN-ZR5M.

27. Association of American Universities, "Top Research Universities Expanding Efforts to Assess, Improve Undergraduate Student Learning," press release, December 12, 2013, which defensively argues that AAU universities are already doing an enormous amount to assess student learning.
28. University Senate Teaching Evaluation Task Force, "Improving How We Evaluate Teaching," January 31, 2018, https://perma.cc/Q2JW-FFZC. See also University Senate, "Implementing a System for the Continuous Improvement and Evaluation of Teaching," May 23, 2018, https://perma.cc/5B85-UKFN; University Senate, "Phase Out Current Student 'Course Evaluations' and Replace with Learning-Focused 'Student Experience Surveys'," April 10, 2019, https://perma.cc/6HQ9-36WQ; and University Senate, "A New System for the Evaluation of Teaching," January 12, 2022, https://perma.cc/YPK4-KAR6. The implementation process is described in Office of the Provost, "Revising [The University's] Teaching Evaluations," August 2018, https://perma.cc/FW8P-LQBV.
29. Although published after this debate at the University, see Lauren A. Rivera and András Tilcsik, "Scaling Down Inequality: Rating Scales, Gender Bias, and the Architecture of Evaluation," *American Sociological Review* 84 no. 2 (2019): 248–74.
30. University Senate Continuous Improvement and Evaluation of Teaching Committee, "Student Experience Survey Response Rate Report," Spring 2021, https://perma.cc/D94M-AGA6.
31. Kristen Doerer, "Colleges Are Getting Smarter About Student Evaluations. Here's How," *Chronicle of Higher Education*, January 13, 2019. Compare that to Beth McMurtrie, "Teaching Evaluations Are Broken. Can They Be Fixed?," *Chronicle of Higher Education*, February 6, 2024.
32. See references and citations in Office of the Provost, "Professional, Inclusive, Engaged, and Research Informed Teaching," https://perma.cc/U2CW-B6RY; and Office of the Provost, "Revising [The University's] Teaching Evaluations."
33. Complete College America, "Complete College America Announces Major Gift From Philanthropist Mackenzie Scott," November 14, 2022, https://perma.cc/2NDR-QWHU.
34. Complete College America, "Four-Year Myth," December 1, 2014, https://perma.cc/UAA4-R9EK.

35. Complete College America, "Four-Year Myth," 66.
36. Office of the President, "The [University] Commitment."
37. Office of Academic Advising, "Flight Paths," ca. 2019, https://perma.cc/5H36-B74B.
38. Office of Institutional Research, "Detailed Enrollment (Undergraduates)," https://perma.cc/TT85-28Z2. Overall undergraduate enrollment went from 18,514 to 18,903 in this period, a net 2 percent increase despite intervening fluctuations.
39. University President, "Five Years of Institutional Governance at the [University]," December 5, 2019, 5, https://perma.cc/6H5L-ZG5X.
40. Board of Trustees, "Meeting of the Board," May 19–20, 2022," 73–74, https://perma.cc/YVP8-GMME.
41. William G. Bowen, Matthew M. Chingos, and Michael S. McPherson, *Crossing the Finish Line: Completing College at America's Public Universities* (Princeton, NJ: Princeton University Press, 2009), 223–38.
42. Compare with "The Equity/Excellence Imperative: A 2030 Blueprint for Undergraduate Education at U.S. Research Universities," https://perma.cc/F7A3-6NRR. This 2022 reform blueprint reworked the 1998 Boyer Commission and contains many of these ideas, plus others.

7. DIVERSITY

1. Letter from University law faculty, November 2, 2016, https://perma.cc/USH7-MMCE; Barran Liebman, LLP, "Investigative Report," December 21, 2016, https://perma.cc/GRL5-SNLF; and Scott Jaschik, "Professor in Blackface Violated Anti-Harassment Policy," *Inside Higher Education*, January 2, 2017.
2. FIRE (Foundation for Individual Rights and Expression), "Scholars Under Fire: The Targeting of Scholars for Ideological Reasons from 2015 to the Present," September 7, 2021.
3. Christine A. Stanley, "The Chief Diversity Officer: An Examination of CDO Models and Strategies," *Journal of Diversity in Higher Education* 7, no. 2 (2014): 101–8.
4. Justice Powell's opinion is excerpted in Wilson Smith and Thomas Bender, eds., *American Higher Education Transformed, 1940–2005* (Baltimore, MD: Johns Hopkins University Press, 2008), 444–45.

5. The diversity rationale predates *Bakke*. See Anthony S. Chen and Lisa M. Stulberg, "Before *Bakke*: The Hidden History of the Diversity Rationale," *University of Chicago Law Review Online*, October 30, 2020.
6. Adam Chilton, Justin Driver, Jonathan S. Masur, and Kyle Rozema, "Assessing Affirmative Action's Diversity Rationale," *Columbia Law Review* 122, no. 2 (March 2022): 331–405.
7. Justice O'Connor opinion is excerpted in Smith and Bender, *American Higher Education Transformed*, 446–48.
8. Matthew Johnson, *Undermining Racial Justice: How One University Embraced Inclusion and Inequality* (Ithaca, NY: Cornell University Press, 2020), 202 (from a draft of the plan).
9. Damon A. Williams and Katrina C. Wade-Golden, *Strategic Diversity Leadership: Activating Change and Transformation in Higher Education* (Sterling, VA: Stylus, 2013), 324–26; compare with the more critical takes in Johnson, *Undermining Racial Justice*, 1–8, 188–214 and Ellen C. Berrey, "Why Diversity Became Orthodox in Higher Education, and How It Changed the Meaning of Race on Campus," *Critical Sociology* 37, no. 5 (2011): 573–96.
10. Ofra Bloch, "Diversity Gone Wrong: A Historical Inquiry Into the Evolving Meaning of Diversity from *Bakke* to *Fisher*," *University of Pennsylvania Journal of Constitutional Law* 20, no. 5 (2018): 1145–1210, comparing *Grutter* and *Fisher* at 1157, 1166–97, with quotations on 1184.
11. Brent K. Nakamura and Lauren B. Edelman, "*Bakke* at 40: How Diversity Matters in the Employment Context," *University of California at Davis Law Review* 52 (2019): 2627–79, at 2632 (for quotation), 2633–35.
12. Rohini Anand and Mary-Frances Winters, "A Retrospective View of Corporate Diversity Training from 1964 to the Present," *Academy of Management Learning and Education* 7, no. 3 (2008): 356–72.
13. Bridget Read, "Inside the Booming Diversity-Equity-and-Inclusion Industrial Complex," *The Cut*, May 26, 2021.
14. Frank Dobbin and Alexandra Kalev, "The Civil Rights Revolution at Work: What Went Wrong," *Annual Review of Sociology* 47 (2021): 281–303, at 285–88, 295–96; Frank Dobbin and Alexandra Kalev, "Why Diversity Programs Fail," *Harvard Business Review*, July-August, 2016; and Frank Dobbin and Alexandra Kalev, *Getting to Diversity: What Works and What Doesn't* (Cambridge, MA: Harvard University Press,

2022). For an exposé, see Pamela Newkirk, *Diversity, Inc.: The Failed Promise of a Billion-Dollar Business* (New York: Bold Type, 2019).

15. Steven W. Bradley, James R. Garven, Wilson Law, and James Edward West, "The Impact of Chief Diversity Officers on Diverse Faculty Hiring," National Bureau of Economic Research Working Paper no. 24969 (August 2018), 10, 29, https://doi.org/10.3386/w24969, showing an inflection point around 2006.

16. Damon A. Williams and Katrina C. Wade-Golden, *The Chief Diversity Officer: A Primer for College and University Presidents* (Washington, DC: American Council on Education, 2007); Williams and Wade-Golden, *Strategic Diversity Leadership*.

17. Raul A. Leon, "The Chief Diversity Officer: An Examination of CDO Models and Strategies," *Journal of Diversity in Higher Education* 7, no. 2 (2014): 77–91, at 77–81, 87.

18. Daniel N. Lipson, "Embracing Diversity: The Institutionalization of Affirmative Action as Diversity Management at UC-Berkeley, UT-Austin, and UW-Madison," *Law and Social Inquiry* 32, no. 4 (Fall 2007): 985–1026.

19. "[University] Battles Discrimination Claims," *[University's Principal Student Newspaper]*, June 3, 2008.

20. Office of Institutional Equity and Diversity (OIED), "Diversity Plan for the [University]," May 14, 2006, https://perma.cc/6CE2-B7EX.

21. OIED, "Diversity Plan for the [University]," 8–10.

22. Ben Gose, "The Rise of the Chief Diversity Officer," *Chronicle of Higher Education*, September 29, 2006.

23. OIED, "Diversity Plan for the [University]," 14.

24. Diversity Advisory Committee, "Recommendations Related to [University] Diversity Plan," May 11, 2006, https://perma.cc/W8YP-4HX8.

25. Division of Equity and Inclusion (DEI) homepage, ca. 2015, https://perma.cc/2SNJ-22DH.

26. The budget for the DEI office grew from $2.1 million to $2.6 million in real (2020) dollars, or 21 percent, which is less than the 24 percent average in the five core categories analyzed in chapter 4, and the 25 percent growth in institutional support specifically.

27. University-Wide Diversity Committee, "2014–2017 [University's] IDEAL Framework for Equity, Inclusion, and Diversity (DRAFT),"

March 11, 2015, https://perma.cc/L6HP-Q7BG; Office of the President, "IDEAL Framework: A Commitment to Equity, Inclusion, and Diversity," June 1, 2016, https://perma.cc/3F52-3LFM; and DEI, "IDEAL Strategies and Tactics," May 1, 2016, https://perma.cc/TN2H-LGUK.

28. DEI, "IDEAL: Our Roadmap for a Fully-Inclusive and Resilient Campus," December 10, 2020, 3, https://perma.cc/S3XF-KCDA.
29. DEI, "L.A.C.E. Resources," ca. August 2020, https://perma.cc/C4V3-TLRV.
30. Office of the President, "Building Renaming Process," 2016–2020, https://perma.cc/3Y7Q-BQ7G.
31. University Senate, "Repeal of Multicultural Requirement and Introduction of US: Difference, Inequality, Agency and Global Perspectives Requirements," May 9, 2018, https://perma.cc/6H6X-HQD4.
32. DEI, "IDEAL Climate Survey: Results 2022," June 2022, https://perma.cc/U75R-ZQMC.
33. College of Arts and Sciences, "[University] Diversity Resources," 2020–21, https://perma.cc/P5QA-LPMV.
34. Office of the Provost, "Field Availability Estimates 101," September 27, 2021, https://perma.cc/T33D-QPRS.
35. Four-year graduation rates for underrepresented minorities grew dramatically from 41 percent (2010 cohort) to 53 percent (2016 cohort, the last for which data were available at the time of writing). See Higher Education Coordinating Commission (HECC), "2020 University Evaluation: [University]," March 5, 2021, 14, table 3, https://perma.cc/5A6N-DMSE,
36. DEI, "IDEAL: Our Roadmap for a Fully-Inclusive and Resilient Campus," 19–21.
37. See Office of Institutional Research, "Detailed Enrollment," tabulation of nonresident aliens; "Report of the American English Institute Task Force," October 15, 2014 (document in author's possession). Disclosure: I sat on this Provost-appointed task force and was later charged with implementing its recommendations.
38. HECC, "[State] HECC Equity Lens," December 15, 2021, https://perma.cc/5USV-F4WT; see chapter 1 on the 40-40-20 goal.
39. HECC, "2017–19 Affirmative Action/Diversity & Inclusion Plan," January 11, 2017, https://perma.cc/T8P8-VPV5; and [State] Education

Investment Board, "Equity Lens," April 15, 2013, https://perma.cc/QP4N-VV6D. On the centrality of DEI to HECC's strategic priorities, see HECC, "Government to Government 2020 Annual Report," January 15, 2021, https://perma.cc/VJ3L-2XHY.
40. HECC, "State Funding and Formula Summary: 2021–23 Biennium," July 15, 2022, 13–19, https://perma.cc/63FG-H63J.
41. HECC, "State Funding and Formula Summary," 14, 22.
42. HECC, "State Funding and Formula Summary," 21, table 23.
43. This assumes a fifteen-credit load and the tuition figures posted at the Office of the Registrar, "Undergraduate 2022 Tuition Cohort Tuition & Fees," https://perma.cc/8RVP-NCF7, for a total of $8,880 in added tuition relative to an in-state student. The University's equity incentive ($6,829) was slightly higher than the statewide average ($6,450) under the SSCM formula.
44. Bradley R. Curs and Ozan Jacquette, "Crowded Out? The Effect of Nonresident Enrollment on Resident Access to Public Research Universities," *Educational Evaluation and Policy Analysis* 39, no. 4 (December 2017): 644–69. Only at the most prestigious public universities, which like their elite private competitors have a strong incentive to cap overall enrollments, is crowding out a problem.
45. Karina G. Salazar, Ozan Jaquette, and Crystal Han, "Coming Soon to a Neighborhood Near You? Off-Campus Recruiting by Public Research Universities," *American Educational Research Journal* 58, no. 6 (December 2021): 1270–1314, at 1295.
46. Ozan Jaquette, Bradley R. Curs, and Julie R. Posselt, "Tuition Rich, Mission Poor: Nonresident Enrollment Growth and the Socioeconomic and Racial Composition of Public Research Universities," *Journal of Higher Education* 87, no. 5 (September-October 2016), 635–73.
47. HECC, "What You Need to Know About: [State's] Educational Attainment Goals," August 3, 2022, https://perma.cc/Z4Z2-9SHR. For an evaluation, see Rob Manning, "[State] Leaders Wanted 40-40-20 By 2025. What Does It Mean and How Close Are We?," [State] Public Broadcasting, October 10, 2022.
48. HECC, "House Bill 3335 (2015): Policy Overview Report," May 4, 2016, https://perma.cc/9VZG-27LR.

49. "[State] Talent Assessment: 2020 Update," Winter 2020, https://perma.cc/497P-VSBZ (see this link for the report's author, a public policy research firm); and HECC, "Senate Bill 1545 (2022): Future Ready [State] Year One Report," December 2022, https://perma.cc/AR9V-W9E4.
50. Organization for Economic Cooperation and Development, *Education a Glance 2020: OECD Indicators* (Paris: OECD, 2020), https://doi.org/10.1787/69096873-en, 243–44, figure B7.1; see also Academic Compass, "A Guide to College-For-All," January 19, 2022, https://americancompass.org/a-guide-to-college-for-all.
51. Kim Parker and Pew Research Center, "The Growing Partisan Divide in Views of Higher Education," August 19, 2019. See also Rachel Fishman, Sophie Nguyen, and Louisa Woodhouse, "Varying Degrees 2022: New America's Sixth Annual Survey on Higher Education: Findings," New America Foundation, July 26, 2022, https://www.newamerica.org/education-policy/reports/varying-degrees-2022/findings; and Thomas B. Edsall, "'There Are Two Americas Now: One With a B.A. and One Without'," *New York Times*, October 5, 2022.
52. See, for example, Howard Dickman, ed., *The Imperiled Academy* (New Brunswick, NJ: Transaction, 1993).
53. Anne Case and Angus Deaton, "The Great Divide: Education, Despair, and Death," *Annual Review of Economics* 14, no. 1 (2022): 1–21.
54. Lisa Camner McKay, "How the Racial Wealth Gap Has Evolved—and Why It Persists," Federal Reserve Bank of Minneapolis, October 3, 2022, https://www.minneapolisfed.org/article/2022/how-the-racial-wealth-gap-has-evolved-and-why-it-persists.
55. For a critique of college for all and an endorsement of vocational training, see Will Bunch, *After the Ivory Tower Falls: How College Broke the American Dream and Blew Up Our Politics—and How to Fix It* (New York: HarperCollins, 2022); on indebtedness, see Elizabeth Tandy Shermer, *Indentured Students: How Government-Guaranteed Loans Left Generations Drowning in College Debt* (Cambridge, MA: Harvard University Press, 2021); on systemic inefficiencies, especially in financial aid, see Sara Goldrick-Rab, *Paying the Price: College Costs, Financial Aid, and the Betrayal of the American Dream* (Chicago: University of Chicago Press, 2016); on dropouts and opportunity gaps, see David Kirp, *The College Dropout Scandal* (New York: Oxford University Press, 2019); on

political interests, see Suzanne Mettler, *Degrees of Inequality: How the Politics of Higher Education Sabotaged the American Dream* (New York: Basic Books, 2014); and on for-profits, but also on the new economy, labor market insecurity, and risk shift more broadly, see Tressie McMillan Cottom, *Lower Ed: The Troubling Rise of For-Profit Colleges in the New Economy* (New York: New Press, 2018).

56. Kelly Nielsen and Laura Hamilton, *Broke: The Racial Consequences of Underfunding Public Universities* (Chicago: University of Chicago Press, 2021); and James M. Thomas, "Diversity Regimes and Racial Inequality: A Case Study of Diversity University," *Social Currents* 5, no. 2 (2018): 140–56.

57. Richard Thompson Ford, "Derailed by Diversity," *Chronicle of Higher Education*, September 2, 2022; David E. Bernstein, *Classified: The Untold Story of Racial Classification in America* (New York: Bombardier, 2022); and Kenny Xu, *An Inconvenient Minority: The Attack on Asian American Excellence and the Fight for Meritocracy* (New York: Diversion, 2021).

58. Natasha K. Warikoo, *The Diversity Bargain and Other Dilemmas of Race, Admissions, and Meritocracy at Elite Universities* (Chicago: University of Chicago Press, 2016).

59. Maria Carrasco, "Record Numbers of Men 'Give Up' on College," *Inside Higher Ed*, September 7, 2021.

60. U.S. Department of Education Office for Civil Rights, "Dear Colleague" letter, April 4, 2011, https://perma.cc/2MF5-3FT6. For a pointed critique of this movement, see Laura Kipnis, *Unwanted Advances: Sexual Paranoia Comes to Campus* (New York: Harper, 2017); and for a wider account of sexual assault on campus, see Jennifer S. Hirsch and Shamus Khan, *Sexual Citizens: Sex, Power, and Assault on Campus* (New York: W. W. Norton, 2021).

61. See Richard Reeves, *Of Boys and Men: Why the Modern Male Is Struggling, Why It Matters, and What to Do About It* (Washington, DC: Brookings Institution Press, 2022); and Richard Reeves and Will Secker, "Degrees of Difference: Male College Enrollment and Completion," American Institute for Boys and Men, March 24, 2024, https://aibm.org/research/male-college-enrollment-and-completion/.

62. Julie Reuben, *The Making of the Modern University: Intellectual Transformation and the Marginalization of Morality* (Chicago: University of Chicago Press, 1996).

8. IMPACT

1. For a deeper theoretical articulation of what I am calling the new instrumentalism, see the account of "Mode 2" knowledge presciently developed in Michael Gibbons, Camille Limoges, Helga Nowotny, Simon Schwartzman, Peter Scott, and Martin Trow, *The New Production of Knowledge: The Dynamics of Science and Research in Contemporary Societies* (Newbury Park, CA: Sage, 1994). Also see the next section where I distinguish the new instrumentalism from the old.
2. As early as 1971, Robert Nisbet used the term "academic capitalism" to excoriate universities for abandoning the pursuit of knowledge for its own sake, which he called the "academic dogma." For him, research centers and institutes were the prime culprit because they severed the classic unity of teaching and research. See Ethan Schrum, "The Prophet of Academic Doom," *Chronicle of Higher Education*, October 19, 2021.
3. "Major Private Gifts to Higher Education," *Chronicle of Higher Education*, as of January 31, 2023. The University's number one ranking comes from treating these two separate installments as a single $1 billion donation.
4. Isabelle Hau, "How Women Billionaires Are Changing the Face of Early Childhood Education and Care—and Philanthropy," *Forbes*, April 1, 2022.
5. Emily Nwakpuda, "Major Donors and Higher Education: Are STEM Donors Different from Other Donors?," *Nonprofit and Voluntary Sector Quarterly* 49, no. 5 (2020): 969–88, at 971, 977, 983.
6. On the new donors, see Holden Thorp and Buck Goldstein, *Engines of Innovation: The Entrepreneurial University in the Twenty-First Century* (Chapel Hill, NC: UNC Press, 2013), 141–50.
7. Board of Trustees, "Meeting of the Board," December 4, 2018," 160–61 [166–67 in pdf], https://perma.cc/5GMJ-SHV2.
8. [New] Campus for Accelerating Scientific Impact, "Strategic Plan," August 6, 2019, 10 [9 in pdf], https://perma.cc/S5DR-B5NN.
9. Board of Trustees, "Meeting of the Board," November 13, 2020, 12–16, https://perma.cc/PU67-T7G5.
10. New Campus for Accelerating Scientific Impact, "Strategic Plan," 10, 11.
11. New Campus for Accelerating Scientific Impact, "Strategic Plan"; Office of the Provost, "TTF [Tenure-Track Faculty] Review and

Promotion Policy," for New Campus for Accelerating Scientific Impact, June 2021, https://perma.cc/9KTH-AR7U.
12. On "JEDI" (justice, equity, diversity, and inclusion) values, see [New] Campus for Accelerating Scientific Impact, "About the [New] Campus," December 2022, https://perma.cc/22ZR-BMUG.
13. Board of Trustees, "Meeting of the Board," March 14–15, 2022," 27, https://perma.cc/3YL3-7K86.
14. Prevention Science Institute, "About Us," April 2020, https://perma.cc/92BE-JG7A; and Prevention Science Institute, "2022 Annual Report," https://perma.cc/939Y-TCYU.
15. Alex Baumhardt, "State Leaders Hope New Behavioral Health Graduates Can Fill Persistent Gaps in [State] Schools," *[State] Capital Chronicle*, April 14, 2022.
16. Roger Geiger, "Organized Research Units—Their Role in the Development of University Research," *Journal of Higher Education* 61, no. 1 (January-February 1990): 1–19; and Burton Clark, *Sustaining Change in Universities* (Berkshire, UK: Open University Press, 2004), 139–53 for case studies.
17. Henry Etzkowitz, *MIT and the Rise of Entrepreneurial Science* (New York: Routledge, 2002); and Henry Etzkowitz and Chunyan Zhou, *The Triple Helix: University-Industry-Government Innovation and Entrepreneurship*, 2nd ed. (New York: Routledge, 2018).
18. Elizabeth Popp Berman, *Creating the Market University: How Academic Science Became an Economic Engine* (Princeton, NJ: Princeton University Press, 2012); Martin Kenney, *Biotechnology: The University-Industrial Complex* (New Haven, CT: Yale University Press, 1985); and on Bayh-Dole, see David Mowery, *Ivory Tower and Industrial Innovation: University-Industry Technology Transfer Before and After the Bayh-Dole Act* (Stanford, CA: Stanford University Press, 2004).
19. Roger Geiger, *Knowledge and Money: Research Universities and the Paradox of the Marketplace* (Stanford, CA: Stanford University Press, 2004), 170–79; also 180–231.
20. It was not until 2013, in *Association for Molecular Pathology v. Myriad Genetics, Inc.*, that the Supreme Court held that a gene could not be patented.
21. Donald Stein, ed., *Buying In or Selling Out? The Commercialization of the American Research University* (New Brunswick, NJ: Rutgers University

Press, 2004); Jennifer Washburn, *University, Inc.: The Corporate Corruption of Higher Education* (New York: Basic Books, 2005); Daniel S. Greenberg, *Science for Sale: The Perils, Delusions, and Rewards of Campus Capitalism* (Chicago: University of Chicago Press, 2007); and Derek Bok, *Universities in the Marketplace: The Commercialization of Higher Education* (Princeton, NJ: Princeton University Press, 2003).

22. Sheila Slaughter and Gary Rhoades, *Academic Capitalism and the New Economy: Markets, State, and Higher Education* (Baltimore: Johns Hopkins University Press, 2004). See also Sheila Slaughter and Larry Leslie, *Academic Capitalism: Politics, Policies, and the Entrepreneurial University* (Baltimore, MD: Johns Hopkins University Press, 1997).

23. Roger Geiger and Creso Sá, *Tapping the Riches of Science: Universities and the Promise of Economic Growth* (Cambridge, MA: Harvard University Press, 2008), 1–3; 118, 140, 144 (on TTOs); 203–10.

24. Brian D. Wright, Kyriakos Drivas, Zhen Lei, and Stephen A. Merrill, "Technology Transfer: Industry-Funded Academic Inventions Boost Innovation," *Nature* 507 (March 20, 2014), 297–99.

25. Steven Brint, *Two Cheers for Higher Education: Why American Universities Are Stronger Than Ever—and How to Meet the Challenges They Face* (Princeton, NJ: Princeton University Press, 2018), 112–14.

26. Holden Thorp and Buck Goldstein, *Our Higher Calling: Rebuilding the Partnership Between America and Its Colleges and Universities* (Chapel Hill, NC: UNC Press, 2018).

27. Office of the Provost, "RIGE [Research, Innovation, and Graduate Education] Report," https://perma.cc/F2MC-7MKH, with further links to the February 14, 2014, "Office of Research, Innovation, and Graduate Education (RIGE) Review Committee Report" and "RIGE Report Appendices." See also Office of the Vice President for Research and Innovation (OVPRI), "Sponsored Project Services Annual Reports," https://perma.cc/34U7-6ZCS.

28. OVPRI, "Startup Planning and Strategy," https://perma.cc/6BM6-RC5A; OVPRI, "Partner With Us: Strategic Initiatives, Research, and Innovation," https://perma.cc/V2J4-H66G; OVPRI, "Conflict of Interest and Commitment," https://perma.cc/ADC6-A7YL; and OVPRI, "[University] Intellectual Property Policies & Guidelines," https://perma.cc/49W5-MTGX, all 2022–23.

29. OVPRI, "Industry-Sponsored Research, Technology Transfer, & Intellectual Property," 2022, https://perma.cc/3JN2-JXW6.
30. OVPRI, "Community Resources," May 24, 2022, https://perma.cc/9VU4-4U3Z.
31. OVPRI, "[University] Startups," April 24, 2023, https://perma.cc/L68A-FJ2W; see also OVPRI, "Innovation and Entrepreneurship," January 28, 2023, https://perma.cc/KVF4-EJLB.
32. Office of the President, "Mighty [University]: Higher Education, Higher Purpose," accessed January 24, 2023, https://perma.cc/C7R3-RQNB.
33. Randolph Hall and Jack Lulich, "University Strategic Plans: What They Say About Innovation," *Innovative Higher Education* 46 (2021): 261–84, at 279, 282.
34. Office of the Provost, "Academic Initiatives," ca. December 2021, https://perma.cc/3UG3-37HL.
35. Office of the President, "Strategic Framework: University-Wide Priorities, 2021–26," May 13, 2022, https://perma.cc/NZA7-NM25.
36. Task Force on the Structure of CAS, "Final Report," May 21, 2019, https://perma.cc/HT53-Y7LJ; and Task Force on the Structure of CAS, "Report from Working Group on External Relations," April 23, 2019, 2 (for quotations), 4, https://perma.cc/XC3C-39EL.
37. Disclosure: I led the creation of a new interdisciplinary school of global studies and languages in 2020–22 which may prove to be an exception to the rule, or the exception that proves the rule.
38. Compare Jerry A. Jacobs, *In Defense of Disciplines: Interdisciplinarity and Specialization in the Research University* (Chicago: University of Chicago Press, 2013), with Harvey J. Graff, *Undisciplining Knowledge: Interdisciplinarity in the Twentieth Century* (Baltimore, MD: Johns Hopkins University Press, 2015).
39. Andrew Abbott, "The Disciplines and the Future," in *The Future of the City of Intellect*, ed. Steven Brint (Stanford, CA: Stanford University Press, 2002), 205–30.
40. Rómulo Pinheiro, Patricio V. Langa, and Attila Pausits, "The Institutionalization of Universities' Third Mission: Introduction to the Special Issue," *European Journal of Higher Education* 5, no. 3 (2015): 227–32; and, Rómulo Pinheiro, Patricio V. Langa, and Attila Pausits, "One and Two Equals Three? The Third Mission of Higher Education Institutions,"

European Journal of Higher Education 5, no. 3 (2015): 233–49, with further citations to the burgeoning literature on the third mission. Also see Lorenzo Compagnucci and Francesca Spigarelli, "The Third Mission of the University: A Systematic Literature Review on Potentials and Constraints," *Technological Forecasting and Social Change* 160 (December 2020): 120284. Much of European universities' "third mission" focus grew out of the Lisbon Agenda adopted in 2000 to make the EU the most competitive knowledge-based economy in the world, paralleling the STEM discourse analyzed in chapter 5.

41. Ridvan Cinar, "Delving Into Social Entrepreneurship in Universities: Is It Legitimate Yet?," *Regional Studies, Regional Science* 6, no. 1 (2019): 217–32. See also the European Commission, "Commission Communication on a European Strategy for Universities," January 18, 2022, https://perma.cc/86BD-TFCE; and the European Education Area, "European Universities Initiative," April 19, 2024, https://perma.cc/SBU2-6A56.

CONCLUSION

1. Alexander Hertel-Fernandez, *State Capture: How Conservative Activists, Big Businesses, and Wealthy Donors Reshaped the American States—and the Nation* (New York: Oxford University Press, 2019); and Michael Goldberg, "Republican Lawmakers Are Backing Dozens of Bills Targeting Diversity Efforts on Campus and Elsewhere," February 10, 2024, https://apnews.com/article/dei-state-legislation-diversity.
2. Steven Brint, "If Trump Wins . . . ," *Chronicle of Higher Education*, March 26, 2024.

INDEX

Italicized page numbers refer to figures or tables.

AAU. *See* Association of American Universities
academic advisors, 187–90
Academic Allocation Model: budgeting system under, 78–81, 159; tuition spending under, 78–79
Academically Adrift (Arum and Roksa), 177–78
Academic Analytics, 153–56, *154*, 158
academic capitalism: arguments against, 240–41; corporate sponsorship and, 244, 246–47; DEI and, 247, 254; entrepreneurship and, 238, 241, 243–45; impact of, 228–29, 237–45; in new millennium, 241–43; origins of, 239–41; overview of, 237–38; power and, 244; public disinvestment and, 241–42; rechristening, 243–45; research and, 239–45; term and first usage of, 312n2
academic depression, 74–75
academic freedom, 111, 259–60
academic labor market, 90–96, 118–19. *See also* job market; labor
Academic Revolution, 93
academic *versus* nonacademic expenditures, 67–68, *68*
accountability: in athletics, 130–32, 295n28; as catch-22, 29; DEI and, 198; through governance, 36; metrics, 28–29; for New Partnership, 26–29; performance funding and, 36–38; performance outcomes and, 176; private donors and, 2–3, 26–27, 29; privatization and, 34–42; public, 17–21, 26–29, 34–42; public missions and, 27–29; RCM and, 59; student success and, 174–76; VSA, 174–75
achievement gaps, 186–91
accreditation, 173–82. *See also* assessment of learning outcomes
adjunctification: of faculty, 90–93, 96, 106–7, 119; job market and, 148

administration: admissions policies and, 200–203, 225; athletics and, 130–32; corruption and, 111; DEI and, 197–98; Delta Cost Project and, 117–18; executives and managers, 109, 133–36; faculty and, 87, 101–3, 110, 113–19; funding and, 125–29; Ginsberg on, 110–11; governance and, 135–36; growth of, 109–11, 113–20, 125–26; job market and, 118–19; leadership and, 109–10, 123–24, 133–35; management and, 133–36; performance metrics, productivity, and, 153–57; power and, 111–12; recruitment and, 120–25; research and, 292n7; restructuring of, 126–27; state appropriations for, 126–27; student retention and, 120–25; tuition spending for, 67–68, *68*; university development and relations, 125–29

administrative spending: administrative bloat and, 56–57, 112–20, 133–36; Baumol's cost disease and, 113–15; for branding and public relations, 127–29; for enrollment, 121–25; on executives and managers, 133–36; faculty spending compared to, 117–18, 133–35; increases in selected core expenditures, by category, 113–14, *114*; for information services, 128–29, *129*; institutional support and, 113–17, 128–29, *129*; New Budget Model and, 56–57; per-student expenditures and, 115–17, *116*; statistics on, 112–16

administrators, 10, 11, 232; budgeting system and, 51–52; expanding power of, 15–16; under RCM, 58;

salaries of, 109, 117–19, 133–35; as stakeholders, 109–36

admissions policies, 200–203, 225

advocacy philanthropy, 175–76

affirmative action, 204–5

AFT. *See* American Federation of Teachers

America COMPETES Act (2007), 145–46

American Federation of Teachers (AFT), 92

anonymization, 8–9, 277n14

anti-discrimination lawsuits, 207

arts and sciences. *See* College of Arts and Sciences; liberal arts

Arum, Richard, 177–78

assessment of learning outcomes, 137, 172–82.

Association of American Universities (AAU), 9; benchmarking, 149–51; founding of, 139; lobbying and, 139; membership, 140–42, 148–49; performance metrics and, 142–43, 147–51; public missions and, 142–43, 149; research universities and, 139–43, 145–49, 163–65; standards of, 141–42, 296n7; STEM fields and, 148, 150; student success and, 179, 185–86, 304n27

athletics, 257; accountability in, 130–32, 295n28; administration and, 130–32; expenditures for, 294n26; funding and, 130; grading athletes, 295n28; public missions and, 131–32; sports-related scandals, 130–31

Bakke, Allan, 200–203, 225
Baumol, William, 73
Baumol's cost disease, 73–74, 92, 113–15

Bayh-Dole Act (1980), 239
behavioral sciences, 235–36
benchmarking, 147–51
bias, gender, 183–84
bibliometrics, 152–53
Biden administration, 80–81
Big Donor, The, 21–22, 43, 126, 130, 230, 282n31
Bill and Melinda Gates Foundation, 174–75
biotechnology, 237–38, 239
Black Lives Matter (BLM), 196, 203, 210–11
Blogger, The, 83, 88, 109–10, 183–85
Board of Trustees, 18, 21, 26–27, 43, 46, 233
Bowen, William, 73, 92, 190–91
Bowen's Law, 73–74, 92
Boyer Commission, 174
branding, 127–29
budgeting system: under Academic Allocation Model, 78–81, 159; administrative bloat and, 56–57, 112–20, 133–36; administrators and, 51–52; Baumol's cost disease and, 73–74, 92, 113–15; Bowen's Law and, 73–74; budget drafts, 53; DEI and, 209, 307n26; enrollment management and, 121–25; general fund and, 52, 55–57; incremental funding model and, 53; institutional resilience and, 78–81; market competition and, 79–81; under New Budget Model, 52–58, 285n17; organizational budgets, 113–16; per-student expenditures as percentage of national average, 115–17, *116*; RCM and, 58–63, 78–79; for research, 150–51; at research universities, 158–62; resource dependency and, 150–51; salaries and, 75–77; selected core expenditures, by category, 113–14, *114*; strategic planning and, 158–62; subsidies and, 51, 54–55, 57, 65; transparency in, 63–64; trouble with, 73–78; tuition flows and, 52–63; tuition rises and, 51, 72–78; tuition spending and, 51; what tuition buys and, 53–72
Bush administration, 28, 172

California: Master Plan in, 34–35, 47, 258–59; tuition in, 75. *See also* University of California
cancel culture, 195–96
capitalism: academic, 228–29, 237–45, 254, 312n2; RCM and, 59–61
Carnegie Foundation, 300n38
CBA. *See* Collective Bargaining Agreement
CCA. *See* Complete College America
chief diversity officer (CDO), 198, 205
Child and Family Center, 235
children's behavioral health, 235–36
China, 145, 214
Chronicle of Higher Education (journal), 118
Civil Rights Act (1964): Title IV, 173, 181–82; Title IX, 224; Title VII, 204–5
Civil War, 49
CLA. *See* Collegiate Learning Assessment
climate change, 2–3
cluster hiring, 160
Coalition of Contingent Academic Labor (COCAL), 91
Cold War, 49, 144

Collective Bargaining Agreement (CBA): description of, 96–97; enrollment growth and, 99–100, 102; faculty and, 96–106, 290n24; faculty workloads and, 105; hiring faculty and, 105–6; management and, 96–106; market competition and, 103–6; non-tenure-track faculty and, 99–102; performance metrics and, 157; on post-tenure review, 98; revisions to, 290n24; shared governance and, 97–99; tenure and, 98–100

college completion: agenda, 171–77; "excellence" standards and, 175–76; leadership and, 172; legislation and, 172; market competition and, 171–72; performance metrics and, 173–74; philanthropy and, 174–76; politics and, 172; public missions and, 171–72; Spellings Commission and, 172–73; student success and, 171–77; Tilghman and, 174

College of Arts and Sciences: DEI and, 254; educational reform in, 249–52; impacts in, 249–54; market competition and, 252–53; neglect of, 71–72, 249; public missions and, 252–53; STEM fields and, 253–54

Collegiate Learning Assessment (CLA), 177–78

community college, 219, 262–63

Complete College America (CCA), 187–89

copyright, 242

core curriculum, 177–82, 186

corporations: corporate management techniques, 58; corporate sponsorship, 244, 246–47; DEI and, 204–6, 247

corruption, 111

COVID-19, 5; faculty and, 101; mental health and, 193–94; online education and, 4, 191–94; student success and, 171, 191–94

creativity crisis, 162–67

credit hours: average amount taken at once, 177–78; monetary value and, 70–72; tenure-related faculty and, 288n5; transferring, 216–17, 219; tuition and, 54–55, 64–65, 70–72, 283n7; tuition spending per credit hour, across divisions, 68–72, 69, 70, 285n21

critical race theory, 5

Crossing the Finish Line (Bowen), 190–91

culture wars, 144; cancel culture and, 195–96; DEI and, 206–15; political polarization and, 5, 264–65

degrees: degree gap and, 22–23; meta-majors and, 189; paradox of choice and, 188; percentage of Americans with bachelor's degree, 3–4; social class and, 222; student success and major choice, 168–70, 188–89, 219–20, 301n2; "unbundling" of, 3, 95; undeclared, 189–90; underemployment and, 219–20

DEI. *See* diversity, equity, and inclusion

Delta Cost Project, 117–18

demographic diversity, 212–15, *213*

discrimination: anti-discrimination lawsuits, 207; gender bias and,

183–85; racism and, 195–97, 214; reverse, 221
diversity, equity, and inclusion (DEI), 5, 261; academic capitalism and, 247, 254; accountability and, 198; administration and, 197–98; admissions policies and, 200–203, 225; affirmative action and, 204–5; background and overview of, 199–200; backlash against, 198–99, 220; Black Lives Matter and, 196, 203, 210–11; budgeting and, 209, 307n26; CDO and, 198, 205; College of Arts and Sciences and, 254; corporate models and practices of, 204–6, 247; as cultural reprogramming, 206–15; definition and meaning of, 199–200; demographic diversity and, 212–15, *213*; diversity training and, 204–5, 207–8; entrepreneurship and, 247; executives and, 198, 205; funding for, 217–19, 221; graduation rates and, 308n35; HECC and, 216–19; hiring and, 204–5, 211–12; IDEAL plan for, 209–10; impact of, 229–30, 234; implementation of, 207–10; international students and, 214–15; Ivy league institutions and, 201–3; in K–12 education, 216–20; law and, 200–205, 220–21; leadership and, 197–98, 204–6, 209; meritocracy and, 201, 229; Michigan Mandate and, 202–3; moral exhortation and, 207–10; politics and, 138, 196–99, 220–22, 225, 259; privatization and, 218–19; public missions and, 138, 197–98, 216–20; race and, 195–98, 200–206, 212–15, 220–26; recruitment and, 212–15; reporting, 209; reverse discrimination and, 221; rise of, 195–98; social class and, 220–26; social justice and, 196–99, 201–5, 207–11, 215, 220–26; SSEM and, 212; state-level policy and, 215–20; strategic planning, 206–10; student success and, 212–15; Supreme Court and, 200–203; systemic problems and, 222–24; unionization and, 211; viewpoint diversity and, 207–8; women and, 210–11, 213, 224
Division for Student Services and Enrollment Management (SSEM), 122–25, 190, 212
dot-com bust, 25
Dreamers, 214–15

economic recessions, 1, 25, 36, 126–27. *See also* Great Recession
educational reform, 2, 5–6; America COMPETES Act and, 145–46; Bayh-Dole Act and, 239; in College of Arts and Sciences, 249–52; 40-40-20 formula and, 32–33, 44–45, 216–19; governance and, 46–47; for K–12 education, 28, 32, 220; knowledge economy and, 239–40; Morrill Act and, 250; No Child Left Behind Act and, 28, 220; teaching and, 183–86; Title IV and, 173, 181–82
endowments, 24–26. *See also* private donors

enrollment, 53, 305n38;
administrative spending for,
121–25; CBA and growth of,
99–100, 102; faculty and, 87,
94–95; management, 121–25,
218–19; New Budget Model and,
57–58; SSEM, 122–25, 190, 212;
strategic planning and, 160–61;
tuition and, 57–58
entrepreneurship: academic
capitalism and, 238, 241, 243–45;
DEI and, 247; funding for, 244,
246–48; growth and adoption
of, 245–46; hype for, 247–48;
innovation and, 228–29, 233–34,
245–50; marketing and, 247
ethnicity. *See* diversity, equity, and
inclusion; race and ethnicity
European universities, 12, 60, 165,
253, 315n40
"excellence" standards: college
completion and, 175–76; in
research, 143–47
executives: DEI and, 198, 205;
governance and, 135–36; salaries
of, 109, 133–36
expenditures: academic *versus*
nonacademic, 67–68, *68*; for
athletics, 294n26; increases in
selected core expenditures, by
category, 113–14, *114*; per student,
115–17, *116*. *See also* budgeting
system

facilities and administration (F&A)
rates, 143–45, 150
faculty, 11, 15; academic labor market
and, 90–96; adjunctification
of, 90–93, 96, 106–7, 119;
administration and, 87, 101–3, 110,
113–19; administrative spending
compared to spending on,
117–18, 133–35; CBA and, 96–106,
290n24; COVID-19 and, 101;
enrollment and, 87, 94–95;
evaluation, 182–86; governance
and, 93–94, 97–99; grievances
of, 86; hiring of, 105–6, 158–62;
instructional support, 116–17; job
market and, 84–85, 91–94, 118–19;
labor law and, 85–86; lessons on
unionization and management
of, 106–8; livelihoods, 82–83;
management of, 82–85, 96–108;
market competition and,
102–6; New Budget Model and,
105–6, 161; organizing, 87–88;
part-time, 86–88, 91; power
of, 82–83; professionalization
of non-tenure-track, 99–102,
182–83; public disinvestment
and, 86; RCM and, 93–94, 105;
at research universities, 94;
restructuring of, 94–96, 100–102;
salaries of, 75–77, 86, 95–96, 102–
6, 107, 133–35, 291n31; scientific
impact and, 233–34; senior, 86–88,
94, 100–101; as stakeholders,
82–108; State Board of Higher
Education and, 82–83; tenure
and unionization of, 82–90,
106–8; tuition spending toward,
66, 66–67, 287n29; types of, 85–88,
95. *See also* tenure; tenure-related
faculty
faculty workloads, 291n33; CBA and,
105; teaching responsibilities
and shift in, 87; technology and,
76–77; working conditions and,
83–84, 86
Fall of the Faculty, The (Ginsberg), 110
federal funding, 144–45, 151, 244

50-30-20 rule, 54–55, 57
flower chart, 153–55, *154*
Floyd, George, 193, 196
40-40-20 formula, 32–33, 44–45, 216–19
"Four-Year Myth, The" (CCA), 187–89
free speech, 259
friend-raising, 125–29
fringe benefits, 87, 135, 295n33
funding: administration and, 125–29; athletics and, 130; breakdowns from 2021–2022, 44; decline in, 35; for DEI, 217–19, 221; endowments, 24–26; for entrepreneurship and innovation, 244, 246–48; federal, 144–45, 151, 244; fund-raising and friend-raising, 125–29; Great Recession and, 9–10, 25, 35–36; incremental funding model, 53; legislation on, 30–31, 35; market competition for, 36–37; under New Partnership, 22–26, 43–48; by Pell Grants, 35; performance funding, 27–28, 36–38, 45, 217–19; performance outcomes and, 44–46; politics and, 35–36; public and, 21–31; by public bond, 24–26; for public universities, 9–10; for research, 143–45, 147–48, 150–51, 298n22; restructuring fund-raising initiatives, 126–29; state appropriations and, 23–25, 30–31, 45–46, 126–27, 260–61, 294n19; State Board of Higher Education and, 30–31; taxes and, 24. *See also* philanthropy; private donors; public disinvestment
future of higher education, 6, 259–66

gender: philanthropy and, 231; teaching and gender bias, 183–85
general fund, 52, 55–57
General Education. *See* core curriculum
Ginsberg, Benjamin, 110–11
global competition, 144–47, 165, 171–72, 219–20, 253
governance: accountability through, 36; administration and, 135–36; admissions policies and, 200–203, 225; Board of Trustees and, 18, 21, 26–27, 43, 46, 233; educational reform and, 46–47; executives and, 135–36; faculty and, 93–94, 97–99; under 40-40-20 formula, 32–33, 44–45, 216–19; The Hat and, 17–18, 26–27, 33; leadership and, 20, 109–10; New Partnership and, 22, 26–27, 42–43, 45–46; policy makers on, 47–48; private donors and, 27; privatization and, 21, 26–33; of public universities, 10, 17–20; of research universities, 20; shared, 84–86, 97–99, 103–4, 108; State Board of Higher Education and, 17–20, 30–31; teaching and, 183; tenure and, 84
grading: athletes and, 295n28; national assessment and, 180–81; student success and, 180
graduation rates: DEI and, 308n35; for minorities, 190, 308n35; performance outcomes and, 45; student success and, 186–88, 190
Great Depression, 1
Great Mistake, The (Newfield), 34, 79
Great Recession, 1, 4, 17; academic depression and, 74–75; funding

Great Recession (*continued*)
and, 9–10, 25, 35–36; institutional resilience and, 78–79; learning outcomes after, 178–79; research after, 144–45; salaries after, 96; student debt and, 3; tuition after, 52–53

Hat, The, 278n1, 280n15; athletics and, 130–31; firing of, 20, 42, 82–83, 90, 141; governance and, 17–18, 26–27, 33; private donors and, 25–26, 29; State Board of Higher Education and, 17–19. *See also* New Partnership
HECC. *See* Higher Education Coordinating Commission
higher education. *See specific topics*
Higher Education Coordinating Commission (HECC), 44–46, 125–26; DEI and, 216–19
h-index, 157
hiring: affirmative action and, 204–5; CBA and, 105–6; cluster, 160; DEI and, 204–5, 211–12; of faculty, 105–6, 158–62; under Institutional Hiring Plan, 160–62; strategic planning and, 158–62, 248
humanities: closure of humanities departments, 71–72; impact in, 250–54; liberal arts and, 2, 168–69, 285n23; STEM majors compared to, 168–69; tuition spending and, 69–72, 286n24

IDEAL plan, 209–10
identity politics, 223
IHP. *See* Institutional Hiring Plan
immigration, 214–15

impact: of academic capitalism, 228–29, 237–45; in arts and sciences, 250–54; in College of Arts and Sciences, 249–54; of DEI, 229–30, 234; impact-driven philanthropy, 230–37; of innovation and entrepreneurship, 228–29, 233–34, 245–50; knowledge economy and, 228–29; metrics, 228; public missions and, 227–30; scientific, 230–36; in social sector, 234–37
income gap, 78; salaries and, 96, 109, 133–35
incremental funding model, 53
inflation, 73–74
information services, 128–29, *129*
innovation: disruption and, 1–6; embracing failure and, 233–34; entrepreneurship and, 228–29, 233–34, 245–50; funding for, 244, 246–48; mindset, 233–34; in science and technology, 232–34, 237–39; in social sector, 234–37
Institutional Hiring Plan (IHP), 160–62
institutional support: administrative spending and, 113–17, 128–29, *129*; fund-raising and, 125–29
instructional support, 116–17
instructors. *See* faculty; non-tenure-track faculty
Integrated Postsecondary Education Data System (IPEDS), *116*, 285n22, 292n8
intellectual property, 242
international students, 214–15
IPEDS. *See* Integrated Postsecondary Education Data System

Ivy league institutions, 2; admissions policies in, 201–2; core curriculum at, 179; DEI and, 201–3; RCM and, 58; research in, 140, 157

job market, 1; adjunctification and, 148; administration and, 118–19; degree choice or major and, 168–70, 219–20, 301n2; faculty and, 84–85, 91–94, 118–19; oversupply of labor and, 84–85; research and, 148, 150; shared governance and, 93; student success and, 168–70, 171, 188; underemployment and, 219–20

K–12 education, 24, 191, 261; children's behavioral health and, 235–36; DEI in, 216–20; No Child Left Behind Act and, 28, 220; P–20 education as alternative to, 32; reform, 28, 32, 220; STEM in, 146
knowledge economy, 4, 22, 171–72, 225–26; educational reform and, 239–40; impact and, 228–29; tuition and, 73–78; views on knowledge and, 227–30
Kuh, George, 176–77

Labaree, David, 282n1
labor: academic labor market, 90–96, 118–19; activism, 91–92; division of, 238; law, 85–86, 92; oversupply in labor market, 84–85; research and, 238; right-to-work states and, 92; science and labor market, 238; structural differences in labor market, 118; tuition spending on, 75–76, 287n29; unionization and labor market, 91–93. *See also* job market
law: anti-discrimination lawsuits and, 207; DEI and, 200–205, 220–21; labor, 85–86, 92; Supreme Court and, 200–203, 225; Title VII of Civil Rights Act and, 204–5
leadership: administration and, 109–10, 123–24, 133–35; college completion and, 172; DEI and, 197–98, 204–6, 209; executives, 109, 133–36, 198, 205; governance and, 20, 109–10; performance metrics and, 153–54; policy makers and, 12–13; SSEM and, 122–25; strategic planning and, 160–61; "A Test of Leadership" report on, 172; turnover, 20; upheaval in, 10
learning: CLA and, 177–78; core curriculum and, 177–82, 186; goals and objectives, 176–82; how teachers should teach and, 182–86; outcomes, 176–77; regional accreditation and, 179–80; SoTL, 185–86; what students should learn and, 177–82. *See also* assessment of learning outcomes
legislation: for America COMPETES Act, 145–46; for Bayh-Dole Act, 239; college completion and, 172; four things to consider moving forward with, 259–64; on funding, 30–31, 35; on New Partnership, 29–31; for No Child Left Behind Act, 28, 220

liberal arts, 2, 70, 71, 142, 148, 150, 169, 193, 249, 254, 285n23, 286n24, 301n2. *See also* College of Arts and Sciences; humanities
lobbying, 139
Lumina Foundation, 174–75, 176

management: administration and, 133–36; CBA and, 96–106; competition *versus* solidarity and, 102–6; corporate, 58; enrollment, 121–25, 218–19; executives and managers, 109, 133–36; of faculty, 82–85, 96–108; fads, 59; how-to guide, 96–106; non-tenure-track faculty and, 99–102; performance metrics and, 153–54; policy makers and, 260–62; politics and, 259–60; restructuring of, 102–6; shared governance and, 93, 97–99, 103–4, 108; unionization and, 106–8. *See also* Responsibility Center Management
market competition, 2, 257–58; academic freedom and, 260; America COMPETES Act and, 145–46; budgeting system and, 79–81; CBA and, 103–6; college completion and, 171–72; College of Arts and Sciences and, 252–53; as driver of education system, 49–50, 282n1; faculty and, 102–6; for funding, 36–37; global competition, 144–47, 165, 171–72, 219–20, 253; institutional resilience and, 79–81; policy makers and, 47–48, 262–64; privatization and, 39–40; public universities and, 7–8, 10–13; salaries and, 77, 102–6; solidarity *versus*, 102–6; stakeholders and, 16; students and, 49–51
marketing: branding and, 127–29; entrepreneurship and, 247; recruitment and, 60
massive open online courses (MOOCs), 3, 4
Master Plan (California), 34–35, 47, 258–59
Matthew effect, 167
Mazur, Eric, 185
men's success, 224
mental health: children's behavioral health and juvenile, 235–36; COVID-19 and, 193–94; of students, 128, 137–38, 193–94
merit, 51–52, 99; DEI and meritocracy, 201, 229; salaries and, 103–4
meta-majors, 189
#MeToo movement, 210–11, 224
Michigan Mandate, 202–3
middle class, 3, 78
minority graduation rates, 190, 308n35
monetary value: credit hours and, 70–72; what tuition buys, 63–72
MOOCs. *See* massive open online courses
Morrill Act (1862), 250

National Academies of Science, Engineering, and Medicine, 145
National Institute for Learning Outcomes Assessment (NILOA), 176
National Institutes of Health (NIH), 143–44
National Research Council (NRC), 145

National Science Foundation (NSF), 143–44, 145
National Survey of Student Engagement (NSSE), 176
neofederalism, 265
neoliberalism, 12, 37, 61, 93, 107, 265
networking and friend-raising, 125–29
New Budget Model, 285n17; administrative spending and, 56–57; enrollment and, 57–58; faculty and, 105–6, 161; 50-30-20 rule and, 54–55, 57; general fund and, 52, 55–57; negative effects of, 54–58; RCM and, 59–63; state appropriations under, 65; student success and, 178–81; taxes under, 56–57, 64–73; tuition spending under, 56–57, 64–72
New Campus for Accelerating Scientific Impact, 230–36
New Faculty Majority, 91
Newfield, Christopher, 34
New Partnership: accountability for, 26–29; criticisms of, 27–29; funding under, 22–26, 43–48; governance and, 22, 26–27, 42–43, 45–46; legislation on, 29–31; performance outcomes under, 44–46; philanthropy and, 21–22, 25–26, 43–47; private donors and, 21–22, 25, 29, 43–44; privatization and, 21–33; public and, 21–33, 42–43; public disinvestment and, 21–33; public missions and, 18, 22, 46–47; three-part plan for, 22
NIH. *See* National Institutes of Health
NILOA. *See* National Institute for Learning Outcomes Assessment

Nisbet, Robert, 312n2
No Child Left Behind Act (2001), 28, 220
non-tenure-track faculty, 288n4; CBA and, 99–102; management and, 99–102; opposition, 89; overview of tenure-track *versus*, 86–88; professionalization of, 99–102, 182–83; support, 89–90
NRC. *See* National Research Council
NSF. *See* National Science Foundation
NSSE. *See* National Survey of Student Engagement

Obama, Barack, 171–72, 196
Obama administration, 4, 171
online education: COVID-19 and, 4, 191–94; MOOCs and, 3, 4
operational expenses, 64–68
organizational budgets, 113–16
out-of-state tuition, 54

P-20 education, 32
paradox of choice, 188
part-time faculty, 86–88, 91
peer reviews, 143, 167, 173; h-index, performance metrics, and, 157
Pell Grants, 35
Perfect Mess, A (Labaree), 49, 79, 282n1
performance funding: accountability and, 36–38; for DEI, 217–19; incentives, 27–28; limitations, 37–38; politics and, 38, 45; privatization and, 36–38; students and, 37–38; two major waves of, 37; whipsaw effect and, 38

performance gap, 38, 170; closing achievement gap and, 186–91; degree gap and, 22–23
performance metrics, 28; AAU and, 142–43, 147–51; Academic Analytics and, 153–56, *154*, 158; administration and, 153–57; bibliometrics and, 152–53; CBAs and, 157; college completion and, 173–74; creativity crisis and, 164–65; "excellence" standards and, 143–47, 175–76; flower chart, 153–55, *154*; h-index and, 157; leadership and, 153–54; management and, 153–54; problems with, 155–56; productivity indicators and, 151–58; public missions and, 137–38; for ranking and benchmarking, 147–51, 157; research and, 142–58, 164–65; unionization and, 156–57
performance outcomes: accountability and, 176; funding and, 44–46; graduation rates and, 45; learning outcomes and, 176–77; under New Partnership, 44–46; student success and, 176–81
philanthropy, 15, 144; advocacy, 175–76; college completion and, 174–76; gender and, 231; impact-driven, 230–37; New Partnership and, 21–22, 25–26, 43–47; power and, 41–42; privatization and, 41–44; public missions and, 46–47; scientific impact and, 230–36; social impact of, 236–37; SSEM and, 190, 212; student success and, 174–76, 190. *See also* private donors

pluralism, 207
policy makers, 11; four things for policy makers to do and not do, 259–64; on governance, 47–48; leadership and, 12–13; management and, 260–62; market competition and, 47–48, 262–64; public and, 45–48; state-level policy for DEI and, 215–20; student success and, 169–71; on tuition setting, 48
political correctness, 144, 197
politics: college completion and, 172; in crisis, 264–66; DEI and, 138, 196–99, 220–22, 225, 259; funding and, 35–36; identity, 223; lobbying and, 139; management and, 259–60; neofederalism and, 265; neoliberalism and, 265; performance funding and, 38, 45; political polarization and, 4–5, 264–65; populism and, 138, 220, 222, 259; privatization and, 35–36; race and, 195–97; research and, 144–47; of shared governance, 97–98; social justice and, 193, 195–97; social welfare and, 222; Trump and, 264–65; wokeness and, 5, 221, 259
populism, 138, 220, 222, 259
post-tenure review, 98, 296n7
power: academic capitalism and, 244; administration and, 111–12; of faculty, 82–83; philanthropy and, 41–42; shared governance and, 84–86; of students, 50; unionization and, 82–84
President Five, 43, 44, 46, 128, 169, 195
Princeton University, 174

INDEX • 329

private donors: accountability and, 2–3, 26–27, 29; fund-raising and, 126; governance and, 27; impact-driven philanthropy and, 230–31; largest, 7, 21–22, 43–44, 282n31; locating, 25–26; negative influences of, 41; New Partnership and, 21–22, 25, 29, 43–44; preconditions and restrictions for, 25–26; public and, 21–22, 42–44

privatization, 15; accountability and, 34–42; adaptations to, 38–41; DEI and, 218–19; governance and, 21, 26–33; market competition and, 39–40; New Partnership and, 21–33; performance funding and, 36–38; philanthropy and, 41–44; politics and, 35–36; public accountability and, 34–42; public disinvestment and, 21, 34–36; revenue streams and, 39–41

productivity: Academic Analytics and, 153–56, *154*, 158; administration and, 153–57; metrics and productivity indicators, 151–58, 164–65; technology and, 76

professors. *See* faculty; tenure-track faculty

public: accountability, 17–21, 26–29, 34–42; funding and, 21–31; future for, 48; HECC and, 44–46; New Partnership and, 21–33, 42–43; policy makers and, 45–48; private donors and, 21–22, 42–44; privatization and, 34–42; as stakeholders, 17–48; tuition and, 23

public disinvestment, 20–21; Academic Allocation Model and, 78–79; academic capitalism and, 241–42; criticism of, 34–35; faculty and, 86; "Great Mistake" (Newfield) of, 79; New Partnership and, 21–33; privatization and, 21, 34–36; tuition and, 23, 23–24, 73, 79

public good, 255–57

public missions: AAU and, 142–43, 159; abandonment of, 6; accountability and, 27–29; athletics and, 131–32; college completion and, 171–72; College of Arts and Sciences and, 252–53; DEI and, 138, 197–98, 216–20; under 40-40-20 formula, 32–33, 216–17; fulfilling, 10–11; impact and, 227–30; New Partnership and, 18, 22, 46–47; performance metrics and, 137–38; philanthropy and, 46–47; research and, 137; STEM fields and, 137

public relations, 127–29

public universities: changes to, 1–6; development and relations, 125–29; funding for, 9–10; governance of, 10, 17–20; ideals of, 7; loss of confidence in, 6; market competition and, 7–8, 10–13; public good and, 255–58; upheaval to, 9–11. *See also specific topics*

race and ethnicity: admissions policies and, 200–203, 225; affirmative action and, 204–5; anti-discrimination lawsuits and, 207; Black Lives Matter

race and ethnicity (*continued*)
and, 196, 203, 210–11; critical race
theory and, 5; DEI and, 195–98,
200–206, 212–15, 220–26; identity
politics and, 223; in Ivy league
institutions, 201–2; politics
and, 195–97; racism and, 195–97,
214; reverse discrimination
and, 221; structural racism and,
196–97; student debt and, 222;
xenophobia and, 214. *See also*
diversity, equity, and inclusion
rankings, 9; performance metrics
for, 147–51, 157; problems with,
155–56; for research universities,
147–52
Readings, Bill, 297n16
Reagan administration, 35
recruitment: administration
and, 120–25; DEI and, 212–15;
marketing and, 60; student,
120–25
regional accreditation. *See*
accreditation
research, 2, 9; academic capitalism
and, 239–45; administration and,
292n7; budgeting system for,
150–51; "excellence" standards
and the rise of STEM,
143–47; funding for, 143–45,
147–48, 150–51, 298n22; global
competition and, 144–47, 165;
after Great Recession, 144–45;
in Ivy league institutions, 140,
157; job market and, 148, 150;
labor and, 238; NRC and, 145;
outcomes, 165–66; performance
metrics and productivity
indicators, 151–58, 164–65; politics
and, 144–47; public missions and,

137; rankings and benchmarking,
147–51; re-examining beliefs
about, 163–65; scientific
stagnation and, 165–66; STEM
fields and, 145–47, 150, 162, 300n37
research universities, 9–11, 12; AAU
and, 139–43, 145–49, 163–65;
creativity crisis and, 162–67;
faculty at, 94; governance of,
20; growth of, 227; performance
metrics and, 142–58; rankings for,
147–52; Research 1 and Research
2 classifications, 140–41, 296n2,
300n38; strategic planning and
budgeting at, 158–62
resource dependency, 150–51
Responsibility Center Management
(RCM): accountability and, 59;
administrators under, 58; basic
idea of, 58; budgeting system
and, 58–63, 78–79; capitalism and,
59–61; demise of, 158; difficulties
in implementing, 62–63; faculty
and, 93–94, 105; negative
outcomes of, 61–63; revenue
streams and, 59; tuition and, 60
revenue streams: privatization and,
39–41; RCM and, 59; from state
appropriations, 65
reverse discrimination, 221
right-to-work states, 92
Rising Above the Gathering Storm
report, 145
risk shift, 35–36
Roksa, Josipa, 177–78

salaries: of administrators, 109, 117–
19, 133–35; budgeting system and,
75–77; of executives, 109, 133–36;
of faculty, 75–77, 86, 95–96, 102–6,

107, 133–35, 291n31; faculty salary comparisons, 133–34, 291n31; fringe benefits and, 87, 135, 295n33; after Great Recession, 96; income gap and, 96, 109, 133–35; market competition and, 77, 102–6; merit and, 103–4; stagnation of, 95; tuition spending and, 95; unionization and, 95–96, 103–4, 107
Sallie Mae, 174–75
scholarships: Pell Grants and, 35; tuition and, 51–52, 283n3
science. *See* arts and sciences; STEM fields; research; technology
science of teaching and learning (SoTL), 185–86
scientific impact, 230–36
scientific innovation, 232–34, 237–39
scientific stagnation, 165–66
SEIU. *See* Service Employees International Union
senior faculty, 86–88, 94, 100–101
Service Employees International Union (SEIU), 92
sexual assault, 130–31
shared governance: CBA and, 97–99; job market and, 93; management and, 93, 97–99, 103–4, 108; politics of, 97–98; power and, 84–86
Smith, Adam, 94–95
social class: degrees and, 222; DEI and, 220–26; education and, 2–3; middle class and, 3, 78; social mobility and, 2–3, 5–6, 220; student debt and, 222–23; student success and, 190–91, 222–23; wealth gap and, 78, 135

socialism, 31, 222
social justice: affirmative action and, 204–5; Black Lives Matter and, 196, 203, 210–11; DEI and, 196–99, 201–5, 207–11, 215, 220–26; moral exhortation and, 207–10; politics and, 193, 195–97
social media, 166
social sector impact and innovation, 234–37
social welfare, 222; welfare state and, 12, 35–36
SoTL. *See* science of teaching and learning
Spellings, Margaret, 172–73
sports. *See* athletics
SSEM. *See* Division for Student Services and Enrollment Management
stakeholders, 15–16; administrators as, 109–36; faculty as, 82–108; market competition and, 16; public as, 17–48; students as, 49–81
state appropriations: for administration, 126–27; funding and, 23–25, 30–31, 45–46, 126–27, 260–61, 294n19; general fund and, 56; under New Budget Model, 65; redistribution of, 31; revenue streams from, 65; tuition and, 52, 64–65, 285n19
State Board of Higher Education, 10; faculty and, 82–83; funding and, 30–31; governance and, 17–20, 30–31; The Hat and, 17–19
state-level policy, 257–58; DEI and, 215–20
STEM fields, 2; AAU and, 148, 150; College of Arts and Sciences and, 253–54; creativity crisis

STEM fields (*continued*)
and, 162–64; humanities majors compared to STEM majors, 168–69; K–12 education and STEM, 146; public missions and, 137; research and, 145–47, 150, 162, 300n37; rise of, 143–47; SoTL and, 185; strategic planning for, 249–50; tuition spending for, 68–72, 286n26

strategic planning: budgeting and, 158–62; DEI, 206–10; enrollment and, 160–61; exercises, 42, 49; hiring and, 158–62, 248; leadership and, 160–61; at research universities, 158–62; revolution in, 160–62; for STEM fields, 249–50

structural racism, 196–97

student aid, 264; scholarships and, 51–52, 283n3

student debt: Biden administration and, 80–81; bubble in, 3; forgiveness, 80–81; Great Recession and, 3; race and, 222; rise in, 3; social class and, 222–23; student loans and, 1–2, 80–81, 174–75; studying, student success, and, 177–78

Student Life, 122–25

student protests, 130–31

student retention, 120–25

students: costs to, other than tuition, 51; decline and demographic dip of, 48; international, 214–15; market competition and, 49–51; as market consumers, 49–51; mental health of, 128, 137–38, 193–94; performance funding and, 37–38; performance gap, 38, 170, 186–91; per student expenditures, 115–17, *116*; power of, 50; recruitment and retention of, 120–25; as stakeholders, 49–81; student services and academic support for, 120–25, 168–69, 187–90; tuition rises and, 15, 50

student success: AAU and, 179, 185–86, 304n27; *Academically Adrift* on, 177–78; academic support, academic advisors and, 187–90; accountability and, 174–76; achievement gap and, 186–91; advocacy philanthropy and, 175–76; as catchphrase, 170; CCA report on, 187–89; closing achievement gap for, 186–91; college completion and, 171–77; COVID-19 and, 171, 191–94; degree majors and, 168–70, 188–89, 219–20, 301n2; DEI and, 212–15; grading and, 180; graduation rates and, 186–88, 190; how teachers should teach, 182–86; job market and, 168–70, 171, 188; Kuh and student success movement, 176–77; learning outcomes and, 176–77; national assessment and, 180–81; new agenda for, 173–77; New Budget Model and, 178–81; NSSE and, 176; paradox of choice and, 188; performance outcomes and, 176–81; philanthropy and, 174–76, 190; policy makers and, 169–71; regional accreditation and, 173–74, 176–77, 179–82; social class and, 190–91, 222–23; student debt, studying, and, 177–78; UESS and, 169–70, 212; VSA and, 174; what students should learn, 177–82

subsidies, 51, 54–55, 57, 65
Supreme Court, U.S., 200–203, 225
systemic problems: DEI and, 222–24; structural racism and, 196–97

taxes: funding and, 24; under New Budget Model, 56–57, 64–73; tax revolts, 39; tuition and, 41, 64–68
teaching: assessment and evaluations, 182–83; core curriculum and, 177–82, 186; educational reform and, 183–86; gender bias and, 183–85; governance and, 183; how teachers should teach, 182–86; online, 192–93; SoTL and, 185–86
technology: accelerating scientific impact and, 230–36; biotechnology and, 237–38, 239; faculty workloads and, 76–77; innovation in science and, 232–34, 237–39; planning, 59–60; productivity and, 76; tuition spending on, 76. *See also* STEM fields
technology transfer offices (TTOs), 239–40, 243
techno-optimism, 3
tenure, 15; academic freedom and, 111; CBA and, 98–100; criticisms of, 84; Ginsberg on, 111; governance and, 84; non-tenure-track opposition, 89; non-tenure-track support, 89–90; shrinkage of, 107; tenure-track opposition, 88–89; tenure-track support, 89; unionization and, 82–90, 106–8
tenure-track faculty, 288n4; credit hours and, 288n5; hiring of,

159–62; overview of non-tenure-track faculty *versus*, 86–88; percentages, from 1979–2013, 289n8; post-tenure review and, 98, 296n7; unionization and, 90
"Test of Leadership, A" (report), 172
Tilghman, Shirley, 174
Title IV, 173, 181–82
Title IX, 224
Title VII, 204–5
TRF. *See* tenure-related faculty
Trump, Donald, 196, 203, 264–65
Trump administration, 4, 214
TTOs. *See* technology transfer offices
tuition, 1–2; in California, 75; composite tuition rate, 284n16; credit hours and, 54–55, 64–65, 70–72, 283n7; declines, 77–78; discounting, 51–52; enrollment and, 57–58; flows, 52–64; after Great Recession, 52–53; knowledge economy and, 73–78; under New Budget Model, 52–58; out-of-state, 54; policy makers on setting of, 48; public and, 23; public disinvestment and, 23, 23–24, 73, 79; RCM and, 60; redistribution of, 31; return on college investment and, 6, 15, 50, 168, 170; scholarships and, 51–52, 283n3; state appropriations and, 52, 64–65, 285n19; taxes and, 41, 64–68; what tuition buys, 63–72
tuition rises, 5–6, 23, 23, 35–36; budgeting system and, 51, 72–78; causes of, 72–78; inflation and, 73–74; students and, 15, 50; yearly, 72
tuition spending, 49–50; under Academic Allocation Model, 78–79; for academic *versus*

tuition spending (*continued*)
nonacademic expenditures, 67–68, *68*; for administration, 67–68, *68*; budgeting system and, 51; toward faculty, 66, 66–67, 287n29; humanities and, 69–72, 286n24; IPEDS and, 285n22; on labor costs, 75–76, 287n29; under New Budget Model, 56–57, 64–72; for operational expenses, 64–68; per credit hour, across divisions, 68–72, *69*, *70*, 285n21; for "rent and taxes," 64–68, *66*; runaway expenses and, 72–80; salaries and, 95; for STEM fields, 68–72, 286n26; on technology, 76; tracking, 63–72; waste and excess, 15–16, 72, 79–80

UESS. *See* Undergraduate Education and Student Success
"unbundling" degrees, 3, 95
undeclared degrees, 189–90
underemployment, 219–20
Undergraduate Education and Student Success (UESS), 169–70, 212
unionization: adjunctification and, 106–7; DEI and, 211; financial burdens of, 104–5; labor activism and, 91–92; labor market and, 91–93; management and, 106–8; passing, 83–85; performance metrics and, 156–57; power and, 82–84; salaries and, 95–96, 103–4, 107; straw poll on, 88; support for, 88–90; tenure and, 82–90, 106–8; tenure-related faculty and, 90; unintended consequences of, 106–8

United Kingdom, 28
United States (U.S.), 200–203, 225
university development and relations, 125–29
University in Ruins, The (Readings), 297n16
University of California, 20, 34–35, 39, 75, 92, 140, 200–01, 240, 258. *See also* California Master Plan.
University of Michigan, 39, 58, 63, 74, 92, 140, 201–3, 225
University of North Carolina, 20, 140, 201, 259
University of Virginia, 20, 27, 58, 140
University Senate's Core Education Council, 180, 183
U.S. *See* United States
U.S. News and World Report, 139–40, 151–52, 157

viewpoint diversity, 207–8
vocational courses, 220, 262–63
Voluntary System of Accountability (VSA), 174–75

waste and excess, 15–16, 72, 79–80
wealth gap, 78, 135
welfare state, 12, 35–36
whipsaw effect, 38
Wieman, Carl, 185
wokeness, 5, 198, 221, 259
women: DEI and, 210–11, 213, 224; gender bias and, 183–85; #MeToo movement and, 210–11, 224; Title IX and, 224
working conditions, 83–84, 86
World War II, 93

xenophobia, 214

GPSR Authorized Representative: Easy Access System Europe, Mustamäe tee 50, 10621 Tallinn, Estonia, gpsr.requests@easproject.com